Date Due

Cue the Elephant!

BY THE SAME AUTHOR

History on the Run, 1984
Times to Remember, 1986
Prime Time at Ten, 1987
Kennedy and Diefenbaker, 1990
Visions of Canada, 1991
The Microphone Wars, 1994

Cue the Elephant!

Backstage Tales at the CBC

Knowlton Nash

Cloth edition published 1996
Trade paperback edition published 1997

Canadian Cataloguing in Publication Data
Nash, Knowlton
Cue the elephant : backstage tales at the CBC

Includes bibliographical references and index.
ISBN 0-7710-6734-8 (bound) ISBN 0-7710-6735-6 (pbk.)

1. Television personalities – Canada – Anecdotes. 2. Canadian Broadcasting Corporation. 3. Radio broadcasters – Canada – Anecdotes. I. Title.

HE8689.9.C3N38 1996 384.54′092′271 C96-931092-7

The publishers acknowledge the support of the Canada Council for the Arts and the Ontario Arts Council for their publishing program.

Typesetting by M&S, Toronto
Printed and bound in Canada

McClelland & Stewart Inc.
The Canadian Publishers
481 University Avenue
Toronto, Ontario
M5G 2E9

1 2 3 4 5 01 00 99 98 97

To the stars and those behind the stars who brought joy and knowledge into the living rooms of the nation.

Contents

Foreword

Cue the Elephant! is an anecdotal, light-hearted, behind-the-scenes glimpse at some of the goofs, gossip, peeves, and pleasures of the stars of Canadian broadcasting.

The title comes from the beginning of Canadian television, when neophyte CBC-TV producer Sydney Newman was urging an elephant to prance and wave its trunk in the opening scene of an experimental television show at the Canadian National Exhibition in Toronto. In spite of the anxious producer's pleas of "Cue the elephant!" the reluctant pachyderm was camera shy; it refused to perform and instead had an elephantine bowel movement. As TV producers would have to do a million times in the years ahead, Newman improvised and got on with the show.

Getting on with the show, in spite of the unexpected, is a theme common to radio and TV programming and is reflected in these pages.

In a sense, this is a companion book to my earlier book *The Microphone Wars*, which traced the history of Canadian broadcasting from its birth. But this book is distinctly different in tone and style, as here the stars themselves talk about the human side of radio and television, and tales are told out of school by producers, directors, technicians, and other backstage co-workers.

Cue the Elephant! also reflects a time that will never return. With the multitude of TV and radio channels now pouring down on us and fragmenting the audience, never again will the broadcasting spotlight be as focused as it has been on individual Canadian stars. The luminaries of yesteryear will remain unique, for rarely in the future will we gather around the office water cooler to talk about how outrageous Max Ferguson had been that morning as Rawhide, how audacious Patrick Watson had been on "This Hour Has Seven Days" the previous night, or how conniving Cynthia Dale had been on "Street Legal." These stars became lasting household names and even our friends.

The current explosion in the number of cable channels, specialized services, satellites and dishes is shrinking star longevity towards the fifteen-minute duration that Andy Warhol foresaw. Through no fault of their own, today's stars do not have the durability or impact that their earlier counterparts had. Inevitably, this saps at Canada's sense of self – but it gives rise to my desire to capture the human qualities of those stars: their challenges and rivalries, beauty spots and pockmarks. I wanted to feature them as part of the heraldry of Canada, something all Canadians once shared at one time, a time that is now disappearing.

But this is, I hope, more a book of joy with a bit of prattle and tattle than a book of woe. My aim is more to tickle than to teach, although admittedly I've tried to do both in places. In the process, if I focus primarily on the CBC, it is because, with some outstanding exceptions, that's where the Canadian stars have been, especially as for a long time there was no other Canadian radio or TV network.

My choice of interviewees was necessarily arbitrary, limited by space and time, but their stories at least provide a taste of the tales so many others could tell. I have to thank the stars and their backstage colleagues – more than 120 on and off the record altogether – who gave so generously of their time and memories.

All have their own versions and visions of history, some viewing the same incident quite differently. But one thing that struck me as I travelled for my research was their strong national pride, no matter whether they lived in Vancouver, Toronto, New York, or Los Angeles. While some are critical of others and of the CBC at times, they all share a devotion to their roots in the CBC. No one puts it better than veteran TV make-up artist Elaine Saunders. "The saddest day of my life," she says, "is going to be when I leave the CBC and the people here, because I've shared their ups and downs and their anger and joy. I've shared their babies and their divorces. I've seen them pull themselves up and drag on. I work with them when their defences are down and they're far more revealing. They're my family – the stars, the directors, the crews. I know it sounds crazy, but I really care. I've become a really good Canadian as a result of all this. We all grew up with these people."

Aside from the stars and their behind-the-scenes colleagues, my thanks must also go to those who so freely gave their time and effort in tracking down interviewees, chasing after details, looking for photographs, and generally making my job much easier. In particular I am grateful for the help of Leone Earls and Anne Mercer of the CBC Toronto Reference Library, Sylvie Robitaille and Diane Martineau at the National Archives in Ottawa, and Tom Curzon and Sandy Homewood of CBC Public Relations in Toronto.

I am also especially indebted to my McClelland & Stewart editor, Dinah Forbes, whose editing talents and personal encouragement once again were invaluable in developing and shaping the manuscript. And, too, thanks must be extended to Heather Sangster, my copy editor, who corrected my errant grammar, spelling, and punctuation among a host of other scripting improvements.

Most of all, I have to thank my wife, Lorraine Thomson, whose rich memory of anecdotes from her days as a pioneer CBC dancer, radio and TV host, researcher and producer is reflected in these pages. Her research help and advice were invaluable.

Frequent reference is made in these pages to "the green room," a phrase that originated with the great English actor and producer David Garrick, whose career flourished in the mid-1700s. He sought to ease the life of actors by establishing a benevolent fund called "The Fund for Decayed Actors" and by improving backstage facilities, which, at the time, were very primitive.

He set aside a room at the Theatre Royal in Bath for this purpose, and it happened to be decorated in green. Ever since, in theatre and broadcasting, such a room has been established and called "the green room."

I

The Golden Years of Radio

Andrew Allan – The Sun King

The sun king of the early years of Canadian radio was a tormented, incorruptible visionary named Andrew Allan, the man who gave Canada its first national theatre. "Broadcasting is one of Canada's principal means of survival," Allan once said, "and only in radio could we have enough drama to make a theatre in Canada."

Frances Hyland, who worked in many of Allan's productions, remembers the days when she was a budding actor in Regina. "We didn't have a whole lot in Regina. Listening to CBC Radio drama was my theatre. The CBC was literally holding the country together, with a couple million people all listening to the same program. I remember Len Peterson's scripts, a lot of Tommy Tweed, and they were doors into fairyland. They were telling my Canadian stories to me." In Timmins, Ontario, a young reporter named Peter Gzowski listened to Allan's plays. "They left an indelible impression on me, and when I came to work at the CBC there were still echoes of them around here." As a young man in rural Saskatchewan, former CBC president Al Johnson was also listening to Allan's plays. "It was our Canadian theatre," he says. "Without it, for me, Canada would only have been Saskatchewan."

Allan was a *bon vivant* outside the studio, but inside it he was a holy terror. "He scared the hell out of me," said actress Mona O'Hearn. Demanding, frightening, and meticulous, Allan insisted on last-name formality in the studio, no matter how friendly he was with the actors. While acting in his first radio play directed by Allan, a nineteen-year-old Don Harron was astonished to find himself addressed by Allan as Mr. Harron.

Lorne Greene, the patriarch of "Bonanza" on TV and the wartime Voice of Doom on CBC Radio news, acted in many of Allan's "Stage" productions, but he was not exempt from Allan's rigidity about presuming on friendship. During a rehearsal Allan, from the control room, could be heard in the studio saying, "Tell Mr. Greene that I would appreciate it if he would read the second half of that line just a bit louder." Greene responded, "Tell Andrew that's fine. I'll get it." A few minutes later, Allan said, "Tell Mr. Greene that I love the reading of the second paragraph." Greene replied, "Tell Andrew that's fine, but I'd like to try it again." All afternoon the last-name first-name messages went back and forth until Allan finally said, "Tell Mr. Greene that Mr. Allan would like him to do it the way Mr. Allan is saying, and when we're finished, Andrew will buy Lorne a drink."

Allan's inflexible studio discipline and godlike aura cowed his performers. The cast of one drama was stunned when Barry Morse, newly arrived from England, spoke up during his first play with Allan. The producer had given the actors a direction, prompting Morse to ask, "Don't you think it might be rather better if we did it this way?" "Suddenly I was aware," he says, "that the studio atmosphere was deathly silent and white knuckles were everywhere. No one ever dreamed of actually questioning something Andrew had said." Allan paused and said in his soft Scottish burr, "Oh yes. Very interesting, Mr. Morse," and carried right on.

Allan was the all-powerful creative overlord whose very presence instilled awe among actors. He always wore well-cut suits, and his ice-blue eyes lent a stern expression to his pink, round face. When Bruno Gerussi was at a Stratford Festival opening night party, someone said to him, "Andrew Allan wants to speak to you." Gerussi, who had never met Allan, was deep in conversation and replied, "Oh Jesus, tell him to wait a minute. I'm speaking to some people here." "All right, you idiot," came the response, "go ahead and starve to death!" "For a couple of weeks, Andrew was frosty to me, but then he softened," said Gerussi.

Allan demanded punctuality of his actors, not all of whom were as prompt as he wanted. "I remember once when a writer and an actor were late for a rehearsal," said Gerussi. "Everybody was sitting there nervously wondering, 'Oh my God, what is Andrew going to say?' "

Perhaps the worst offender in this regard was Jane Mallett, one of Canada's leading dramatic performers. She was almost always late for rehearsals, breathlessly saying, "Oh, I'm so sorry," and inventing tales such as, "You know, on my way, I was cornered by a squirrel in the park." In the middle of summer, she'd explain, "I got caught in this terrible snowstorm," or in the spring, she'd say she'd been delayed by the Santa Claus parade. Tommy Tweed was another culprit, once offering the excuse, "I'm sorry I'm late but I just ran over a fool of a boy." Mavor Moore was also often late, and although he made no excuses, he says, "I always made sure I looked extremely harried."

Other actors also had problems keeping track of time. Ruth Springford was never late for an Allan production but once left too early. "She was driving home, listening to her car radio, when she tuned into the middle of this play," Barry Morse says. "Suddenly she realizes it's a play – live of course – in which she has played a role, but now remembers she hasn't made her last entrance yet, and she's halfway home. She turned around, but couldn't get back in time. The producer had grabbed a woman walking down the hall, stuck a script into her hands, and had her read the lines."

John Drainie, whom Allan viewed as the best radio actor in Canada, didn't keep track of time because he didn't usually wear a watch. On one show he had the opening lines, but reckoned he had a few minutes to go to the bathroom before it began. Unfortunately he miscalculated, and the program went on the air with Drainie still out of the studio. Fletcher Markle, also in the show, realized what had happened, grabbed a script and dashed to the microphone, and, trying to imitate Drainie's voice, delivered the opening lines. Two minutes later an embarrassed Drainie arrived and did the rest of the show.

Lister Sinclair, who was watching from the sidelines, remembers that Allan later read the riot act to Drainie, saying, "No more of this! You've got to buy a watch and wear it." Drainie did, but six months later he was again late. Allan demanded, "Mr. Drainie, I requested that you buy a watch and wear it at all times." "I did," said Drainie. "Here it is. But look, the hands have fallen off. They came off quite a while ago." Drainie's punctuality never really improved, and once he arrived two days late for a meeting with Sinclair. He also occasionally took naps in the studio. Barry Morse recalls that one time Drainie could not be aroused from his slumber, "so I played the whole scene by myself with two voices."

In spite of his constant losing battle with time, Drainie became one of Canada's most esteemed actors of the twentieth century. Although triumphant on radio, he never effectively transferred his talents to television. As a youngster he had been hit by a car, badly injuring his leg; the resulting limp made him feel awkward on television. "He was always self-conscious about his limp," says fellow actor Lloyd Bochner.

"John was the master of radio. He was magical," says Frances Hyland. "He taught me to play to the microphone as if it were a human. He could tilt his head a tiny little bit and literally transform the sound." Mavor Moore was also given advice on humanizing the microphone. "Make love to the microphone, laddie, it's closer than the girl," a Scottish director once told him.

Practical jokes were frowned on by Allan, but they happened nevertheless. Once when Drainie was on live delivering a narration, Tommy Tweed, one of broadcasting's great pranksters, crawled into the booth on his hands and knees and set fire to the bottom of Drainie's script. "There were flames leaping up," says Morse, "clouds of smoke, and he's coughing, trying to grab another script, all the while being live on the radio. A short time later, Tweed came on with a long speech, and Drainie, seeking revenge, sat behind him snoring loudly to unnerve him." When veteran actor Frank Peddie was similarly delivering live a lengthy narration, his fellow actors undressed him down to his undershorts.

Mavor Moore says that emotional problems often delayed productions. He remembers the time the Hollywood star Merle Oberon ordered a chicken sandwich during the meal break, but was brought an egg sandwich instead. "She lay on the studio floor and screamed," Moore says. On another occasion, during a rehearsal for a CBC production, Orson Welles was told, "Mr. Welles, Miss Del Rio is on the line from Hollywood." "Oh God!" sighed the weary Welles. "Tell her I love her."

In the days of live radio drama, timing was crucial. "Sometimes," says Morse, "you had to die more slowly or more quickly, depending on how much time was left." Mavor Moore recalls doing *King Lear* with the great American actor Walter Hampden, who had played Lear so many times he didn't need a script; as he spoke he just dropped the pages on the floor. Unfortunately, however, the script had been edited for timing, and Hampden, performing from memory, restored all the cuts that had been made. In a scramble, whole scenes had to be eliminated to get the program off the air on time.

To Allan, words were holy, not to be tampered with by actors, and he built the "Stage" series on scripts by Len Peterson, Lister Sinclair, Fletcher Markle, Harry Boyle, W. O. Mitchell, Joseph Schull, Hugh Kemp, and some seventy other Canadian writers. It was a writer's theatre, and Allan was the impresario of words, pulling out of his actors the pacing and inflections that brought the scripts alive. "He had an incredible ear," remembers Frances Hyland. "He would say to me, 'There's a little echo in your character, and you made a choice yesterday that seems to me better because you connected the scene with your inflection with the way you played the first scene.' "

"I had awe for Andrew – gratitude and fondness," says Lloyd Bochner, who first performed for Allan when he was ten years old. "But for all that, he inflicted a feeling of tension on the actors. Andrew couldn't stand it if anyone made a mistake. He was somewhat bald, and just like a thermometer he would turn beet red if something went wrong, which only increased our nervousness." "He was a very savage producer," Lister Sinclair says, "and he would accept no excuses if you stumbled or made a slip. You would be dropped from next week's line-up." Actor Larry Mann remembers Allan once telling him as a rehearsal began, "I know exactly how you should do this role, dear boy, so consequently that's how we will do it."

But for all his martinet tendencies, Allan's immense creative talents and his charm outside the studio drew both enormous admiration as well as apprehension from his actors and writers, who, in turn, sought to please the master with their work.

"When a piece of work is performed . . . something exciting must happen," Allan once said. "If it doesn't, something is wrong." It was a philosophy he brought to his teaching in Toronto at Lorne Greene's Academy of Radio Arts, a school Greene established just after the Second World War for aspiring broadcasting producers, directors, and performers. It offered a one-year course in which Allan taught production, Lister Sinclair taught writing, Mavor Moore offered drama instruction, and Greene taught announcing techniques. "Lorne was a fatherly but forceful teacher," says Don Brown, a onetime student and later director. "You would never question what he said." Leslie Nielsen, Fred Davis, Gordie Tapp, producer Drew Crossan, and actors such as Alfie Scopp, future "Star Trek" officer James Doohan, and Paul Soles were among the graduates.

The academy was on Jarvis Street just across from the CBC, and Fred Davis and his wide-eyed fellow students would go over regularly to the CBC cafeteria. "We used to call it 'the Jarvis Street Sardi's,'" he said. "We were fledgling radio people, and it was just like going on Broadway. In the cafeteria, we saw people like Allan McFee and Byng Whittaker, who were all the stars of the day."

Andrew Allan, the Scottish-born son of a Presbyterian parson, immigrated to Canada at the age of seventeen. After university, where he focused more on the student newspaper and theatre than on classes, he began his radio career as a dance-band announcer in Toronto. He wrote plays for the CRBC, forerunner to the CBC, for twenty-five dollars each and in the late 1930s went to England to produce radio plays. The most traumatic moment of his life coincided with the beginning of the Second World War when he, his fiancée (the actor Judith Evelyn), and his father were returning to Canada from England on the *Athenia*. The ship was torpedoed in the Irish Sea, and in a bungled rescue attempt, their lifeboat was slashed by the propeller blades of a freighter coming to their aid. Allan's father and many others were chopped to pieces. When Allan and Evelyn were at last rescued, they were among the six survivors of the eighty-five people originally in the lifeboat.

When he finally got back to Canada, Allan went to work for the CBC in Vancouver, where he encountered the tall and tweedy Lister Sinclair, also newly arrived from England. When they first met, Sinclair refused Allan's offer of a cigarette, saying, "No, thank you. I never indulge in non-cooperative vices." Allan was bowled over by Sinclair's brilliance and later made him a key writer and performer in the "Stage" series. The Bombay-born, London-raised Sinclair had been writing and performing at the University of British Columbia, and had co-starred with fellow student Pierre Berton in a play called *The March of Slime*. Allan's total professional dedication is shown in advice he once gave to Sinclair: "You mustn't let your work suffer. Let everything else suffer, but not your work."

Sinclair worked with Allan through all the golden years of CBC radio and went on to a successful television career, a bruising and frustrating senior executive role, then finally returned to radio as the velvet-voiced polymath host of "Ideas." In old age, he describes himself as "a young fogey" and says he would like to have on his gravestone, "He Died Learning."

While in Vancouver, Allan met others who became lifelong colleagues and who played a part in his drama revolution, including John Drainie, Fletcher Markle, Len Peterson, Arthur Hill, and Bernie Braden. Summoned to the CBC in Toronto in 1943, Allan's first challenge was to develop a national radio theatre series to be broadcast on Sunday nights. One of his first tasks was to come up with a name, and while contemplating a bottle of Scotch, he decided he liked the simplicity of the Vat 69 label and so called his series "Stage 44," changing the year every new season.

Allan had replaced as the head of radio drama Rupert Lucas, whom Mavor Moore says had "no brains in his head, a flabby soul, and an ambition exceeding his endowment." Allan regarded Lucas as a rival, even though he was replacing him and Lucas had been dispatched to Montreal. "Andrew was always very edgy with Lucas," says Lister Sinclair. "Among the actors it was generally held that if you'd been successful in Montreal under Lucas, Andrew would not hire you, or at least would let you languish for a while."

Allan's discomfort with Lucas was one of several rivalries that steamed under the surface of his career. "I'd very much wanted to be a producer, but Andrew wouldn't make me a producer," says Sinclair. "He didn't want any competition. The two people he kept at arm's length were me and Esse Ljungh."

Esse Ljungh, a Swedish-born producer who worked on the "Stage" series, was immensely popular and was eventually appointed Allan's successor. As a youth he'd herded cattle in Saskatchewan, and he began his radio career in Winnipeg in the late 1930s, acting for $1.50 per performance.

"Andrew shafted Esse consistently, and Esse was very bitter about that," says Sinclair. "He felt Andrew had not given him a fair shake and was always standing in his way. Andrew was steely and ambitious to control the drama area. He was always flicking off the heads of the tall poppies – his perceived rivals."

Most actors felt that Ljungh was the better director of performers, but that Allan was unmatchable in his technical mastery of radio and his overall creative genius. "Esse was a primitive, really, someone who did most things by instinct," says Barry Morse, "while Andrew was more cerebral. There was always a certain amount of fragility in one's relationship with him."

A similar assessment is given by Hollywood comic Leslie Nielsen, who worked with both Allan and Ljungh. "Esse was a moody Swede but with so much vitality. Still, I think Andrew could end up being more deadly when he wanted to be."

The clash between Allan and Ljungh was inevitable given the patrician, icy style of one and the emotional, sensitive nature of the other. "Esse would rant and rave and swear in Swedish and march up and down the office cursing," says Mary DePoe, an administrative clerk in the radio drama office at the time. "But we didn't understand what he was saying because it was in Swedish. Andrew would just sit there in cold fury."

"We all loved Esse, but Andrew we respected," says DePoe, who remembers Ljungh derisively calling Allan "The Legend."

Allan worried about the popularity of his "Stage" series, which at one point was second in audience ratings only to Foster Hewitt's "Hockey Night in Canada." Popularity has its liabilities, he felt, because "having more listeners means you are subject to more pressure groups. This can be inhibiting, you grow cautious." To overcome the pressures, he would follow a particularly provocative play with something bland. He would eliminate profanity as a trade-off for keeping controversial themes such as abortion, politics, racial discrimination, or sex. At one point words such as "hell," "God," "damn," or "brothel" were formally blacklisted by the CBC. Even in a warning about profanity, program director Charles Jennings refused to write the word "goddamn," spelling it "G-d d-m." The CBC chairman at the time complained he'd heard four "hells," one "bloody," and four "damns" in a single show. "All profane, indecent or blasphemous language is absolutely forbidden," a head office memo instructed. Occasionally the CBC allowed "darn" to be substituted for "damn," or "heck" for "hell." Allan and the chief news editor, Dan McArthur, got nowhere in pointing out the feebleness of saying, "Out darn spot," "War is heck," or "Till heck freezes over."

"I remember 'Gee' was cut out of one of our scripts because it was felt it was short for 'Jesus,'" says Lloyd Bochner.

The same fear of offending the audience led CBC executives to worry about sexual allusions in music. Jennings, a convivial man of the world, nevertheless sought to eliminate such suggestive lyrics as "I want to be loved." He said it was "lamentable" that 40 per cent of popular music had sexy inferences. Even after much discussion and many meetings, the CBC failed to find the dividing line between sexy and romantic.

As absorbed as he was by his work, Allan still took time to enjoy drinking and women. He was married and divorced twice, and, says Pierre Berton, who had known him since his Vancouver student days, "Andrew drove a lot of women mad. They were crazy for him because he was charming, witty, and lots of fun."

Frances Hyland remembers drinking with Andrew after rehearsal when she and other actors would gather to sip and listen to him. "He would hold court, drinking his Scotch and displaying his knowledge and his anecdotes. He spoke so well, words were what he relied on for his wooing. He was powerful and charming, and I don't wonder that women fell for him."

Writer, broadcaster, and social activist June Callwood, who had never finished high school, sat at Andrew's Celebrity Club table soaking up his conversation. "I paid attention and I learned a lot from him," she says. "He knew everything. He sort of took me on, told me what authors I ought to be reading. To hear Andrew put together a sentence changed the way you phrased your own thoughts, and you tried to rise to the level of the company you were in. He was a kind man, but there was also a deep sadness in him."

Andrew would entertain his office girls as well as female actors and writers. Mary DePoe remembers when she was a young, impressionable office clerk that "he'd take us off and ply us with pink ladies, a dreadful drink of gin and cream and pink colouring, which you drank with a straw while he had his Scotch on ice. But he was a wonderful raconteur with stories about actors and plays and what he had done."

"A pretty face had a fatal attraction for him," says Mavor Moore. Allan delighted in a sign hanging in the CBC announcers' lounge that had been left over from the building's days as the Havergal Girls School. "The sign was over a bell pusher," remembers Barry Morse, "and it said, 'If you want a mistress in the night, ring the bell.'" It was rung a lot by the announcers, but nobody ever came.

Allan always seemed to be attended by beautiful women, but Berton says that Allan's real problem was that he was impotent. DePoe remembers Allan's wife complaining to her friends about his impotence and talking about it at parties. Lister Sinclair says the sexual weakness added to Allan's woes as the years rolled by. "There would be embarrassing parties," says Sinclair, "where his wife would loudly explain to everyone about Andrew's sexual failings. It was not only embarrassing but it was boring, and it was always the same speech. She really gave him a very hard time."

Allan had always drunk and smoked heavily, but his drinking got out of control after he made a fatal plunge into television a few years after its beginnings in Canada in 1952. He had been the cock of the walk in radio for nearly two decades, one of the world's masters of radio drama. Now he viewed sourly what he felt were TV barbarians taking over the CBC with clichéd programming that soaked up everybody's attention and money and smothered radio. "When television came along, Andrew lost his path," says Hyland. "He really didn't like it at all." Sinclair says, "Andrew was determined not to like television – he was afraid of it." Most of the radio producers and stars also initially scorned television. "Everybody spitballed television as being vulgar and crude," says pioneer TV producer Sydney Newman. "It was never regarded as enlightening."

"Andrew shut himself off deliberately, almost violently, from television, pretending it didn't exist," says Morse. "But it became more and more evident that radio was diminishing in its impact and television was increasing. Then, very bravely, he decided to have a go at it."

He was almost fifty years old, an exhausted volcano, but still with a few sparks left that he tried to use for television. He handed over the "Stage" productions to Esse Ljungh in 1955 and, swallowing his pride and many of his principles, called the head of TV drama, Sydney Newman, whom he regarded as an intellectual inferior. "Sydney, I've been a damn fool all these years," Newman remembers Allan saying. "I should have gone into television years and years ago. I would like now to get into television."

Newman was thrilled to have the giant of radio drama move to TV and gave him a courtroom drama to produce. "But I made it clear I was going to be boss," Newman says. He told Allan he would vet all scripts because of concerns of the advertising agencies.

Television was a whole new world for Allan, technically and creatively, but his first show was a success. Trouble brewed, however, with the second show. "I went to the rehearsal and was making notes," Newman says, "when suddenly he says out loud, 'Well, look who's here. The head of drama to tell me what to do.'"

Lloyd Bochner was performing in that second show and remembers everything going wrong. One of the cameras failed during the live production, which led to an argument between the technicians and Allan that was so raucous it almost drowned out the play's dialogue. "The screaming, the frantic gestures, the tearing of hair," says Bochner. "One could hear Andrew rending himself to pieces. It was terrible, horrendous."

Newman was appalled both at the disdainful treatment he was getting from Allan and by the production itself. "He was just so fucking arrogant," says Newman. "And then after that he just degenerated – failed miserably. It was sad, sad, sad. He had been such a lustrous, wonderful man and then suddenly to be a nobody with nobody giving a shit about Andrew Allan anymore. Imagine swallowing that bitter bile."

"It was television that really did Andrew in," says Morse. "I never saw him impaired by booze until he got into television. He went from omniscience, omnipotence, and infallibility to being a rather frail and uncertain beginner."

Allan had burned out. He sought to escape through alcohol from what he called "a dark time living on the edge of despair." Lister Sinclair says, "He was the kind of alcoholic who would have three double Scotches at lunch and then rehearse all afternoon as if he were stone-cold sober and then would go back to drinking after rehearsal." Almost every night he would sit sipping at his own table in a corner of the Celebrity Club across the street from the CBC, where he would be joined by people wanting to talk to him or, more likely, listen to his stories.

Heavy drinking and heavy smoking were widespread among the stars of radio's golden age, including John Drainie, Tommy Tweed, and J. Frank Willis, with the handsome Willis the leading toper. An icon in Canadian broadcasting since his dramatic reportage from the Moose River, Nova Scotia, mine disaster of 1936, Willis was known as Peck's bad boy of radio. His wife once admonished him about his drinking, warning, "We're having a dinner party tonight, and if you come home and you've been drinking, I'm going to cut off half your mustache." He came home drunk, and while asleep that night, she did indeed cut off half his mustache. While co-hosting a show with Willis, Don Harron watched Willis give the opening line and then fall forward on his face. He didn't awake until the program was over.

Boozing seemed an integral part of the radio business at the time. Even the head of the CBC, Gladstone Murray, had a reputation for often being drunk before noon. Mavor Moore recalls first seeing Murray, whom he describes as "a stoned ostrich," rising to make a speech at a Canadian Club luncheon in Toronto, beginning, "Ladies and gentlemen . . . ," and then slowly sliding out of sight under the table.

For performers, however, drinking and live radio didn't mix. This was vividly demonstrated in a radio production involving Frank Willis, Broadway star John Carradine, and several others. Between rehearsal and the live show, Willis and his colleagues had a highly liquid dinner, during which they offered repeated toasts to Shakespeare, the Queen, President Roosevelt, Mackenzie King, King's dog, and each other. On the show,

Carradine, who was used to acting on a full quart, was appalled at Willis's slow and mumbling pace and whispered loudly, "Speak up, for Christ's sake! Speak up!" Meanwhile, trying to compensate for the performers' slowness, maestro Sir Ernest MacMillan sped up his orchestra, sounding, Mavor Moore says, "as if he had a train to catch."

Half a dozen years after his television failure and the subsequent dark days of alcoholism, Allan was helped back to sober creative productivity by CBC Radio program director Harry Boyle, a writer for many of Allan's productions who had himself climbed out of an alcoholic black hole. For Allan, it was a conquest of intelligence and determination over alcoholism and despair. With characteristic ceremony, he took his last drink at the Celebrity Club just as the bar was closing, saluted his friends, and the next day poured all the liquor he had at home down the sink.

Boyle steered Allan into writing stylistic essays for the radio network morning show hosted initially by Bruno Gerussi and later by Peter Gzowski. "At first he was nervous and apprehensive, but he did it extremely well," said Gerussi. "For me, sitting across the table," says Gzowski, "there was the literacy of his essays, all the tradition he brought, his great sense of storytelling and great sense of delivery. His essays were filigrees of the lightest sort. I felt such awe and respect for him. One awful morning in the winter of 1974, he did not show up at the studio. We sent a messenger to his apartment. He had had a stroke." A few days later, at age sixty-six, he died.

"I wish I had told him how much what he had put on the radio had meant to me, as it must have meant to so many thousands of others," says Gzowski.

Reflecting on Allan's contribution to radio, Mavor Moore says, "There are lots of people with vision without the craft to make it happen. Andrew had both. But he was a loner, really. A man so very much alone."

Shortly before he died, Andrew Allan had said, "To survive you need a good capacity to absorb disappointments. You also need a phone-answering service."

Your Old Pal Rawhide

The national bonding provided by the dramas of Andrew Allan was reinforced by the single most controversial character of radio's golden age – Rawhide, an eccentric old coot invented by Max Ferguson, a toothy imp with an Irish heritage. Rawhide was born out of Ferguson's hatred for the country music he was forced to play on a morning show in Halifax in his début as a CBC program host in 1946.

"I will do the housekeeping around here, dust the desks, wash the floor, anything, but take me off that show," he begged his boss. Ferguson, who originally had wanted to be a teacher, was mortified at the prospect of introducing tunes like "I Rapped on the Hearse Window, Granny, But You Did Not Look Out," and he was appalled at having to introduce a musical request for "We Shall Gather by the River" that came from a mother who said she wanted it played "in memory of my daughter what was drowned there." The program, called "After Breakfast Breakdown," was one of the most popular in the Maritimes at the time, and Ferguson's bosses were unmoved by his pleas.

"Well," he warned them, "I can't be responsible for the way I'm going to do it," and on the spur of the moment as he began the program, he lowered his voice to a wheezing cackle, called himself Rawhide, and proceeded to pan every country singer in sight. One of them was the legendary Hank Snow – the Yodelling Ranger and idol of the Maritimes. Rawhide called him the Yodelling Village Idiot and after playing one of Snow's songs said, "And there goes Hank moseying off down the trail into the flaming sunset not realizing there's a four-hundred-foot drop at the end of the trail waiting to claim him for that Great Studio in the Sky, and not a moment too soon."

Ferguson's boss, Syd Kennedy, burst into the studio, white-faced with anger, and warned him to leave the studio quickly to avoid being lynched. He also told him to apologize. "I just made a very unfortunate mistake," Ferguson told his audience the following day. "I meant no disparagement of Hank Snow. I was talking about another yodelling idiot I once knew in Upper Canada."

To Ferguson's consternation, Snow once insisted on coming to the studio to be interviewed by Rawhide. "He was about five feet tall, wore a ten-gallon hat, and had a tiny, little face," remembers Ferguson. "He drove up in a huge limousine and asked me, 'Rawhide, is there any song you'd like me to sing?' I said, 'Hank, would you happen to know "The Strain from the Opera Hernia"?' 'I don't believe I know that one,' Hank replied, and he sang one of his wretched cowboy songs."

Ferguson also got into difficulties with another country music hero, Wilf Carter. "Wilf and Hank hated each other," says Ferguson. Once while interviewing Carter, Ferguson said he'd heard a report that Carter had been killed in a car accident and wondered how the rumour had started. "That son of a bitch Hank Snow spread the rumour around and I'll get him for it," snapped Carter.

Carter's mother lived in New Brunswick and regularly listened to the Rawhide show, often to her consternation when Ferguson would make fun of her son. "Wilf's recordings always opened up with him saying, 'Throw another log on the fire, boys, and I'll tell you about my grey-haired mother,'" says Ferguson. "So I'd imitate Wilf's voice and talk about throwing his grey-haired mother on the fire."

"I don't think Wilf would like that type of thing," Mrs. Carter wrote to Ferguson, who had to send her a letter of apology. He also had to apologize after a complaint that he was favouring Wilf Carter over Hank Snow was brought up in the House of Commons. A brother and sister in Lunenburg, Nova Scotia, had written their MP protesting that one morning Rawhide had played two Wilf Carter songs to one of Hank Snow's. Ferguson was warned to stand by in case he had to fly to Ottawa to face a parliamentary inquisition about his alleged Carter favouritism. "It finally blew over," he says. "But thereafter I tried to balance Carter and Snow because they were neck and neck in popularity."

Responding to a letter from a New Brunswick woman who also accused him of shamefully neglecting Snow in favour of Carter, he lashed back, privately hoping to stir up a controversy that would lead him to be taken off the show. He read her letter and her name and address on the air and then, sniffing and blowing his nose in feigned remorse, responded, "I would be within my rights to say something nasty, but I'm just not built that way. Instead, I'm merely going to turn the other cheek and ask you, in the spirit of true Christian friendship, to drop dead!" To his astonishment, the woman wrote back, "Well, 'Rawhide' old pal . . . I asked for it. No hard feelings."

Ferguson didn't get off so easily, however, when he offended the CBC music librarian by playing "Fella from Fortune," a Newfoundland song about a woman who has an illegitimate baby by a man from Fortune. "He came charging in," says Ferguson, "and said, 'I want that record destroyed!' Then he grabbed it and smashed it."

Ferguson's seemingly uncontrollable mischievousness got him into trouble sometimes when he filled in for the Maritimes farm and fishery commentator, Keith Morrow. In reporting fish landings, Ferguson would say, "Five thousand pounds of haddock were landed in port, three thousand pounds of hake, six thousand pounds of cod, twenty-seven pounds of shit . . ." and on he would carry with the report. Sometimes his ad lib would slip by listeners, but sometimes they would call in to ask, "Twenty-seven pounds of *what*?"

Ferguson also added spark to station breaks, as when he once came on after an NBC announcer had said, "This is NBC, the home of ninety-nine million American listeners." Ferguson followed immediately with, "This is CBC Halifax, where there are just two of us listening – me and my engineer."

Ferguson disliked country music so much that he tried to make his morning show pass more quickly by creating a cast of characters around Rawhide. "Not knowing or caring who might be listening and strictly for my own amusement," he says, he introduced a range of people who came into the studio through a creaking door. There was Granny, sweet-voiced, corrupt, and malicious, who hated everybody. Marvin Mellowbell was pompous and self-adoring, and the Gomer Brothers were farmers who ran an illegal hard-cider bootlegging business and on the side sold 155-proof eggs from white Leghorns stoned on fermenting apple mash. There was also Little Harold, an imaginary black widow spider who once sank his fangs into Granny and was promptly pulverized by her umbrella and rushed to hospital. "A plucky little patient," said Rawhide, "who spun his own oxygen tent." Harold seemed so real to listeners that Ferguson got dozens of get-well cards for him, several knitted miniature suits, and food parcels, three of which included praying mantises "in case he didn't like the hospital food."

In another medical skit, Ferguson had Granny and a friend at the Toronto General Hospital try to save the CBC some money by grafting several performers' heads onto one body, thereby requiring only one performance fee to be paid. The hospital demanded an apology and several CBC performers did as well. This and other skits were literate lunacy, and Ferguson played all the roles with his different voices, settling arguments among the characters with his Rawhide voice and adding in his own sound effects. He let his imagination fly, following only the sketchiest of notes for the skits and ad libbing his characters in and out of confrontations and hair-raising misadventures.

The inspiration for the loony Rawhide characters came from Ferguson's first announcing job at CFPL in London, Ontario, where he met a practical joker named Doug Trowell, who later became a senior radio executive. Trowell imitated on the air everything from an elephant to a priest. One of Ferguson's jobs at CFPL was hosting "In the Chapel," a fifteen-minute program of hymns and Bible stories told by a guest minister. As one program went to air, the minister hadn't turned up. Ferguson was in the middle of an apology when in through the studio door burst what Ferguson assumed was the minister. "Jesus, Max," he said, "I'm sorry. I ran like a son of a bitch down from St. Paul's." Too late, Ferguson realized it was Trowell, who had removed his tie and put a white cloth at the front of his shirt. Trowell continued, "Well, I'll start off the morning with a couple of dirty Bible stories that really break me up."

"I was terrified," says Ferguson. "He was swearing and telling lewd stories, and when our time was up I said ever so sweetly, 'Won't you join us next week for another quiet moment in the chapel?' then on came the hymns, and I just collapsed."

Only the next day did Ferguson realize it had all been a hoax by Trowell and the technician, who had switched them off at the beginning of the show. The station had been playing religious music while Ferguson was listening to Trowell's scatological biblical stories.

As Rawhide, Ferguson ridiculed every VIP in sight, broadening his targets from country singers to political, business, and religious leaders, farmers, and Hollywood stars. Nobody was safe from the pungent wit of Rawhide and his pals. "Meaningless ravings and tripe, couched in the poorest possible illiterate English and an insult to the intelligence of the Canadian public," fumed Toronto Conservative MP Douglas

Gooderham Ross. "A boorish sort of nincompoop," said another MP, and Rev. Stuart Ivison, an Ottawa Baptist minister, said Rawhide was spouting "sacrilege, blasphemy, evil . . . something that Godless Soviet Russia could hardly improve on." What made it worse for the more stolid listeners was that when Rawhide and his demented friends were moved to Toronto in 1949 and put on the full CBC network, the show followed the morning devotion program.

As a result of a storm in Parliament over something he had said, Ferguson was asked by the Parliamentary Press Gallery to come to its annual dinner in 1949 – a long night of heavy drinking, raucous singing, and sharp-tongued roasting among journalists and politicians. Prime Minister Louis St. Laurent, Conservative Leader George Drew, and Governor General Viscount Alexander were among the guests who joined in the frivolity and saw Ferguson imitate Winston Churchill in one skit. The entire evening was a scene not dissimilar to the chaos of a Rawhide sketch, only this was real. "I circulated at the cocktail party before the dinner and stumbled onto CBC chairman Davidson Dunton," says Ferguson. "As we were chatting, a cabinet minister, Chubby Power, lurched towards us with his hand outstretched to shake hands, but he missed by a foot and went crashing into the wall behind us with his hand still out. Two commissionaires carried him out.

"Then George Drew came over, and he was shaking my hand when all of a sudden a *Time* reporter who had written a scathing article about Drew came over. Drew dropped my hand and ploughed the reporter in the mouth.

"They had two commissionaires there who did nothing all night but pick up bodies and carry them out. It was like the final scene in *Hamlet*."

Playful moments for Ferguson were not confined to Parliament or his programs. He and his announcing colleagues had more than their share of mischievous off-air moments. One victim of their devilry was the head of the CBC in the Maritimes, a spit-and-polish wartime navy captain and hero named Ted Briggs. Built like a mix of British bulldog and Japanese sumo wrestler, Captain Briggs, who was called "Uncle Bulgy" behind his back, enjoyed his rum and his own practical jokes. One time he went with Ferguson and CBC Halifax executive Syd Kennedy on an assignment to cover the Annapolis Valley Apple Blossom Festival. As a prank one night,

Briggs sawed the legs of Kennedy's hotel-room bed so that when Kennedy climbed in, it collapsed. The next day, while Briggs was taking a shower, Kennedy and Ferguson hatched a retaliatory plot. "I went into the bathroom," says Ferguson, "and yelled at the tubby figure with water splashing all over him, 'Captain Briggs, there is quite an attractive young blonde girl at the door who wants to speak to you.' 'I'll be out in just a minute,' the captain said.

"He came out, wrapping a towel around his middle, and as he opened the door to peek out, we shoved him from behind, pulled the towel back, and locked the door. Then we phoned the front desk and complained, 'There is a nude man running about the hallway, pounding on the doors and shouting.'" Briggs later commented, "Damned embarrassing out there in the hallway." After much commotion, the punctilious, all-powerful CBC Maritimes director was allowed back into the room, but for years thereafter the CBC was banned from that hotel.

None of Max Ferguson's CBC colleagues was more mischievous, however, than Allan McFee, a legendary practical joker, misfit, and onetime star athlete and choirboy at Toronto's élite Upper Canada College. When they first met after Ferguson had moved to Toronto from Halifax, Ferguson said to McFee that he brought greetings from his old friend Captain Briggs. "Oh God, that piece of excrement," McFee responded. "You'll hate it here. You have my sympathy." It was the beginning of a friendship and partnership that has lasted into their retirement years.

Ferguson was transfixed by the things McFee would do. "I would sit in with him on a broadcast he did for hospitals and sanitariums. He'd say, 'This recording goes out,' and he'd mention a name and then say, 'and we certainly hope you enjoy this because, you son of a bitch, you probably won't live to hear it another time.' I was petrified, but I didn't know until later that he would shut his mike off just before speaking the offending words."

A particular joy for McFee was introducing an afternoon soap opera called "Terry and the Pirates" that was fed in from New York. The program would open with a street scene evoked by the sounds of rickshaws and gongs and a multitude of Chinese voices. McFee's job was to announce "Terry and the Pirates," and then the recorded sounds would play for half a minute or so. Amid the cacophony, however, McFee would open his mike, adopt a sing-song accent, and castigate his bosses, saying, "Oh crazy knucklehead Ernie Bushnell, he one stupid man. Velly dumb, velly useless. He not earn his money. Oh Charlie Jennings, he sit on big fat bum all day. Big dumb Charlie Jennings," and on he would rant, adding in the names of all his bosses and rivals. His comments were mixed in with the street noises and could be understood only by particularly sharp-eared listeners. On one occasion as McFee was spouting his Chinese-accented invective, the broadcast line from New York failed. McFee did not find out until later that only his voice had been going out over the air.

He also would interject noises into newscasts, invent odd-sounding towns for weather reports, and on the "Ma Perkins" radio serial, he'd belch into the microphone in the middle of Ma's conversations. He'd open his mike and noisily blow his nose during a French horn passage in a symphony, and sometimes he would interrupt with the sounds of throat clearing, breaking wind, or vomiting into a poetry reading or a musical recital. "His uninvited appearance was in just about every program that went out over the CBC Toronto transmitter," says Ferguson. Although frequently suspected, he was rarely caught in the act, and the interruptions would be covered up by technicians who reported "unidentified noise on the line."

Ferguson remembers that when he and McFee worked on the Rawhide program together, "he would say some awful thing and break me up just as I tried to say, 'Good morning.' McFee then would say, 'Max, enough is enough. You're not being professional, and you owe it to your audience to shape up and stop laughing.' He would do that to me about every second morning." Whenever they did a show together, Don Harron was terrified McFee would make him laugh on the air. "McFee would do anything," says Harron. "He wouldn't bring out his private member, but close to that."

Not infrequently McFee would be late for live newscasts, leaving dead air for a minute or so. His tardiness got so bad that the radio assignment officer would occasionally pin a note on his jacket that read, "My name is Little Allan McFee. If you find me wandering the halls at airtime, send me to Studio H."

When McFee and Lorraine Thomson co-hosted a morning talk show, his late arrivals often caused problems. Once when a station break was coming up, McFee was nowhere to be found, and the technician told Thomson she would have to do it. At the time, she was new to radio and, as a performer, technically not supposed to do station breaks. She was forced to do it this time, however, nervous as she was, but instead of saying, "Stay tuned for the CJBC News" she said, "Stay stuned for the C.J. Boo Soo Knees." "McFee came in laughing and I could have killed him," she says. Thomson had an equally traumatic broadcast misadventure a couple of decades later co-hosting Eaton's Santa Claus parade with sportscaster Ted Reynolds. Opening the show, she enthusiastically welcomed viewers to "the seventy-sixth annual Simpson's Santa Claus parade." "Ted's eyes practically popped out of his head, and I realized I'd said Simpson's, the deadly rival of Eaton's. I hoped the street would open and swallow me up. I hoped I was dreaming. But I wasn't. After that, I said Eaton's a hundred times to try to make up. They never did ask me to do the parade again."

While McFee's on-air gaffes were mostly premeditated, those by Thomson and others were spontaneous, such as when host Neil Leroy, while opening the show "Court of Opinion," complimented colleague Kate Aitken for being on Canada's best-dressed list, saying, "I want to congratulate our panellist in having been chosen as one of Canada's ten best-breasted women."

A similar blunder was made by Peter Whittall, who gained fame as TV's Mr. Fix It but earlier had been a farm broadcaster in Winnipeg. While doing his noon program, Whittall got word that his wife had just given birth to a rather small baby. "Gosh," he exclaimed to his farm audience as a note was slipped to him, "you don't hardly get your seed back anymore."

If Whittall's comment was unexpected, so was that of a five-year-old listener to veteran CBC announcer Harry Brown's "Uncle Harry" phone-in program in St. John's. When, on air, Brown asked the youngster what was the first thing his father did when he came home, the boy replied, "Pee in the sink!"

One morning when he and McFee were working together, Ferguson arrived at the CBC to find the hallways and windows smeared with green and yellow slime. McFee admitted he was responsible, telling Ferguson, "Getting a can of asparagus tips out of the refrigerator last night, I spilled some on the floor and made such an obscene splatter that I thought I'd bring some tins down to the CBC, and I went around the building last night smearing them all over the place."

Inside or outside the studio, McFee would verbally harangue his superiors, much to his colleagues' apprehension. Ferguson and McFee once stepped outside on a fire escape for a breath of fresh air when they noticed Ernie Bushnell, the CBC general manager, walking below them. "You down there," McFee said. "Yes, you! You red-faced excrement. Get inside and make an effort to do something for the money you're being paid." Bushnell looked up, scowled, and walked away, saying not a word.

One boss he couldn't bamboozle, however, was Keith Morrow, who had come from the Maritimes to run the CBC Toronto operation. When Morrow asked him, "What are you trying to prove?" McFee replied, "I'll tell you exactly what I'm trying to prove. I think management is so craven around here that it's become a game with me to see how far I can push them before they stand their ground." "Well," Morrow said, "I'm going to stand my ground now. I'm dismissing you for two weeks."

"From then on he just idolized Keith Morrow," says Ferguson.

Of all the legends about McFee, none is more memorable than his continuing, bitter feud with Elwood Glover, a handsome, smooth-talking fellow announcer. "He just hated Elwood," says Ferguson. "McFee always said to everybody that he had nothing but contempt for Elwood and the way Glover did things," says Lloyd Robertson, who worked with both men at the CBC. "Glover was very smooth and took himself very seriously. But with McFee, you always knew something crazy was going on in his head."

Once, on his noontime television show, Glover had both Ferguson and McFee on to mark a Rawhide anniversary. He totally ignored McFee, however, addressing not a single question to him. Finally Ferguson said, "Allan, do you want to say something?" McFee replied, "No. I don't talk to him."

"Elwood was petty and bad-tempered," says Mary DePoe. "And that probably set McFee off. McFee was just McFee. He could be charming, but he was totally mad. There was one time when McFee had his hands on Elwood's throat in the studio. They were right up against the control-room window, and McFee was threatening to strangle him."

McFee once tried to asphyxiate another perceived enemy at the CBC, producer Drew Crossan, who had riled McFee by criticizing him for not picking up his cues quickly enough. "When I point my finger at you, you speak," Crossan had lectured him after a program. McFee determined to have revenge and decided he would kill Crossan by asphyxiation.

"McFee backed up his banged-up old car to the air intake at the radio building, stuck a hose on his exhaust pipe, and ran it into the building's intake," says Lloyd Robertson. "McFee vowed he was going to kill Crossan," Ferguson says. "When I saw his car running in the parking lot, I told him, 'You forgot to turn off your ignition.' He said, 'No, no. Leave it alone. That goes right into the studio where Crossan works, and it's worth a tank of gas a day to get him.' This went on for a week." In the end the carbon-monoxide gas was detected by another producer, John Kannawin, who was working in the studio and who ordered everyone out. McFee was not fond of Kannawin either, and when he discovered he'd been gassing the wrong target, he was philosophical. "Oh well, if I didn't get Crossan, Kannawin was second best," he told Ferguson.

Among McFee's numerous hates was his car, which he would frequently kick and swear at. Once, he got so angry at the car he drove it to work in second gear and told fellow announcer Alex Trebek, "I taught it a lesson, boy! It won't misbehave again."

Bruno Gerussi remembered McFee telling him that he refused to shovel the snow in front of his home. When the elderly woman who lived next door complained to McFee, he said, "Why don't you clear it yourself?" The next day as he was leaving for the CBC, McFee saw the frail old woman chipping away at the ice on his sidewalk. "You're doing very well, my dear," he said cheerily. "Keep it up and be sure it's done by the time I get home."

Once, McFee and Tommy Tweed arrived early for their program "Hohner Harmonica Hour" and set all the studio clocks two minutes fast. The unknowing producer cued them at what he thought was the correct time and heard McFee say, "This is the Horror Hormonical Hour," followed by McFee and Tweed launching into obscene abuse of each other. Two minutes later when the real program start time began, they carried on smoothly, while the producer lay paralysed on the control-room floor.

Larry Mann, a veteran CBC performer now in Hollywood, swears he once heard McFee do a station break by saying, "This is the Canadian Backbusting Constipation." He would sometimes terrify colleagues when announcing a station break by saying, "This is the fucking CBC Radio network," but punching the microphone off just as he swore. Sometimes, however, he wasn't quite quick enough, and he was almost always the leader in what was known as the CBC "fault report," which recorded the miscues of all announcers.

McFee's final years of broadcasting saw him hosting a late-night radio show appropriately called "Eclectic Circus" for "all those out there in vacuum land." In his old age, living in a retirement home, he still nursed his hatred for Elwood Glover. With his memory failing, he had little comprehension of the incidents Ferguson regaled him with on his visits until one day Ferguson mentioned Glover. "I'm sorry to have to tell you this," Ferguson said, "but Elwood Glover died recently." "Oh, that's too bad," said McFee, recognizing the name. Ferguson was pleased with the recognition but puzzled by McFee's new concern for his old enemy. "Yes, it's too bad," McFee mused. "It would have been so much better if he'd lived a few more years and suffered a bit more."

For all his success and prominence as Rawhide, in 1954 the CBC was paying Ferguson $2,700 a year as a staff announcer and refused to give him any further annual salary increments, or "excrements" as he called them. Frustrated, he quit, but program director Harry Boyle, stage-managing in the background, organized it so that after Ferguson resigned he continued with the program and sold it to the CBC. That gave him $15,000 a year.

He took the money and his show back to Halifax, where he continued to host it before finally retiring Rawhide after seventeen years. Ferguson then plunged into television as host of the local CBC dinnertime news program, "Gazette." "Those were the best years of my life," he says. They were also the most adventuresome thanks to all the things that can and do go wrong with live television. Once, an English submariner brought his pet monkey named Clement Attlee to the studio. It promptly bit Ferguson's finger and fled to the ceiling, where it swung and chattered all over the studio before being caught. The time he was sliced by a fencing master, it was Ferguson's own fault. "*En garde!*" he said as he began a demonstration with the expert. "I'd always imagined that if I just kept my foil going rapidly enough, like a windshield wiper, it would be very difficult to get through." It wasn't. Within a few seconds, a sword penetrated Ferguson's defence, and, he says, "I looked down to see blood pouring out of my side. They'd forgotten to put protectors on the end of the swords. The producer, Bill Langstroth, was furious. But I was bleeding."

He also had a close call while interviewing a 350-pound Japanese sumo wrestler famous for his "sleeper hold." "Let's try it," said Ferguson, whereupon the wrestler grabbed him and Ferguson went out like a light. "The first thing I knew, his arm was around me and he cut off my windpipe," recalls Ferguson. "It was an awful feeling of smothering. I couldn't get any air. My head was throbbing, my lungs were burning, and I was sure my eyeballs were going to burst. My last conscious thought was that this was a psychopathic killer. Then I thought a month had gone by. Slowly a little red light came into focus, and I realized I was lying on the studio floor. Langstroth quickly put up a slide and played music while the CBC switchboard lit up with five hundred phone calls. They and everyone in the control room were scared stiff and thought I was dying." Langstroth burst into the studio and shouted at the wrestler's manager, "You get that ape out of here or I'll call the police."

One Christmas Ferguson brought his British bulldog, Toughy, to the studio. For most of the program, the dog snoozed contentedly under a sofa. Then towards the program's end, Santa Claus came rollicking into the studio shouting, "Ho! Ho! Ho!" and carrying a lighted plum pudding. Toughy snarled, bared his fangs, and leapt at Santa, clamping his frothing jaws on Santa's rear end. They both crashed into the Christmas tree, which caught fire from the lighted plum pudding. "We said, 'Have a Merry Christmas,' and went off the air," Ferguson recalls.

Another awkward TV moment involved an Irish jumping horse and a boxer dog. They came into the studio with their owner, whom Ferguson interviewed. The producer wanted to have the camera focused on the animals at various times, and so the camera operator took a close-up the Irish hunter. "The only trouble was," Ferguson recalls, "the horse had an erection right down to the floor. It was a horse with five legs." The operator quickly panned over to the dog who, by strange happenstance, also had a highly visible erection. After that, the camera stayed focused on Ferguson and his guest.

On the program "Tabloid," Ferguson once interviewed the author of a book on pornography. When the interview was over, his colleague, the announcer John O'Leary, congratulated him. "It was so informative and I learned so much," O'Leary said. "For instance, I always thought fellatio meant stamp-collecting and cunnilingus was an Irish airline."

A highlight of Ferguson's career was meeting the Queen and Prince Philip at an Ottawa dinner. It was marred slightly, however, by his tablemate, the Liberal cabinet minister Judy LaMarsh. Amid the stiff formality of the dinner, LaMarsh, in a loud voice heard by the prime minister and the Queen, said to Ferguson, "God, I'll never forget my first royal dinner. I didn't have a pot to piss in, and Mike Pearson said he wanted me to come reasonably dressed. So I tried to get into my brassière, but I couldn't make the damn thing hook up at the back since I'd put on a little weight. I went across the apartment hall to my neighbour, but he couldn't hook it up either. So I said to myself, I don't give a damn if my tits fall into the soup, I'm just going to go without a brassière." "She was so boisterous, the Queen was looking over at us and Pearson was frowning," says Ferguson, "but she never stopped talking."

At the same dinner, Ferguson, for no apparent reason, provoked the wrath of Prince Philip, who, on shaking hands, remarked, "It's my opinion that every CBC announcer should be taken out and shot!"

Over the years many a politician, church minister, and VIP thought that Rawhide should be taken out and shot, but for most Canadians, he was one of our national symbols thanks to his incisive irreverence. He let us laugh at ourselves while learning about ourselves.

The Unhappy Happy Gang

Rivalling the popularity of Rawhide and the plays of Andrew Allan in the golden years of radio was that "slaphappy, Hap, Hap, Happy Gang."

Two million Canadians tuned in to "The Happy Gang" in its heyday to listen to emcee Bert Pearl, Canada's first entertainment superstar, lead his Gangsters through an early afternoon half-hour of frenzied effervescence, corny jokes, syrupy sentimentality, and sprightly music. Beginning on the CBC Trans-Canada network in 1937, the Gang's happy talk, giggling, and patriotic fervour – they played "There'll Always Be an England" almost every day during the war – lifted the nation's spirits through the last throes of the Depression, the Second World War, and the postwar recovery.

Their own spirits, however, were often assailed by backstage jealousies, bickering, and bitterness. Pearl was a skinny little bundle of nervous energy whose on-air enthusiasm hid his own obsessive worries, tensions, and autocratic style. On the air he was called "that slaphappy chappie" and "Old Pappy," but he always worried he was going to crack up, which he eventually did. Still, despite the anxieties and discord, "The Happy Gang" was a delightful program Canadians shared each weekday, matched only by the later and more sophisticated slapstick comedy of Wayne and Shuster.

As a six-year-old, Bert Shapira was plunking the piano in his Winnipeg home. Not long afterwards he was on local radio doing impersonations, earning himself the nickname Radio's Cheerful Little Earful. As he grew older, he crooned into a megaphone like Rudy Vallee and played the piano in dancehalls and vaudeville shows. In between shows he was a scholarship-winning student who dreamed of becoming a brain surgeon. The dream didn't last. He gave up his pre-med university studies, changed his last name to Pearl, and swept into show business, touring Western Canada as a pianist with a fan dancer and winding up in Toronto in 1934 playing piano for a CRBC house orchestra. Three years later the CBC asked the eager, bright-eyed Pearl to put together a summer replacement half-hour musical show. With Kathleen Stokes, who was known as Canada's Sweetheart of the Organ, Toronto Symphony violinist Blain Mathe, and trumpet player and composer Robert Farnon, Pearl began "The Happy Gang," which went on to captivate Canadian listeners for more than two decades.

Farnon was an ebullient man and a superb musician who later became famous in England as a composer and arranger; Mathe was a quiet, gentle soul who would play a mediating role in many of the future Gang squabbles; and Stokes provided both organ music and a multitude of infectious giggles. At the beginning Pearl was paid twelve dollars per show and the others five dollars.

To their surprise, and the CBC's, their frothy concoction was an instant hit, despite the competing and immensely popular radio soap operas of the day. Soon the Gang expanded, including over time the original four members plus: tenor and accordionist Eddie Allen, nicknamed the Swoon Goon; bass player Joe Niosi; clarinetist Cliff McKay, known as a Ton of Fun; trumpeter Bobby Gimby; band leader Bert Niosi; pianists Jimmy Namaro and Lou Snyder; and announcers Hugh Bartlett, Herb May, and Barry Wood.

One of the program's features was the Joke Pot, a repository of hokey, hoary old wisecracks and knee-slappers, such as Pearl's announcement "I think I'll go out and have my shoelaces pressed."

The banter was largely spontaneous. Chirping, "Remember, keep happy," Pearl led "the kids," as he called his cast, on frequent train tours of Canada, in one month performing twenty-eight one-night stands. In the Toronto studio, each show day they entertained 750 fans who would line up for hours before broadcast time at 1:15 P.M. Over the more than two decades of "The Happy Gang," two million fans came to watch the show, which always began with the signature sign-on of Blain Mathe rapping on his violin as a sound effect and the Gang shouting, "Knock, knock. Who's there? It's the Happy Gang! Well, come on in!"

Pearl was named Chief Happy Voice in the Sky by the Blood Indian band, and Manitoba named him to the Order of the Buffalo Hunt, the province's highest honour. The CBC had never before seen such a flood of fan mail as poured in for "The Happy Gang," whose members became instant nationwide celebrities and, because they all were highly talented, were much sought after by entertainment impresarios and orchestras. Several, in fact, had their own orchestras.

Busy as they were, they didn't have much time for horseplay, but occasionally a practical joke was played on Pearl. Once, in the years before they had a studio audience, the Gang set all the clocks fifteen minutes ahead. To the unknowing Pearl, things seemed to go wrong as soon as he opened what he thought was the live show. Eddie Allen, who always began by saying, "Hi, Mom," was introduced for his song, and instead of his usual greeting, he made a nasty crack about his mother. "And," he added, "I don't want to sing that damn song." Announcer Hugh Bartlett refused to read the commercial and told off-colour jokes, while the musicians all blew sour notes. Pearl was staggered, but soldiered on until the cast broke into laughter and told him of the joke. It didn't seem so funny to Pearl, however, and Kathleen Stokes said later, "We thought Bert was going to die."

It was not the practical jokes as much as the unrelenting pressures of the show, dissension among the Gang, and his own obsessive, anxiety-ridden style that drove Pearl into nervous exhaustion. "I died three times a day," he said, worrying, "I'm at the top and there's only one way to go." His bubbly on-air personality was "a difficult thing to live up to," he later said. "It's hard to know where the synthetics end and the real begins, where the person is and where the performer begins."

Pearl's worst moment was when *Maclean's* magazine writer June Callwood exposed the inner turmoil of Pearl and his Gang. " 'The Happy Gang,' " she wrote, "has one outstanding peculiarity. When it's not on the air, it isn't happy." The Gang, she said, was beset by burning jealousy and rivalry, adding, "It is entirely possible one half of the 'Gang' would cheer happily if the other half were fired." She said Hugh Bartlett lusted after Pearl's job and described Gang members scowling at one another over who got how much airtime, complaining about insufficient rehearsal time, and resenting Pearl's sarcastic criticisms of their work. "I think I was at least as tough on myself as I was on anybody else," Pearl later said. "There was disillusionment, disappointment both in myself and a few people. . . . It's not so unusual in show business where there are so many different temperaments." "We weren't the same kind of people," Bobby Gimby admitted.

In the Callwood article, Pearl said, "The kids cut me up at times, but they don't quit." Later he said he had been deeply hurt by the article because "perhaps it was touching on some truths too closely." "There were the pressures of doing the show five days a week, dissension among the Gang, and this caused a certain amount of bitterness," he told TV interviewer Charles Templeton.

With his nerves frazzled and the Gang rebellious, Pearl cried to friends, "It's inhuman. I've got to get away before I crack up." But the brightest entertainment star in Canadian history to that time didn't get away. He had a nervous breakdown in 1955 and wound up in a sanitarium north of Toronto. As soon as he had recovered sufficiently, he fled from the show and from the country. He wanted anonymity, but what he found was oblivion. He flew to Hollywood, hoping to start afresh, hoping for a prominent role in American television, and all the time hoping the CBC would call him back to do a TV version of "The Happy Gang."

But none of that happened.

Living in an apartment a block from Grauman's Chinese Theatre in Hollywood, he found work as a rehearsal pianist for the network show of a fellow Winnipegger, singer Gisèle MacKenzie. He also played for her in a Las Vegas act and was a lounge pianist around Los Angeles. Later he got an administrative job with the Quality Light Meter Company in Los Angeles. In 1961 he did a "Where Is He Now?" interview for the CBC-TV show "Close-Up" and did a skit with Lorne Greene for a show marking the CBC's twenty-fifth anniversary. In the skit, Pearl was playing the piano when Greene, à la "Bonanza," rode up on a horse and commanded, "Play faster!" Pearl promptly did.

About the same time, Pearl's nephew persuaded him to go to Winnipeg to do a TV show produced by future "Front Page Challenge" producer Ray McConnell. "Bert was just wonderful until ten minutes to air," McConnell says. "I went into the make-up room, and he was sitting there with his head in his hands, sobbing, 'I can't do this. I just can't go on.' We spent the next eight minutes convincing him to go on, and at the last instant, he did."

In the late 1960s, producer Don Brown reunited the original four "Happy Gang" members, Pearl, Kathleen Stokes, Bob Farnon, and Blain Mathe for an interview on "Flashback." Before doing the show, Pearl sent Brown page after page of questions and instructions about the program. "He was a very precise person, a nitpicker," says Brown. The producer also found him "very conscious about being gay." Pearl told Brown that one reason he went to Los Angeles was that he felt more comfortable there than in Toronto, with what he called "my peculiarities." "A person who is different sticks out in Toronto, but not in Los Angeles," he said.

In his Los Angeles years, Pearl's bright blue eyes dulled and his eager assertiveness turned to wary defensiveness. A lifelong bachelor, he infrequently partied with Canadian friends, such as Lorne Greene or game-show host Monty Hall, who had achieved success in Hollywood. He later told another Winnipegger, singer Juliette, that when he did go to a party, "I stand in the corner, not even a member of the fringe, and ask myself, 'What am I doing here?' After the first six people come over and say, 'What are you in?' my answer is, 'I think I'm in trouble.' . . . I'm the only Canadian who came here and didn't make it. . . . When I was all harassed and pressed, I hoped for some anonymity, to be let alone for a while. Before I knew it, the anonymity became almost utter oblivion. . . . I've been disillusioned about many things, but when your own country forgets you, that's a real blow."

"There was a lot of tension on 'The Happy Gang,'" Juliette says. "Bert was very hurt the CBC didn't transfer the show to television, and he carried that chip on his shoulder to the day he died. He left Canada angry and bitter, and it affected his whole life from then on. He became reclusive."

Once when producer Norman Campbell was in Los Angeles directing "All In The Family," he accidentally dropped his light meter in the ocean. He gave it to a CBS colleague to see if it could be fixed. "The next day," Campbell says, "the production manager comes over and says, 'Your light meter is fixed.' I go over to a guy who has it in his hands, and it's Bert Pearl. Bert Pearl with my light meter? I paid him and found he worked for a little optical instrument company. We talked, and he seemed a very bitter person, very upset about what had happened to him at the CBC."

When Pearl abruptly left "The Happy Gang," tenor Eddie Allen took over as host for four years until, in June 1959, the CBC cancelled the program after twenty-two years and nearly five thousand shows – the longest-running program in Canadian broadcasting history to that time. As a replacement, the CBC brought in an up-and-coming young country singer, Tommy Hunter, who had made guest appearances on "The Happy Gang." He was known as the Singing Guitarist, and he featured Juliette on his first show.

Pearl made a nostalgic and briefly successful return to Canada in 1975 when he and several members of the Gang had a public reunion at the bandshell of the Canadian National Exhibition in Toronto. Thirty thousand die-hard fans – the biggest crowds ever at the bandshell – saw two presentations. Pearl had been afraid no one would come, but with his eyes sparkling and his voice chipper again, Pearl told the crowds, "I've waited for this . . . and right now I feel as if it was only yesterday." Kathleen Stokes was given two standing ovations, Eddie Allen sang 1940s tunes, Bobby Gimby trumpeted vintage "Happy Gang" melodies, and the shows ended with almost everyone in tears, singing "Those Were the Days."

But the triumph was only momentary and those days would never return. Pearl went home to Los Angeles and slipped back into the obscurity he so hated. He died alone at age seventy-three in 1986.

He shoots! He scores!

All through the golden age of Canadian radio and beyond into the television era, there was one ever-present, recognizable voice that did almost as much to galvanize a sense of Canadian identity as the national anthem. For decades, Foster Hewitt captivated Canadians with his "Hockey Night in Canada" broadcasts from Maple Leaf Gardens in Toronto. His excited, high-pitched, nasal shout of "He shoots! He scores!" ricocheted across the country. In big cities and small communities, streets emptied as families sat down together for Hewitt's Saturday night ritual. It was a weekly shared experience like no other in Canadian history.

Foster William Hewitt's fascination with radio began in 1921 when he was a teenager listening to the Dempsey–Charpentier boxing match from Jersey City, New Jersey – Hewitt himself was a title-holding lightweight boxer at university. Later he worked in a factory for twenty-five cents an hour making radio sets and in 1922 became a technician for the Toronto *Daily Star*'s experimental radio station. That same year he became the *Star*'s radio editor, and on March 22, 1923, although worried that he would be "a flop" broadcasting hockey, Hewitt reluctantly agreed to broadcast an Ontario Hockey League play-off between Toronto

Parkdale and the Kitchener Seniors. Seated at rinkside, Hewitt, for the first time, yelled the unforgettable phrase "He shoots! He scores!"

Perched on a milk stool and broadcasting from a tiny box glassed in on three sides, Hewitt shouted into what was essentially a telephone. One distraction for listeners was provided by a phone company operator who occasionally broke into the broadcast to ask, "Number please. What number do you want?" A more serious problem was that the carpenter had forgotten to punch air holes into the box and Hewitt nearly suffocated. Fortunately he found the glass was fogging up and opened the door to see the play – and let in some air. The game went into three periods of overtime before Toronto won.

"If I had been permitted free choice that would have been my first, last, and only hockey broadcast," he said later.

Far from being his only hockey broadcast, it was the start of a national obsession and half a century of fame for him. By 1933, a million Canadians were regularly listening to Hewitt's broadcasts, and at his zenith, six million were tuned in and he was getting ninety thousand letters a season.

Former NHL coach and current "Hockey Night in Canada" star Don Cherry recalls, "When I was a kid I'd get into my pyjamas, have some cocoa ready, and at nine o'clock, there was Foster." Hewitt was an idol, too, for CBC sportscaster Brian Williams. "He wasn't afraid to be excited," Williams says. "He didn't embellish, he was just simple and straightforward. He was maybe the quintessential Canadian. His voice reached out over the whole of Canada and drew people together."

Through the Depression and the war years, Hewitt lifted the nation's spirits as his sometimes almost-falsetto voice captured the hockey magic of Howie Morenz, King Clancy, Charlie Conacher, Syl Apps, Gordie Howe, and "Rocket" Richard. His broadcasts were wartime morale builders for Canadian troops overseas, and once when he mentioned briefly that the RCAF Coastal Patrol was in need of binoculars, more than a thousand sets were mailed in.

Over the decades the short, thin, chipmunk-faced Hewitt sat in a wooden chair in front of a small table amid a maze of wires and cables in what was called the Gondola – a twelve-by-four-foot steel tank suspended fifty-four feet above the ice of Maple Leaf Gardens. The three associates he worked with, plus an occasional guest, crowded the Gondola. "It was a pretty precarious perch," remembers Ted Hough, an advertising executive who later ran "Hockey Night in Canada." As a teenage rink rat, Hough sat in the Gondola giving scoring notes to Hewitt. "You got to the Gondola by creeping out over girders. It was kind of scary," he says. "A few years later they built a catwalk."

One who tiptoed across the catwalk to join Foster was writer and broadcaster Gordon Sinclair, who was a mid-1930s version of Don Cherry. Unlike Cherry, however, Sinclair's iconoclastic comments got him thrown off the job after only one season.

For more than three thousand games, sometimes sipping a sore-throat remedy of honey or glycerine and warm water, Hewitt made even the dullest game seem exciting, and yet privately he was anything but a showman. He was an introverted worrier, always on time and frustrated by people who weren't. He was a quiet family man, set in his ways. He made millions speculating in the stock market, but appeared to be a penny-pincher. "While he was not tight in doing things for people," says Hough, "he would complain about the high cost of things. Looking at a restaurant bill, he'd say, 'Gee, it never used to cost this much for a toasted western sandwich.'"

Brian Williams remembers once being in a taxicab with Hewitt on their way to a game in Boston. Hewitt was clutching a brown paper bag full of sandwiches for his dinner. "The guy who said you have to spend money to make money never heard of Foster Hewitt," said one of his co-workers. Later, when Hewitt ran a Toronto radio station, he was famous for his tightfisted approach to salaries. One employee, seduced by Hewitt's simple charms, said, "The sort of guy he is, you end up thanking him for refusing you a raise."

Nor did he spend a lot of money on stylish clothes. "Foster was not a dandy. He was one of those people who dressed well, but looked like a ragbag," says Hough.

A graduate of Upper Canada College, Hewitt was a political right-winger who had imbibed all the prejudices of the 1930s WASP world he lived in. He couldn't imagine blacks as sports heroes, and he couldn't get his tongue around the names of Quebec hockey players. He could never pronounce the name of the Montreal Canadiens star Yvan Cournoyer, calling him Corn-y-aye or another variation. After a number of tries to get it right, he gave up. "I just said t' hell with it," he said later.

When television came along, Hewitt found he didn't like himself on camera, and his usual pre-game anxieties increased. The program producer tried to get him to shed his look of an unmade bed and managed to persuade him to wear a "Hockey Night in Canada" jacket and make-up.

"Hewitt was self-conscious," says hockey's first producer, Sydney Newman. "He insisted on being in his bloody little box up in the rafters, and I had to shoot him with a telephoto lens. I always got him in profile. He quickly found out he had a very weak chin. And he drove the make-up girl crazy getting her to strengthen the appearance of his chin."

"Foster was not a television performer," says Hough. "He felt uncomfortable and he didn't look good. He wasn't photogenic, as he was very jowly. He was also teased about getting made up by his hockey colleagues who thought it was a sissy kind of thing to do."

While Hewitt was painfully learning about television, Newman was just as painfully learning about hockey. "I never did know what icing the puck meant," he says. "There was nothing more important in Canada than hockey and Foster Hewitt, but it was a bloody nightmare getting that show on the air. I was trying to understand the game, and my concern was not to lose the goddamn puck. The ad agency executives, all of Foster Hewitt's friends, Hewitt himself, team owner Conn Smythe, and even my cameramen kept telling me what to do. I went absolutely nuts."

Hewitt told friends that Newman initially told him, "This is going to be easy. It's just like ballet." Some years later ballerina and choreographer Celia Franca and star player Frank Mahovlich did an intermission feature on hockey as a form of ballet, but the first game Newman did was anything but choreographed. The players, as usual, went after each other as well as the puck. "The ad agency tried to keep the camera off the fights," Newman remembers. "They interfered all the time. They didn't want to despoil the game. They wanted it portrayed as a gentlemanly sport."

After a few years, Hewitt found doing both radio and TV was too much, and his son Bill took over the TV play-by-play. Then Hewitt retired, half a century after his reluctant beginning at rinkside, shouting into a telephone.

He came out of retirement in 1972 for the last and most exciting game of his career, one that turned out to be a defining moment in Canadian twentieth-century history. From Moscow a perspiring, slightly hoarse Hewitt screamed, "Henderson scores for Canada!" as Paul Henderson, with thirty-four seconds to go, broke a tied final game between Team Canada and the Soviet Union. Just as Americans alive at the time know where they were when Kennedy was assassinated, Canadians of that generation know where they were when they heard Hewitt's triumphant shout of victory.

Hockey was never quite the same for Hewitt after that. He became disillusioned with the expanding number of NHL teams and the increase of violence in the game. "It's not hockey," he said. "It's something else, and I don't like it." Typical of the new era, TV producers had put a microphone at the players' bench at rinkside as an experiment to catch their excitement and intensity. What the microphone picked up, however, was their profanity. The word "fuck" was repeatedly hurled at the referee and opposing players and was heard across the nation as it never had been before. The mikes were quickly pulled.

Hewitt's old-fashioned civility was a quality out of step with the new brand of slam-bang hockey and totally different from the style of the coach-turned-commentator who catapulted to prominence on hockey broadcasts a few years after Hewitt left the TV stage – Don Cherry.

Don Cherry is everything Hewitt wasn't – a showman with outrageously controversial comments, a love of the combative style of hockey, and a spectacularly outlandish sartorial fashion. "He looks like Liberace's estate has been settled, and he's wearing it," says Brian Williams. Whereas Hewitt was revered by all hockey-loving Canadians, Cherry is popular with the macho, beer-drinking fans who identify with him. "Cherry is not illiterate by any means, but he's hockey's Dizzy Dean, twisting his syntax and deliberately fracturing the Queen's English," says Ted Hough. "But he's a very clever man and a very nice man."

"Don, you don't speak English, but you speak hockey," producer

Ralph Mellanby once told him. Williams has worked with Cherry in radio and TV and recalls bearing the brunt of a Cherry onslaught. "Don and I are hosting a Canada–Russia world junior championship game and a fight breaks out," Williams remembers. "They turn out the lights. They're swinging sticks. He's died and gone to heaven. I say, 'This is a black mark. This is a disgrace.' He says, 'Oh yeah? You say black mark or disgrace one more time, I'm going to punch you on the air. Don't say disgrace. You're a Commie!' " When the two went off the air during a commercial, the cameraman said he thought it would be fun if Cherry had his hands around Williams's throat when they came back. "I couldn't do that," Cherry responded, "because I'd never let go of the little prick!" Williams says, "At that point I knew I was in trouble. But I have a lot of respect for him. It's all real, what you see is what get. But he's a very generous guy."

Williams, Cherry, and their colleagues all trace their sportscasting roots back to the pioneering Foster Hewitt, whose voice from the Gondola exclaiming, "He shoots! He scores!" remains one of the most treasured and defining symbols of the nation.

Bert Pearl, Max Ferguson, Andrew Allan, and Foster Hewitt were the stars of the golden age of Canadian radio. Through sports, drama, comedy, and music, they helped define what it meant to be a Canadian and provided touchstones for the nation. But as the one-eyed monster of television surged onto the Canadian scene, all of them became yesterday's men.

2

"Cue the Elephant!"

The Dawn of Television

"Cue the elephant! Cue the goddamn elephant!"

Sydney Newman's frenzied cry to floor director Harry Rasky in the late summer of 1952 signalled the dawn of Canadian television. Rasky and Newman, the exasperated TV producer, were trying to broadcast an experimental live show from Toronto's Canadian National Exhibition. The elephant, slated to perform in the opening scene, was being uncooperative. Ignoring the urgings of Rasky, Newman, and its trainer, it declined to prance and wave its trunk and instead left a large deposit on the set.

"It was a monster thing just standing there. It dropped a very large load of waste material and then slowly lumbered off," says Desmond Smith, who became a senior producer but was then a script assistant.

The elephant was a harbinger of live television's capricious nature. TV, too, would prove to have a mind of its own and be unstoppable in its march to becoming the most powerful agent of information and entertainment the world has ever known.

CBC producers, directors, and technicians had begun training for TV in the early months of 1952 under the creative guidance of Mavor Moore, veteran radio producer and boy wonder of Canadian theatre. Among his trainees were Norman Jewison, Ross McLean, Murray Chercover, Ted Kotcheff, Arthur Hiller, Harvey Hart, Don Hudson, Sydney Newman, and Drew Crossan. "We were trying to give them a vision," says Moore. "We had the perfect medium for uniting the country. We considered ourselves missionaries."

Moore and his trainees were intoxicated with television's potential. "We thought we could change the world," says Rasky. "We were going to change the way people thought and felt." To reinforce this attitude, Moore brought up from New York the American broadcaster, author, and social commentator Gilbert Seldes. Seldes warned the trainees that television "may stimulate us to thought, but it may also put our minds to sleep. . . . We must make sure that it serves by disturbing our complacency as often as it lets us escape from our problems." His outlook jibed with the recently released Massey Commission report, which had spoken out for culture that "enriches the mind and refines the taste." It was a lofty objective that television would only sometimes reach.

Moore had taken philosophy at the University of Toronto before serving as a captain in intelligence during the Second World War, and now, on the front line of television, he felt he was launched on the creative adventure of his life. Not everyone agreed. One day he met his old philosophy professor, who put his arm affectionately around Moore's shoulders and said, "So, Moore, what are you doing with yourself these days?" "Well, sir," Moore replied, "I'm putting a television network on the air." "Ah, Moore," his professor said, "when are you going to quit fucking around?" "It was," Moore says, "a good example of the attitude of academia towards television."

The TV trainees studied far harder and longer than most university students, learning both about the philosophy of television as an instrument for enlightenment as well as entertainment and the practical details of program production. They spent their days studying techniques and their nights arguing about television's role in society. As well, they studied shows from New York such as Milton Berle's "Texaco Star Theater," "The Ed Sullivan Show," and "Studio One."

They practised everything from running the cameras and being stagehands to directing and going on camera. They were on the leading edge of the TV revolution, excited, confused, overworked – and young.

Lister Sinclair wasn't allowed to go on the training course because he was too old. "To sign up for the course on television you had to be under thirty," he says. "They said television is a young man's job, and if you were over thirty, forget it. I was three months over." He learned about television by sitting at the back of the control room observing how drama producer Bob Allen directed.

Like all the soon-to-be producers, Norman Campbell was tremendously excited about the imminent arrival of TV when he came to Toronto from CBC Vancouver in the early summer of 1952. As Campbell rode in a cab along Jarvis Street to the CBC studios, the driver said, "You're on the street of broken dreams." For Campbell, though, Jarvis was the street of dreams, and he immediately signed up for an afternoon course in titling and special effects. Later he was given the job as director of CBC Toronto's first TV show.

Through the summer Campbell and his colleagues practised in makeshift studios, producing experimental coverage of hockey and baseball games, dramas, and variety shows.

Everyone, said Ross McLean, was in a "state of disintegration and panic as the going-on-air date of early September loomed."

Sharing their fears and challenges, the fledgling TV programmers scrambled to get ready for September. Soon singers, actors, musicians, and dancers were auditioned for future TV shows. Lorraine Thomson was the first chorus girl hired; she, Anna Wilmot, and Lloyd Malenfont were to be the chorus backup for a variety show called "The Big Revue." The starstruck dancers were chosen out of 110 who auditioned. Hundreds of other performers were tested before the cameras as producers searched for the right cast members.

"We walked into this big barn of a place just off Jarvis Street," Thomson says, "with cables and wires all over and an open ceiling, and we had to dance on a cement floor. I thought, 'My goodness, this place isn't finished yet. They'll never finish it in time.' It was the first television studio any of us had ever seen, but we were so excited we were all walking on air."

"We were all so nervous," says Norman Campbell. "There was terrific pressure on us all. We were called into the office of our boss, Fergus Mutrie, and he told us we all had five years to live. We would be burned out by then."

Like ringmasters cracking the whip, Mavor Moore and program director Stuart Griffiths drove their producers, performers, and technicians relentlessly towards the September 8 start date for English-language television in Canada. While most trainees regarded them as the dynamic duo, they didn't get everyone's approval. "Mavor was always a flibberty-gibberty character, flitting about like a bee looking for a flower to shove his nose into," says Sydney Newman. "Griffiths also kept his nose in everything and drove me crazy. He was such a ruthless guy in making TV a success. He operated by the seat of his pants, but he was a very dynamic leader."

Others were more appreciative. "Stu Griffiths was my idol," says Norman Jewison, at the time a trainee studio director. "He had great enthusiasm and great confidence in the ability of Canadians to create their own television."

Griffiths was a controversial figure at the CBC. While a student in prewar Munich, he had been beaten up by the Nazi SS, and the incident led the RCMP to sticker him with a "red" label. Later, after he joined the CBC, the RCMP checked into his background and was told that his first wife and his secretary both had Communist connections. He was refused security clearance, and External Affairs and the RCMP contacted CBC executives, asking that he be dismissed. Producer trainee Gunnar Rugheimer recalls that the McCarthyist paranoia, and Igor Gouzenko's revelations six years earlier of a Communist spy ring operating in Canada, put terrible pressure on CBC general manager Ernie Bushnell, who eventually could stand it no more, saying he wanted to "fire the bastard!" There was no proof of the charges against Griffiths, however, and CBC chairman Davidson Dunton came up with the idea of moving Griffiths out of the International Service and over to television, where, it was thought, he wouldn't pose a security risk. In view of the shadowy Communist accusations against him, it is somewhat ironic that Griffiths later left the CBC to become a private TV entrepreneur.

Mavor Moore says, "He ended up as one of the dirtiest old capitalists I knew." Later his name was placed on a list of possible candidates for the job of CBC president.

Moore called Griffiths "an enthusiastic chipmunk," while Griffiths called Moore "the poor man's Leonardo da Vinci." Griffiths's drive and exuberance were ideally matched to Moore's wide-ranging creative genius. Moore, as the son of Canada's theatrical matriarch Dora Mavor Moore, had been performing onstage since age six and was a playwright and songwriter, radio and stage producer, and Rhodes Scholar nominee. After university he'd been offered a job at the National Film Board and one at the CBC, and chose the CBC because the salary of $35 a week was $5 more than what the NFB offered. Just after the war, he went to work for the United Nations broadcasting service and was about to take a job at CBS for $1,500 a week when Griffiths called him offering $165 a week as senior TV producer. "I convinced myself that my duty lay in coming back to Canada and that prostitution lay in the other direction if I sold myself to the Americans," he says.

First Night

Inauspicious is the only word to describe the beginning of English-language television in Canada. On opening night the first image viewers saw was an upside-down CBC logo. A few seconds before airtime, a technician, wanting to be sure the logo slide was absolutely clean, pulled it out of its holder and shined it. "Don't do that!" came the anguished cry of the opening night co-ordinating producer, Murray Chercover, later president of CTV. The technician quickly shoved the slide back in, but, alas, upside down. When it flashed up on the screen, there were cries of agony from all of Chercover's CBC bosses, who were standing behind him – Stuart Griffiths, Mavor Moore, chairman Davidson Dunton, general manager Ernie Bushnell, and TV head Fergus Mutrie. Chercover remembers that they all simultaneously thumped his shoulder, and Dunton blurted, "What'll we do?" Other than throw up, Chercover had no idea. He got rid of the slide in a couple of seconds, and the evening of TV began.

The upside-down logo wasn't the first awkward incident of that night. Moore had been assigned to escort the CBC board of directors and the cabinet minister responsible for the CBC, J. J. McCann, into their seats in the studio before the program began. By five minutes to air, they had not appeared, so Moore closed the studio door. A few minutes later they arrived in a great bustle, and Dunton said, "We're terribly late. Is it okay?" "No," said Moore. "I told them that they would have to wait for a break when we cut to the other studio for a commercial. Then I said I would let them into the studio. The minister, McCann, who was a revolting, pompous man, came up breathing brandied fumes on me and said, 'What the hell is this?' He bumped me with his large belly, saying, 'Do you know who we are? We are your bosses!' I said, 'Well, sir, there probably are a million Canadians tuned into this program tonight, and I think they are really more important than you are tonight. They are my bosses.'"

Dunton laughed, said Moore was right, and the VIPs waited.

Making their television début that night were, among others, a twenty-year-old, relatively unknown pianist, Glenn Gould, comic Don Harron, singer Jan Rubes, the Leslie Bell Singers, the Howard Cable Orchestra, popular singers Wally Koster and Terry Dale, the Geoffrey Waddington CBC Orchestra, actor Barbara Hamilton, weatherman Percy Saltzman, the puppets Uncle Chichimus and Hollyhock, commentator John Fisher, and Lorne Greene hosting "Newsmagazine." It was 100 per cent Canadian. But the evening's program was not the first that viewers saw. The CBC had been on the air before the formal opening at 7:15 P.M. with a breaking news story on the escape that day of the notorious Boyd Gang from Toronto's Don Jail, making gang leader and bank robber Edwin Boyd the first real star of Canadian television.

Girls, Girls, Girls

On CBC-TV's opening night there were only 146,000 TV sets in the country, but soon millions of Canadians were enjoying a short-lived golden age of television variety shows and drama. Because everything was live, the early years of television have left a rich, often bizarre legacy of gaffes and indiscretions.

Nowhere is that more evident than in early variety programming, which provided the best years of song-and-dance TV we've ever had, a showbiz heyday that lasted about a decade and a half. A sunburst of singers, especially girls, radiated from TV screens across Canada, highlighting shows that also featured crooners, dancers, and musicians. Almost overnight Canada had its own stars, challenging although not surpassing the popularity of Milton Berle, Dinah Shore, Sid Caesar, Jackie Gleason, and Ed Sullivan. Singers dominated the tube, including Phyllis Marshall, Joyce Hahn, Shirley Harmer, Joyce Sullivan, Lorraine Foreman, Sylvia Murphy, the Hames Sisters, "Our Pet" Juliette, and the Leslie Bell Singers. Male singers and comedians included Jackie Rae, Wayne and Shuster, Cliff McKay, Billy O'Connor, Jack Duffy, Wally Koster, Robert Goulet, Denny Vaughan, and George Murray.

"Canada really didn't have show business until television came along," says pioneer variety producer Len Starmer, nicknamed Starmaker. "And TV variety was far easier to do than drama."

It may have been easier, but since it was all live the miscues and goofs shone through the glamour, and every show had the tensions of an opening night. Lorraine Thomson, who had trained as a ballerina, was one of those who danced their way across the nation's small screens, first as a chorus girl backing up soloists Allan and Blanche Lund and then as a featured dancer. Dancers were used as sex symbols, and once, clad in a slinky black sequin dress, Thomson lay atop Duke Ellington's piano as he played "Satin Doll." He told her, "I'm going to tickle the ivories and I hope to tickle you." Dancers would accompany stars such as Nat King Cole as he sang love songs, and Thomson worked frequently with Canada's most popular baritone, Robert Goulet, flitting across the set while he sang "Laura," "Gigi," or some other ballad. "We were kind of moving pieces of furniture, beautiful girls in beautiful gowns, very much in the Ziegfeld style," Thomson says

Emmy Award-winning producer Norman Campbell remembers the CBC's rehearsal halls being alive with music, laughter, and dancing. "A walk past the halls was like a stroll down Tin Pan Alley or down the streets of a film studio like MGM," he says. "You'd hear opera in one hall, jazz in another, and a poorly tuned piano plunking out pop music for the dancers of variety shows in yet another hall."

"Nobody knew what they were doing," says Norman Jewison. "But what was happening was a wonderful burst of creative energy." "It was exciting, but it could be dangerous too," Thomson says. Once, her dress fell off in the midst of a dance number, several times doors didn't open when they were supposed to, and a couple of times she was nearly knocked unconscious.

Once, as Jewison signalled Thomson to go on, the set fell down, hitting her on the head. Jewison stood her up and pushed her into camera range, "and I did the dance, although I had no recollection right after of having done it," she says. Another time, a huge boom mike swung out, hitting her just as she was dancing into view, leaving a large lump on her head. Thomson's hatred of pigeons grew out of her early days on "The Big Revue," the CBC's first TV musical show. Thomson was dressed in feathers from head to toe and carrying two live pigeons on her outstretched hands. "We're on live and I'm hanging on to these pigeons, my feathers are swaying, and I'm walking down a staircase," she says. "Then the pigeons started pooping all over my hands. The audience couldn't see it, but, trying to look glamorous and smiling all the way, I had pigeon poop all over my hands. I have not liked pigeons to this day. But it was fun being live. There was an adrenalin that you don't get when everything is taped and, in a way, it's a shame everything is edited now and all the goofs are cut out."

One goof that distressed dancer Allan Lund happened when he was dancing and singing "I Left My Hat in Haiti." The song and dance ended when he ran down towards the camera and slid on his knees with his legs spread out. "It was a wonderful, dynamic ending," says Campbell, who produced the show. "But just as he went down his trousers ripped up the middle completely. He was furious at the costume people for giving him too-tight trousers."

Steve Hyde was puzzled once when floor-directing a live program with the blind Puerto Rican guitarist José Feliciano. As the program went to air, Hyde was instructed by the director to cue Feliciano. "Suddenly I realized, how the hell do you cue a blind guy?" Hyde says. "You can't point your finger at him as you usually do. So I said out loud, 'Cue!'"

Veteran announcer Elwood Glover refused to go on television for years after doing a live TV commercial in what turned out to be "the case of the poisoned ice cream." In the commercial, Glover talked about the joys of Borden's French Vanilla ice cream. Just before going to air, a stagehand noticed the ice cream was attracting flies, and, not realizing Glover was going to eat a spoonful during the commercial, he sprayed it with fly tox. As Glover ended his pitch, he took a big spoonful of the pesticide-loaded ice cream, swallowed it, and, smiling wanly, said, "If it's Borden's, it's got to be good!" But he felt like throwing up and was terrified he'd been poisoned. Len Starmer was in the studio at the time and recalls, "They rushed him to hospital, and I believe his stomach was pumped out just in case because he'd had a snootful of fly tox. That was the last TV commercial he ever did, and he swore he'd never do television again. He did, but it was years later."

Flies were often buzzing about the CBC-TV studios, and once when announcer George McLean was anchoring a newscast, a fly flew into his mouth. He simply swallowed it and carried on.

Off-air problems also arose occasionally for program sponsors. After one show in which a number of Westinghouse refrigerators were featured in a commercial, a truck showed up late the same night and the driver explained to the studio guard that he had come to pick up the refrigerators. He signed a sheet, loaded up the truck, and took off. The next day another driver arrived, this one really from Westinghouse, only to be told the refrigerators had already been taken. "Nobody knew who took all the stuff. They just cleaned out the whole studio," says Larry Mann, who had performed in the studio the night before.

The prime-time variety series "The Big Revue" featured a hypnotist in one of its early shows. "We thought it would be great fun to put to sleep some of the cast, including the emcee, Peter Mews," says Mavor Moore, who produced the series. "The hypnotist did so, and he was to wake them up right after we cut to a commercial in the adjoining studio. The trouble was that Mews had been particularly susceptible to the hypnotist and had not yet come out of it when we cut back to the program. He was still two-thirds asleep, and I had to cut back to the commercial studio and tell them to invent something." Equally serious, says Moore, the hypnotist had also actually put to sleep some viewers. "There was a hell of a row, and as a consequence, the CBC board of directors ordered that hypnotism could not be used on the air," says Moore.

On-air problems of another kind struck Allan Blye when he was singing on "Cross Canada Hit Parade." The plan was for the camera to take a wide shot, then zoom in slowly on Blye's face, and finally pull back for another wide shot. As he began singing, the camera rolled in surprisingly quickly. He knew something was wrong when he saw he was on a very close-up shot and the cameraman suddenly snuck over to him on hands and knees and reached up to his crotch. "I had forgotten to do up my zipper and my fly was gaping open," Blye remembers. "I felt the guy's hands on my zipper, and I was trying to be cool as I'm singing 'No Other Love Have I.' " Blye was zipped up, the cameraman went back to his position, and then ended on the wide shot as planned.

Blye was the victim of a prankster on the program "Summer Showtime," when he sang live part of "Return to Sorrento" in Italian, reading from a cue card. As a practical joke, a technician set fire to the card. Blye tried to speed up his singing before the flames consumed the whole card, but failed. "So I just did double-talk words that sounded Italian," he says. "Some Italian viewers later called in asking what part of Italy I came from since they couldn't recognize the dialect or the words."

In the seat-of-the-pants style of so much early variety programming, remembering lines was always a challenge. These days were long before teleprompters, and some performers went to extraordinary lengths to have lines and song lyrics copied out somewhere in sight. Billy O'Connor, host of a late-night variety show, had a notorious "forgettery," says producer Norman Campbell. "He would hide his lyrics in different places. If we had a scene beside a tree, the script would be pasted on the tree. Once, Billy was singing with George Murray, who was wearing a suit of armour, and Billy had his lyrics written in pen on George's armour. Another time they were doing a song sitting in a rowboat in real water, and it was live. They had their script lying at the bottom of the boat, but the boat sprang a leak. Their scripts were floating around and they couldn't read them, so they ad libbed, trying to figure out what to do. But they got through it."

Canada's first true country music star of the TV era, "King" Ganam, used to scribble his lines on his wrists and palms, but he was usually nervous and his perspiration would wipe out his lines. Campbell encountered line problems when he produced *The Mikado* with the improbable casting of the Metropolitan Opera's Helen Traubel and Groucho Marx. Marx used cue cards, but in the scenes with the more than ample Traubel – "She looked like a statuesque gorilla, towering over him," says Campbell – her bulk blocked out his view. "Poor

Groucho kept peeking around her trying to see the cards, and he slowed down the performance."

Anna Cameron, who hosted an afternoon show called "Open House" with Fred Davis, once forgot the unusually long name of her guest, a Spanish guitarist who had five names. Smiling into the camera, she simply invented five Spanish-sounding names. "The guy looked surprised, and turned around to see who the other person was, then shrugged his shoulders and started to play," said Davis.

Alex Trebek, host of the American game show "Jeopardy!," has almost a photographic memory, but once when he was host of the CBC's "Music Hop" in early TV days, his mind went blank as he was introducing the number-one hit song of the country. "I turned to the piano player and said, 'Norm?' and he gave the title," says Trebek. "It happened another time, and when I turned to Norm, he said, 'I give up, what is it?' I just said, 'Whatever it is, here's somebody to sing it.'"

"I try to memorize the idea, not the specific words," says comedian Dave Broadfoot. "I've seen actors when they blank out and it's frightening. They're in a state of panic. You can see stark horror in their eyes."

American guest stars sometimes caused dramatic moments behind the scenes. Douglas Fairbanks was "just a horror," says Mary DePoe, a script assistant at the time. "He had I don't know how many young girls and women up in his room. Then his wife arrived, and we were getting this girl out of here and that girl out of there. He was like a sheepdog, and just seemed to know which girls he could get out of the flock – two or three at a time. He was something else."

Johnny Cash, DePoe says, "was awful. No one could go near him. They just kept him separate in his dressing room. They were fearful he'd go berserk. I don't know what the matter was." On the other hand, DePoe says that George Burns was "just a sweet, dear, little old man," and Harry Belafonte "was a delight."

Producer Paddy Sampson also has good things to say about Belafonte, who starred in some early CBC television shows and became Sampson's close friend. They met after Sampson went to New York to persuade Belafonte to do a show for the CBC. In the 1950s, black performers had few opportunities on American network television, but the CBC frequently offered shows to people such as Belafonte, Duke Ellington, Nat King Cole, and Sammy Davis, Jr., among others. Belafonte kept Sampson waiting all day outside his office, but then took him home to dinner. Upon seeing a recording of Sampson's previous shows, the singer was so impressed he agreed to accept a scale rate of $200 to $300 for doing the program.

In one show with Belafonte, which also featured the famous raven-haired Greek singer Nana Mouskouri, Sampson ran into racial discrimination. As the show was ending, Belafonte impulsively kissed Mouskouri. CBS had originally wanted to air the program, but when the network's program director, Mike Dann, met with Sampson and Belafonte, he said, "That's a hell of a show. But, Harry, we're not ready for the kiss." CBS never did air it.

Over the years Belafonte starred in several CBC programs and, at one point, according to June Callwood, had a romantic fling – "a serious one," she says – with Canadian TV host Joyce Davidson.

Davidson's blonde, pale, cool beauty made her a natural for TV stardom, hosting talk shows and major productions. She was one of the early Canadian "talking dolls" Ross McLean recruited as program hosts. Davidson enraged the Canadian establishment, however, a few years after TV began by telling Dave Garroway on his NBC morning show on the eve of a royal trip to Canada, "I, like most Canadians, am rather indifferent to the Queen's visit." The ensuing uproar included denunciations in the House of Commons, threats of acid being thrown in her face, and suspension by an apoplectic and apologetic CBC. Nearly forty years later, Callwood admitted that she feels responsible for Davidson's comment. "We were having lunch, and I was talking about a piece I was writing for *Maclean's* magazine on the Queen. I told Joyce the right word for the way Canadians felt about the Queen is indifference. A few days later, she was on the Garroway show and used my comment."

It certainly caused a flash of excitement in the broadcasting world, as, on a lesser scale, did the chicken prank pulled by a group of musicians on the show "Á La Carte." "We thought the show needed something," says Jimmy Dale, "so we went to Kensington Market and bought a live chicken. The show was live, and we hid the chicken until the last number and then released it, and it strutted across the stage, cackling loudly. We thought it made a lively ending, but I can't imagine doing that kind of thing now."

Don Harron

When television began in Canada, Don Harron was on the first night as a comic; a few days later on "The Big Revue," he presented his character Charlie Farquharson. "I used my father's old suit and borrowed a peak cap from Norman Jewison, who was a floor director and wore a cap all the time," says Harron. Harron had been on network radio in the mid-1930s as a child actor but was fired by the CBC in 1936 at the age of eleven. After wartime service with the RCAF, he acted for Andrew Allan's "Stage" series with Tommy Tweed and Lister Sinclair and in 1950-52 performed onstage in London and the United States before coming back to Canada.

A comment by actor Jane Mallett was the inspiration for Harron's character Charlie Farquharson. Harron used to do political humour as a warm-up for her shows in rural Ontario. When Harron mentioned to her that he felt his patter wasn't as effective as he hoped, she told him, "You have to have a mask. People don't want some young punk telling them what to think. You've got to get an old image." So Harron developed Charlie. Later he based his character Valerie Rosedale on a combination of Jane Mallett and her sister. Charlie's first performance was in *Spring Thaw* in 1952. Norman Jewison, who was also working on the revue, gave Harron his father's hat. He says, "All my family talked that way, and, in a sense, Charlie was partly modelled on my dad." A few months after *Spring Thaw*, Charlie was introduced to the television audience on "The Big Revue" when it débuted in September 1952. For nearly half a century, Harron has been giving out political advice in the character of this old codger, saying things he would never himself say.

Besides playing Charlie, Harron has acted in everything from "Hee Haw" to Shakespeare, performing at the Stratford Festival, where he shared the stage with James Mason, Helen Hayes, Katharine Hepburn, William Hutt, and other classical actors. Two men who shaped his life were literary critic Northrop Frye and British director Tyrone Guthrie, who wooed Harron to Stratford. One bit of Guthrie advice that Harron has never forgotten is "You are very good with the audience, but you have a paucity of gesture." Harron found he was able to gesture more freely as Charlie Farquharson than as any Shakespeare character.

Once while playing the unshaven, unkempt Charlie, he ran into the famed actor Anthony Quayle, who, having seen his name on the billboard, asked him, "Excuse me, but are you any relation to Don Harron of the Stratford Shakespeare Festival?" "I'm him!" Harron proclaimed. "Good God, man," Quayle replied, "whatever happened? How did you come to this?"

"Sometimes the character comes home with him, and I'm not sure whom I'm married to," says his wife, singer Catherine McKinnon. "There is this old guy with a stubbly face and ragged clothes. Sometimes a character becomes more real than you want it to be. Don's also the epitome of the absentminded professor, forever losing his glasses when they're on his head. He could get lost in a turnstile. Once, he got into his car and was absolutely outraged because, he said, 'Someone has stolen the steering wheel! The steering wheel is gone.' He was sitting in the backseat."

Harron's character Valerie Rosedale gets him into more trouble than Charlie Farquharson, much of it caused when he finds he has to go to the men's room while dressed as Valerie. At a posh golf club in Burlington, Ontario, where he was appearing, he was standing at the urinal wearing a dress, pearls, and furs when several startled men came in. "Don't mind me," Valerie said haughtily. "I'm just standing up for my rights." Once, at a women's press club ball, a drunk asked him for a dance, but Valerie declined, saying, "I'm terribly sorry. I'm spoken for." Another time, when he was waiting in the lobby of the Lord Nelson Hotel in Halifax, he was mistaken for a prostitute. "The desk clerk came over and said they had complaints about me and that I should be out on the street with the rest of the girls," says Harron. "He thought I was an old hooker."

Norman Jewison

The early years of TV sired a galaxy of star producers and directors who helped make the new medium *the* entertainment stage of the era. None shone brighter than Norman Frederick Jewison. A wanna-be actor from east-end Toronto, Jewison didn't make it on the stage, but made it instead on the studio floor. As a TV director, he was a rare, if not unique, model of gentle authority and creative effervescence. On the set, he would steer performers on and off camera with an impish smile and a quick, encouraging word, and in the control room, he was a whirlwind of flailing arms and soft-spoken instructions.

"Jewison had great enthusiasm," says fellow director Don Brown. "He would act out every part, standing most of the time behind his director's seat in the control room. He enjoyed every second of it, for he was an actor after all."

While directing a jazz show, Jewison would hum aloud and beat on the table, and whenever he directed a comedy show, he'd be the first to burst out laughing. "He was just a delight to watch," says Sydney Newman. "He also was very shrewd. He sort of disappeared around late November, and it turned out that he had a side business selling Christmas trees."

"Norman never said, 'You've got to do this,'" says Len Starmer. "He just wrapped his arms around the performer and assured them they could do it. That was his magic; that was his success. I've never seen him bawl out a performer. He has an authentic gentility. It's not in his nature to yell and rant and rave."

"We used to call him Sammy Big because he was so persuasive," says writer and performer Alex Barris. "He could talk anybody into anything."

"Directing, in many ways, is manipulation because you're dealing with a lot of egos," says Jewison. "You have to manipulate people into thinking it was their idea, to get them to do what you see as being the best, to edit them without their knowing they're being edited."

He'd first been onstage at age five when, before about five hundred people at the Masons, the Elks, or Rotary clubs, he'd recite the endless stanzas of the Robert Service classic "The Shooting of Dan McGrew," complete with arm-waving gestures and dramatic voice changes. "Two guns blaze in the dark. A woman screams!" he'd emote. For his curtain call, he'd recite "Willie Gets the Neck" – a poem about a boy in a large family eating turkey dinner whose big brothers get the legs, wings, and breast, but Willie gets only the neck. Whenever he was on an excursion boat on Lake Ontario, he'd go to the ship's microphone and recite stories or sing. At high school and university, he acted on the stage, and after graduation he performed for Andrew Allan on CBC Radio while earning his living by driving a Diamond cab.

When he first saw television, he was totally enchanted, and at age twenty-four, he went to New York to learn about TV. He wrote for the old Dumont Network and then went to England, where television was far more advanced. Canadian expatriate Bernie Braden gave him a job on his late-night BBC show "Bedtime with Braden." Earning about thirty dollars a week, Jewison wrote school broadcasts for the BBC and lived in a fifth-floor cold-water flat in London until the day he got a letter from Stuart Griffiths, the new CBC-TV program director, offering him a job. Jewison had talked to Griffiths before going to England, and Griffiths had told him, "When we get around to it, we'll think about you, kid." Jewison came back to Toronto in the spring of 1952, took the TV training course, and was floor director and writer for "The Big Revue" when it went on the air in the first week of Canadian TV. He started wearing a peaked cap almost at once to keep the studio lights out of his eyes, and it became his trademark. To this day he wears a baseball cap while he's working on the set of his movies.

In the early years, Jewison was the only director who got on smoothly with Wayne and Shuster and Tommy Hunter, all of them notoriously hard on directors. Hunter recalls a scene on "Country Hoedown" that he and singer Tommy Common had bungled in rehearsal. "We were singing a song called 'I Saw Esau Sitting on a Seesaw,'" says Hunter. "We had to saw a log and sing at the same time, and we had to cut through the log just as we stopped singing. But we were awful. We couldn't get it right. We braced ourselves to hear the producer, Jewison, scream his head off. Then we heard, 'Supper break,' and Norman walked across the set, looked over at us with a big smile, and said, 'Getting dark, guys.' He didn't blow, and it was the best thing because we did it right for him after the supper break. He was just fabulous."

While he was producing "Hoedown," Jewison received a letter from a woman who said she was crazy about the long, shiny boots worn by Hunter. "It was some kind of sexual thing with her," says Jewison. "So next week, I did a lot of close-ups of boots. She wrote fifteen letters saying what a wonderful experience it had been to see Tommy's boots."

Larry Mann was the target for Jewison's sense of humour once when Mann was walking down a street on a set in a live production. He was supposed to say a brief hello to a man at a newspaper kiosk and then walk on. "When I got to the guy to say, 'Hi,' he says, 'I've got a message for you,' and hands it to me. I say to myself, 'Hello, what's this? It's not in the script.' I open the message and it's a note from Jewison that says, 'Stretch for two minutes.'" Mann invented some dialogue with the newspaper seller for a couple of minutes and then walked down the street, having accomplished his "stretch."

Doors that don't open properly on live TV are a nightmare for directors as well as actors, and Jewison faced one of his worst on-air moments in the première of "The Denny Vaughan Show," a variety program whose star had become a Canadian heartthrob. The set for the big opening number was the front façade of an ivy-covered house. Vaughan was supposed to come bursting through the front door, smiling and singing, "Hi neighbour. Hi neighbour. What do you know? What do you say . . . ?" As the show opened, the orchestra began, the audience applauded, the announcer said, "Ladies and gentlemen, Mr. Denny Vaughan," and the camera moved in on the door. "The door began to rattle and the whole set began to shake, and I realized the door was stuck," says Jewison. "I called to the floor director, 'Somebody help him with the door, for God's sake!' But they couldn't budge it. Now Vaughan was getting panicky. Then I saw him come crashing through the ivy at the side of the set, singing, 'Hi neighbour' with the most terrified look on his face. And just as he was coming through the ivy, a piece of it caught his toupee. Here I had one of Canada's romantic idols singing and grimacing, and now one end of his toupee is sticking straight up! I got hysterical and couldn't stop laughing, and we cut to another studio for a commercial. I said, 'Calm him down and fix his toupee,' and we went on with the show. The next day, the reviews came out. They thought it had been a comedy sketch that didn't really work."

A similar door challenge once faced Leslie Nielsen when, in a live TV drama, he was in a room with actor Albert Decker. As he tried to leave the room, the door wouldn't open, no matter how hard he pulled. "Your door seems to be stuck," he said to Decker. "Oh," said Decker, "it's always doing that." Speaking louder in hopes that a stagehand would hear him and kick the door open, Nielsen said, "Yes, you're right, the door really is stuck." But it was to no avail, and his co-star finally ad libbed, "Well, you might as well use this other door," and with that Nielsen opened a closet door and stepped inside, where he stayed until the scene changed.

Jewison could be quietly tough, as Harry Belafonte found out when Jewison was directing one of his shows. Just before the rehearsals began, Belafonte gathered the performers around and started telling them how the show was going to be done. Alex Barris, who was at the rehearsal, says, "Norman was very concerned about who was going to control the show because he was, after all, working for Belafonte. Norman was across the floor from Belafonte, and he got up and said, 'Excuse me' and dragged his chair across the floor directly behind Belafonte. Then Norman got up on the chair and began talking, and Belafonte stopped. That was the moment Jewison got control of the show. If he hadn't done that, Belafonte would have thought he had a weak director, but then he backed off and let Norman take over."

Ever since, Jewison and Belafonte have been close friends. Jewison is proud that the program was the first black special on American network television. Jewison also got black performers on "Lucky Strike Hit Parade" for the first time.

Barris recalls another show Jewison directed that saw a fight between Danny Kaye and Lucille Ball, two performers with huge egos. Ball asked Kaye if he would mind her making a few suggestions for the script. "She kept giving more and more suggestions, and people were getting very testy," says Barris. "Finally, Danny Kaye said, 'Who the hell do you think you are coming in here to tell me how to do my show?' Nobody had ever talked to Lucille Ball that way, and she said, 'Who do I think I am? You're full of shit, that's who I am!' "

Many of the shows Jewison produced for American TV were award-winning successes and led to him doing more work south of the border. In 1963 he turned to making movies, which have won him Academy Awards and made him the most celebrated director Canada has ever produced.

Robert Goulet

Another luminary on the early Canadian TV screen was Robert Goulet, whose good looks and golden-toned baritone voice made him an international star. Audience surveys of shows Goulet appeared in alerted the CBC to his enormous potential, and for half a dozen years he starred in Sunday night's "General Electric Showtime" first with Shirley Harmer and later Joyce Sullivan, whom, Goulet says, "I used to call juicy." His commanding artistry made Goulet Canada's first male sex symbol, and his appeal sometimes ranged further than he wanted. A horse once fell in love with him on the set of "Showtime." The horse was held in a stage corral while Goulet was singing a romantic western ballad. Just before the show began, Goulet had fed some sugar cubes to the horse and put several remaining cubes into his back pocket. While he was singing, the horse came over and started pushing his nose into Goulet's rear end to get at the cubes, shoving him about in the process. "What the hell was I going to do?" says Goulet. "It was live television. If I gave the horse a shot, he would have clobbered me. So I kept on singing, and he kept on pushing me in the ass."

It may have been unnerving, but not as much as the first time he sang as a child at a family gathering. "I was frightened to death," Goulet says. "I didn't want to do that. When they applauded I ran, and I never sang for my family again."

Goulet was born in Massachusetts and brought up in Alberta. His family was originally from Quebec, and he still speaks French. On his deathbed, his father told him, "Robert, God gave you a voice. You must sing." Goulet says, "I was twelve years old and I said, 'Okay, Dad.' My father died that night. Those were his last words to me, and I knew I had to become a singer." His first job on radio was not as a singer, however, but as an announcer for the University of Alberta station CKUA, reporting high-school news.

He went to the Royal Conservatory of Music in Toronto on a scholarship, arriving with fifty dollars in his windbreaker, and he and a fellow student at the conservatory shared a room in a downtown boarding house to save money. "We had a place on the second floor with one little window overlooking a wall," he says.

While taking singing lessons, Goulet earned pocket change in walk-on acting jobs, including the CBC's "Howdy Doody" show. He was Lucky Pierre, a lumberjack, appearing with Barbara Hamilton, who was the Good Fairy, and Alfie Scopp, who was Clarabell the Clown. "Goulet didn't have a nickel, and every now and then Peter Mews, who played Timber Tom, would fake being sick so Goulet could get a job," says Larry Mann. Goulet says he only worked on the show for one two-week period as a favour to his friend Mews. "I was continually broke," says Goulet, "but I didn't want to make a career in 'Howdy Doody,' for God's sake!"

Goulet went on to perform in several Mavor Moore productions, including *Spring Thaw*, as well as an increasing number of television roles, working with Hamilton, Lloyd Bochner, Leslie Nielsen, Toby Robins, and Don Harron, among others. Not known for his acting ability at the time, Goulet once saw Bochner walk by a studio where Goulet and Robins were rehearsing. Mischievously he called out, "Lloyd, come in here and see what acting is really all about." "I was joking, and Toby gave me a daggers look," says Goulet. "Lloyd and I never spoke again until we met on the set of *Naked Gun*. Lloyd said he didn't even remember the incident."

After dropping out of the conservatory, Goulet landed the job of lead singer in "Showtime," which became his launching pad for international stardom. Jim Guthro remembers thinking it was a mistake for Goulet to give up the conservatory. "He had a lot of promise, but he stopped taking lessons and his voice never developed," says Guthro. "He could have been a really rich baritone. He became a good singer, but only for Broadway stuff, but then, he only wanted the pop stuff anyway."

Guthro and other producers who worked with Goulet at the time say he was no prima donna, never had a tantrum, and was easy to get along with. "Hell, I was always easy and I loved the work," says Goulet. He also enjoyed women, drinking, and joking, in that order. "Goulet was an innocent, naive, good-looking guy who liked women," says Norman Jewison. "He was always playing tricks," says Lorraine Thomson, who danced in many of his TV shows. "He had a very naughty, bawdy sense of humour. Once, he was singing 'Laura' and I was Laura, dancing and running all around him. In rehearsal he'd be singing and then would chase after me, shouting between lyrics, 'I'm going to get you yet!' and getting hold of me so I couldn't dance."

"In the early days," says Len Starmer, "Goulet was shy, but he quickly outgrew that. He was a devilishly handsome guy, affable, and one of the boys. As he developed professionally, his world with the ladies became more and more active." Goulet remembers that girls would throw hotel-room keys and brassières at him onstage. "I'm a little too old for that now," he says today, at age sixty-three. "He was a real tomcat," says Alex Barris. "If there was a girl around, he was going to get her – and the girls would just flock to him."

As Canada's foremost romantic singer, Goulet was having the time of his life, starring in his own show and guesting on other programs. But in 1959 his life changed forever because of Don Harron. Harron had been asked to audition for a new Broadway musical called *Camelot* that was being put together by Moss Hart, Alan Jay Lerner, and Frederick Loewe. "What? Me sing?" exclaimed Harron to the show's New York agent. "Are you guys crazy? Call this guy Goulet in Toronto." The agent did, but Goulet was reluctant to audition. "I don't have any time to go to New York," he said. "I've got a weekly TV show." Still, Goulet thought about it overnight and, the next day, encouraged by his "Showtime" producer, he called back to say he could squeeze in a quick trip. "Imagine saying to Moss Hart and Lerner and Loewe that they had to stop whatever they were doing to hear this kid from Canada," he says. To make it worse, when he got to New York, he lost his luggage and arrived for the audition wearing a leather jacket, a T-shirt, and blue jeans. "I see you've come prepared," said Hart. He sang "Maria" – "I gave it a good solid blast and let it fly" – and then a song in French. "A fat little kid who'd been playing the piano said, of all things, 'I think you've got it!'" Goulet remembers. The kid was right. "This is the deal," they told him. "$750 a week for the first nine months, $900 a week for the next nine months, and $1,000 a week for the next six months."

"Years later," Goulet says, "I met Don Harron and said, 'Thanks for mentioning my name and starting my career in the U.S.' He didn't even remember it."

Harron also was instrumental in getting Larry Mann on Canadian television. Harron had been approached about a role in a new show and had suggested to the producers that Mann would be more effective working with puppets than he would be. So the CBC hired Mann for

"Uncle Chichimus," the first program ever seen on English-Canadian television, starting Mann on a career that would lead him into many a Canadian TV performance and finally to Hollywood.

When Goulet left "Showtime," he was hurt that there was no farewell party for him. "I was never so despondent in my life," he says. He remembers leaving the studio for the last time and driving up what was then Toronto's sin strip on Jarvis Street, near the CBC. He was hailed by "a delightful, beautiful black lady" and lowered the window of his 1956 Corvette, naively thinking that she wanted directions. But she had something else in mind and said, "Ten dollars in the car, twenty in the room." "What the hell does that mean?" Goulet wondered, and then, realizing what it did mean, he reached into his pocket and found he had only seven dollars. "What can I get for seven dollars?" he asked. "I'll see you later, sonny," she replied as she walked away. "There went my big chance," he says.

When Goulet left Canadian television, he joined Richard Burton and Julie Andrews in one of the century's great musicals. *Camelot* débuted in Toronto before going to New York, and Goulet got a taste of what it was like to be a big star. "I was walking down Yonge Street, and just for fun I went into one of those nick-nack stores, and for about a buck I bought a tiny little frog," he says. "I met someone who noticed the frog and asked if I collected them. For some reason, I said yes, and word got out that I was a frog collector. Since then, I've been sent about five thousand of them from all over the world. I've got frogs coming out of my yin-yang."

Shortly after *Camelot* opened on Broadway, several of Goulet's old "Showtime" colleagues came to see the show. Dancers Connie Campbell, Pauline Ross, Andy Body, and a friend, June Sampson, went backstage after the performance and were chatting with Goulet in his dressing room when Richard Burton walked in. "Bob caught Burton's roving eye looking at Connie, who had just broken up with her husband and was miserable," says Paddy Sampson, June's husband. "So Bob invited the girls and Burton to dinner and, at the appropriate moment in the evening, Burton takes Connie to his home. She got back to her hotel at two in the morning, and the other girls, who were all sharing a room, excitedly asked, 'What happened with Burton?' 'Nothing happened,' she said. 'Except, you know, he tried to get fresh with me.' 'Well, what the hell did you expect?' they said."

Earlier that night, says Sampson, the other girls had "had to pour Bob back to his apartment," a sign of Goulet's love affair with booze, which almost ruined his career. "He became obnoxious when he was drunk," remembers Mary DePoe, a CBC-TV script assistant. "In the early days, he was just a nice young guy, but when he was drunk, he wasn't nice."

Some time later Sampson met Goulet for lunch at the Beverly Hills Hotel in Los Angeles. "He always had a case of vodka because he did vodka commercials, and he'd obviously been into it," says Sampson. "I'd seen him drunk at a party, but never this bad. He was off to court for his divorce from Carol Lawrence. 'You're going to court like this?' I said. 'You're hammered!' 'It's the only way to go,' Goulet said."

The nadir of Goulet's career came when he forgot the words to the American national anthem in front of a huge audience. Tales of that and talk about his excessive drinking dogged him for years. Remarriage some years later transformed him. He overcame his alcoholic demons and relaunched a successful singing career.

In the early years of television, viewers were enthralled by Goulet's rich renditions of pop songs and those of other performers on shows such as "The Big Revue," "Cross Canada Hit Parade," "The Denny Vaughan Show," "The Jack Kane Show," "Pick the Stars," and "The Jackie Rae Show." But there was a whole other musical world that also found a place on the box: country music.

Fiddlin' and Stompin'

CBC-TV tiptoed into country music with former Gangster Ton of Fun, clarinetist Cliff McKay, who hosted a Saturday night show called "Holiday Ranch," supposedly set on a dude ranch. Real fiddling, foot-stomping country music arrived a few years later with "Country Hoedown." The program was headed by "King" Ganam, a shy fiddler from Saskatchewan who had quit "Holiday Ranch" in a dispute with McKay. With his thin riverboat-gambler's moustache, western hats, and string ties, Ganam was an instant hit when CBC starred him and his band as a summer replacement for "Holiday Ranch."

Ganam was known as the fiddler with a wink because he ended every number with a smiling wink. The signature twinkle began by accident when his eyes twitched in the bright lights during his first performance onstage. "By popular demand, I've been twitching them ever since," he said.

Although he was pleased the program was renewed after its summer run, Ganam was disappointed that it was not named after him. The CBC had decided that he wasn't a good host and gave the job to Gordie Tapp, a fast-rising performer. For the show, Ganam, who stayed on as band leader, hired a stringbean guitar player from London, Ontario, seventeen-year-old Tommy Hunter. "Grab your toothbrush, laddie, and polish up your pearly whites, you're going on television," Ganam told Hunter. For Hunter and Tapp, this was the big-time beginning of lifelong careers, although at first Tapp was uneasy about his country image, feeling it might hurt his marketability as a performer. "Gordie didn't really want to be associated with the country image," Hunter says. "Back then you'd never admit being in 'country.' It was like being in the closet. He told me, 'This country image has cost me because some advertisers didn't want their product to have a country image.' He didn't mind sort of hiding behind 'Cousin Clem,' but he didn't want Gordie Tapp associated with it. He made a great career on 'Hoedown' and later on 'Hee Haw,' but back originally, he absolutely didn't want any part of it."

"Gordie would have been appalled at the thought he would ultimately end up doing so well in country music," says Len Starmer, who went to Lorne Greene's Academy of Radio Arts with Tapp. "He worried about losing work by becoming too corny. But then corny came in."

Before he started with "Country Hoedown," Hunter worked on and off with Ganam, supplementing his income from music by selling paint at Eaton's. He was paying $7.50 a week for a room he shared with a former Greek Orthodox priest at Toronto's West End YMCA. On "Country Hoedown," despite his billing as "young Tommy Hunter, the Singing Guitarist," he still wasn't paid very much. He usually played from a place on the bandstand and says that whenever he stepped off the bandstand for a solo he was paid an extra $5. "I didn't wear any make-up, and I had pimples all over the place so I sort of put powder on myself," he says. "But

I had to stand to do it because, under union rules, if I sat in the make-up chair, I had to be paid another five bucks."

Hunter often lip-synched his songs, using a recording done earlier and, on camera, mouthing the words. This could lead to problems, however, as it did when he and Tapp were singing a song together called "Mush On You Malmamute" about a half-dog, half-wolf loping through the night. Thinking their words could not be heard, they made up the lyrics, and Tapp sang, "I hate this dumb song and I'm gonna get real drunk tonight." Hunter says, "One of the cameramen was trying to tell us that we were on live, but we just went right on. The producer thought we'd all be fired." They weren't, they were too popular.

With his talent for improvisation and practical jokes, Tapp made dress rehearsals an endurance test for his producer. "He would say awful things and tell awful jokes that you hoped would never get on the air," says Mary DePoe, who used to time the show. Once during a Halloween show, a coffin was placed on the set for a Frankenstein number. To celebrate a cast member's birthday, DePoe says, "Gordie had hired a stripper, and in the dress rehearsal, when the coffin was opened, the stripper jumped out."

Hunter quickly became a star, soon outshining his boss, "King" Ganam, and the CBC hired him to replace "The Happy Gang" when the long-running radio show was finally cancelled in 1959. For a while he starred on both radio and TV, but when "Country Hoedown" ended, Hunter was given his own television show. "The Tommy Hunter Show" lasted twenty-six years, far longer than its closest rival, "Don Messer's Jubilee."

Don Messer

Messer, who had been a popular Maritime fiddler since the 1930s, began his TV career in 1957 and shortly afterwards shot to stardom as host of a summer replacement for "Country Hoedown."

No Canadian TV performer was more loved by his fans than this shy, pudgy, middle-aged fiddler from Tweedside, New Brunswick. His unashamedly corny, toe-tapping style struck a chord in rural Canada that most big-city critics never understood.

One value he epitomized was being careful with money. Messer was more than careful, he was downright stingy. One day in mid-rehearsal, he suddenly stopped with an odd expression on his face and put down his fiddle. He walked to the far corner of the studio and bent over and scooped up a ten-cent piece, which he tucked into his pocket. Patting the pocket, he chuckled and said, "Every little bit helps." Then he went back, picked up his fiddle, and carried on with the rehearsal. Catherine McKinnon, who sang on his program, recalls Messer's wife telling her, "Mr. Messer is so tight that when his hearse comes down the road, there'll be a Brink's truck coming right after it."

Messer's penny-pinching was in sharp contrast to the generosity of the former New Brunswick lumberman, Charlie Chamberlain, a singing star on the Messer show. A lovable old rascal and gentle giant, Chamberlain never kept a nickel of his money. "Charlie would get his paycheque and cash it in for a huge wad of five-dollar bills, and then start spending," says McKinnon. "He'd give you the shirt off his back. He was a great, sweet man, and for extra cash and for pleasure he used to pump gas on weekends in his home town. He'd call me darlin' and always had a little glint in his eye."

"Charlie gave all his money away," says Bill Langstroth, who worked closely with the Messer troupe. "He was generous beyond description. Charlie and Don had nothing but good to say about each other, but they couldn't stand each other's habits. Don couldn't stand the fact that Charlie was drinking himself to death and wasn't careful with his money."

When he was really angry with Charlie or someone else, Messer's pink face would turn red, but the worst he could bring himself to say would be "tarnation poop!" "That's the harshest language I ever heard him use," says Langstroth, "but he was given to little mutterings and growling to himself."

Messer didn't like the sound of his own light voice, and hardly ever spoke more than a few words on the show. "He spoke through his fiddle," says McKinnon. "Even so, he was very much the man in charge. He was focused and ran a tight ship. I always called him Mr. Messer because he never told me to call him anything else. He knew his audience well. He knew what they wanted, and that was the key to the magic of the show."

Singer Marg Osburne, a soft-spoken, sensitive soul, was the other star of "Don Messer's Jubilee." "I felt Marg Osburne was the woman next door," says another Maritime singer, Anne Murray. "She was kind, witty, a woman of great dignity who was always concerned with others," says McKinnon. "But she herself didn't have an easy life, and her husband really didn't hold a job." Her daughter had medical problems and, says Langstroth, there were marital problems Osburne didn't want to talk about. "She suffered a sense of guilt for not being home as much as she wanted, and her husband didn't enjoy being a house-husband very much," he says.

For a decade "Don Messer's Jubilee" was in the top ten, but by 1969 it was fading in popularity. The network entertainment program director Doug Nixon cancelled what he called "those geriatric fiddlers," setting off one of the biggest firestorms of audience protest in CBC history. It pitted country music fans who loved Messer against city-slicker decision-makers at the CBC in Toronto. Despite protests in the House of Commons and picket lines at the CBC, Nixon's cancellation stood. "It was a shame," says Langstroth, "for Don Messer was more than a television show. He was an institution."

Tommy Hunter

Another institution began when "Country Hoedown" was replaced by "The Tommy Hunter Show," which would run longer than any other musical show in CBC-TV history. Hunter, who became known as the Country Gentleman, was a true believer in the emotions and simplicity of country music, and for a quarter-century he was disparaged by the same blasé critics who had attacked Messer and who could not understand the popularity of country music. As a result, he had a never-ending battle with producers who tried to change his style.

Hunter had started guitar lessons at age nine, paying a dollar a lesson and getting a free guitar as part of the package. He was mesmerized by Roy Acuff and his Smoky Mountain Boys and Girls at a concert they gave in London, Ontario. He heard what he said was "a beat that filled me with so much excitement I could hardly stay in my seat. When Acuff sang of tragedy, you could hear the pain and tears in his voice. I suddenly knew that what I wanted more than anything else was to make music like that for the rest of my life."

As a teenager he sang and played at birthday and Christmas parties, hoping for a chance to sing on the stage and on the radio. His determination overcame, but did not wipe out, the ridicule he felt at age fifteen when auditioning in London for the stage role of a singing hillbilly. "I started to sing and they all laughed," he says. "I was totally stunned at why they were laughing at me. I put the guitar away and that was it. The audition was over." More than forty years later, the memory of that moment still hurts. Despite the laughter, the day after the audition, the producer offered him the role, and Hunter was on his way.

Wearing his trademark yellow cowboy boots and red stetson, the six-foot-four Hunter played around London and even played briefly in New York City. Then "King" Ganam heard about "this skinny kid" and brought him to Toronto where, not yet out of his teens, he played with Ganam on "Country Hoedown." One of Hunter's "Hoedown" colleagues was Gordon Lightfoot, who, in his spare time, played drums and sometimes guitar in a downtown Toronto bar.

Hunter learned a great deal from his "Hoedown" appearances. "While I was sitting on the bandstand, I watched everything: what the producer did, what the set designer did. And I watched the lighting guys and the choreography," he says. Before long, he knew what worked for him in the studio, and, through his travels with Ganam's band, he knew what people in as diverse places as Manitoulin Island, Ontario; Pincher Creek, Alberta; or Antigonish, Nova Scotia, wanted to hear.

In the fall of 1964, the CBC gave Hunter his own program. With his "Hi, folks" opening and his ending of "Be the good Lord willing, we'll be talking to you again next week," the program rapidly became one of the most watched shows, particularly appealing to older people. Joan Tosoni, one of the first female TV directors, directed the show for ten years. She says the crew used to call the live audience "a sea of blue hair." Some came in wheelchairs, some even with respirators. Says Tosoni, "One technician I was standing with while the audience filed by looked at the wrinkled faces and doddering souls and said, 'What the hell is this, Lourdes?' "

"An ambulance would sometimes come," says make-up artist Elaine Saunders. "Once in a while they would resuscitate someone in the audience, and occasionally one of the audience would have to be hauled away. Nobody actually died, though." Once, Tosoni remembers, someone in the audience threw up in the middle of the show, provoking a band member to say, "Gee, I didn't think we played that bad."

Hunter had, at best, a fragile memory for new song lyrics, and to compensate, he says, "We used to put lyrics on the edges of guitars or stick lyrics on the side of the set or put them down on the floor beside the cameraman. Sometimes I made up lyrics when I forgot them."

Studio director Steve Hyde says everything for Hunter was written in big letters on cue cards. "One time Tommy was introducing the Rhythm Pals, Mike, Mark, and Jack, and we just had one card and no room for 'Jack.' He just stopped after 'Mark' and later told us, 'Well, the card didn't say Jack.' "

"There used to be a joke," says producer Paddy Sampson, "that you had to hold up cue cards that said, 'Good Night.' "

Still another challenge for Hunter was choreography. "Moving around on the set never came easy to me," he says. "I could practise and practise, but I never got it. I was very awkward. In a little dance when everybody would move to the right, I would go left." Another problem for Hunter was his own face. "He was very hard to make up because he had skin problems and would sweat a lot," says Saunders.

"But Tommy got more fan letters than anybody at the CBC," says Hyde. "He could sell himself terrifically, but there was no love lost between Tommy and the crew. Some of the guys loathed him. And he was tight with a nickel. He told me once, 'Take the guys over to the Red Lion Pub and buy them a drink for me.' The bill came to forty dollars, and he said, 'Bring me a receipt so I can put it on my taxes.' But I never saw the forty dollars."

"Everybody made snide remarks behind Tommy's back," says Saunders. "And yet, I will say he was a good host." "You'll get a different story from different people about Tommy," says Tosoni. "Sure, people might say he was the biggest jerk in the world. But that was not my experience. For me, I saw a very easy, down-to-earth manner. But Tommy does generate anti as well as pro feelings from people, and I'm not sure why. And when he didn't trust the people around him, he became a monster to some."

One guest on the show who grew to detest Hunter's love affair with the Nashville style of country music was "Stompin' Tom" Connors. "To him, 'The Tommy Hunter Show' was a travesty of the Canadian airwaves because of the American guests," says Tosoni. "To him, it was unforgivable. It was like shit on his boot." When a retrospective of Hunter shows was being compiled, Tosoni says, Connors threatened to sue if a "Stompin' Tom" clip was shown.

"Connors is a character and a half. Holy man, there's just no one like him," says Tosoni. "He's a rabid nationalist. He's passionate and he has an opinion about everything. You might think he has a bit of a hick reputation singing his 'Bud the Spud from the Bright Red Mud' and 'Sudbury Saturday Night,' but he's no hick. He has a very extensive knowledge of politics and philosophy and religion, reads all the time."

Connors is rarely without a bottle of room-temperature Molson's beer in one hand and a cigarette in the other. "I don't even know if he eats, and I think the guy probably never sleeps," says Tosoni. He also has his own dress code. When he was doing a TV show with Tosoni, she suggested he change his brown shirt because the background was brown. "I haven't changed my shirt for a week or so," he said. "So I don't see as how I'd be doing that now. No. Just think of it as 'Stompin' Tom' camouflage."

But "Stompin' Tom" never achieved the national popularity of Tommy Hunter.

Despite Hunter's fame, John Diefenbaker had never heard of him. They met when both were on "Front Page Challenge." Diefenbaker said, "How do you do, young man, and what kind of work are you in?" Slightly disappointed at the lack of recognition, Hunter said, "I'm in the communications business, sir." "Well, I hope you'll be very successful at it," said Diefenbaker as he walked away. Five minutes later Diefenbaker ran into Hunter again and asked the same question. Hunter replied, "Oh, I'm still in communications, Mr. Diefenbaker." "Well," said the forgetful Diefenbaker, "I hope you'll be very successful at it."

This was not the only time Hunter's appearance on "Front Page Challenge" had an awkward moment. Once, he was in a live commercial for Polaroid, demonstrating the wonder of instant cameras. He took a picture of the "Front Page Challenge" panel, then held it up, smiling and saying, "There, isn't that a great picture?" The only trouble was the photograph was completely blank. "What could I do?" he says. "We were live. Finally they just faded to black."

Hunter had a special appeal to women, many of whom sent him marriage proposals and romantic propositions. "Yeah, you get a lot of letters like that," he says. "Sometimes there would be lipstick on my car window saying, 'I love you.'" His biggest problem came when a woman he didn't know sued him for divorce. "After we'd done a show, a lady asked to talk to me privately," he says. "'Tommy, it's about the divorce,' she said. I thought, 'Gosh, the poor gal is going through a divorce and she has no one to talk to.' I told her I was sorry and urged her to get a real good lawyer."

She did, and three days later she showed up with the lawyer at Hunter's rehearsal. "Good to see you again," Hunter smiled a bit warily. "How are you, Jim?" she said. "It's Tommy," Hunter replied. "Oh, it's Tommy now, but it used to be Jim," she said. "Now, Jim, here are the divorce papers." "Divorce papers?" Hunter exclaimed. "What in the world are you talking about?"

At this point Hunter's rehearsal colleagues were snickering and heading for various corners of the room. "Your friends can laugh, but here are the papers. This is very serious," she said, throwing the documents on the floor when Hunter refused to take them. Hunter was stunned. After the woman left, he called his wife and told her, "I've just been served with divorce papers." Mrs. Hunter, who at that instant was having a new refrigerator delivered at home, paused for a moment and said, "Does that mean I have to give the refrigerator back?"

When he convinced her it was serious, they contacted his lawyer, who, on reading the papers, said the grounds were "drinking, gambling, and chasing women." It was a nightmare, however, as the woman's lawyer pressed the case. Finally, Hunter discovered the woman had been married briefly years earlier and was convinced Hunter was her husband. Both were roughly the same age and build, and the husband had also played guitar and sang. Eventually Hunter's lawyer found the military record of the husband, and Hunter had his fingerprints taken to prove he was Tommy Hunter, not Jim, the woman's husband.

"What the great fear in all this was that while there is humour, you could see this hitting the papers: 'Tommy Hunter sued for divorce and bigamy,'" Hunter says.

Hunter's biggest worry, however, was not strange women but producers and directors. The war waged between them was almost neverending. He wanted to stick to the tried-and-true Nashville, Grand Ole Opry country style, but his producers wanted more sophisticated songs, comedy, dancers, and elaborate sets. "They were trying to reach a broader audience, but Tommy knew his audience, and his attitude was, why not please the audience that wants to see him," says Joan Tosoni. "He knew in his heart that there was a whole pile of people out there who wanted what he wanted to give them."

"I kept visualizing," Hunter says, "some poor old guy out in Rosetown, Saskatchewan, who'd worked hard all day and he wanted to just put his feet up and listen. I wanted it simple." He didn't want rock music, Hollywood patter, or a city-slicker's idea of rubes down on the farm. Some of his directors and producers, in contrast, felt Hunter was hopelessly hokey and too stubborn in his ways.

In essence, Hunter felt the producers wanted Cecil B. DeMille while he wanted Roy Acuff. "I couldn't get to square one in explaining my concepts," Hunter laments in criticizing his first producer, Dave Thomas. "I felt the show was becoming more and more unrecognizable. I'd come home most nights dead tired, feeling battered and beat, wondering how much longer I could go on and wishing there was some way out of this nightmare. At the same time, I was drinking too much for my own good."

Hunter learned to be tough with his producers and directors in part from Juliette, whose own battles with producers were legendary at the CBC. "She was very forceful and she knew her audience, so I could relate to that," he says. His determination, however, caused a great deal of conflict. "It was certainly not a happy ship," says Ray McConnell, who directed the program for a year before leaving in frustration. "Dave Thomas, the producer, wanted Hunter to become Robert Preston in *The Music Man*. You would go into rehearsals and there'd be factions everywhere. Tom suspected everyone of competing with him and trying to change him. He was very conscious that he had to be the star, and nobody was allowed to upstage him. I only did one season because I couldn't take any more."

Thomas tangled endlessly with Hunter and brought in comedy writers who had contempt for Hunter's style. Hunter tried to get Thomas fired, and their war escalated. "Either you're going to leave or I'm going to leave," Hunter said. In the end, in a fight over comedy, Thomas quit. "Tommy had been after me to get rid of Thomas for some time," says Jim Guthro, then head of the variety department. "They were giving Tommy a role like L'il Abner, and the comedy was dying. Thomas told me, 'I have to get my way or I resign.' I said, 'Fine, we accept your resignation,' and he was gone." One of the writers, Bill Lynn, became producer but, says Hunter, "He understood very little about country music and the kind of country show I wanted. What we were left with was a show in total disarray." Lynn was replaced by another producer, David Koyle. Again Hunter was unhappy with his producer because, Guthro says, "The show was getting too jazzy, too uptown," and on Hunter's request Koyle was removed. "Tommy was a pushy guy," says Joan Tosoni. "But if he trusted you, he would relax. It was all a matter of trust." Finally, when Les Pouliot took over the job, Hunter got the producer he wanted – a country boy from Saskatchewan, a singer and guitar player himself, who held the same country values as Hunter.

Hunter was now doing the show he wanted to. He didn't even mind when critics called him Lawrence Welk in cowboy boots because, he said, like Welk, he believed in family values in his program and knew his audience.

In spite of all the wars with his producers, "The Tommy Hunter Show" was drawing huge audiences. "Tommy has this ability to communicate on camera," says Guthro. "He's perceived as a nice guy. He was never a great singer, but he is a good singer. His whole package was just nice."

After more than twenty-five years as the star of his prime-time hit show, Tommy Hunter was flying high. While vacationing in Florida in the spring of 1992 prior to his next season, he got a phone call from the network in Toronto advising him that an executive was coming down to talk to him. He thought it was simply to discuss the terms of renewing his contract and was staggered when he was told over lunch in

Sarasota, "The Hunter show will not be coming back in the fall line-up." It had dropped some audience, but it was still drawing close to a million viewers. Still, the network wanted to move him out. The CBC did not want Hunter to complain to the media, however, and he says, "I was told if I didn't go to the press, they would offer me two television shows a year for the next four years. 'But if you do go to the press, forget it,' they told me. They really wanted me to stay away from the media.

"I'd had a wonderful run and had been on TV with my own show and 'Country Hoedown' for thirty-six years. So I was hurt. Only a couple of months before, people at the CBC had told me that the show was safe as long as I wanted to be there. I was hurt mostly because the people I had dealt with didn't have the guts to tell me the news. They sent the news with somebody I hardly knew. I thought I was part of the family. I was told, 'Ivan [Fecan] sends you his love,' and I thought, 'They haven't enough balls to meet me.' I just blew sky high. It was all over."

Nowadays Hunter tours the country, singing for his fans and saying he'll never get in front of the TV cameras for a series again. "It's a pressure-cooker I don't need," he says.

3

TV Drama's Sunshine Days

Variety programming dominated the early years of Canadian television, but drama, too, was enjoying its heyday on the screen.

The first week of TV featured a thirty-minute adaptation of Stephen Leacock's *Sunshine Sketches of a Little Town*, a ninety-minute drama, and a couple of adventure dramas. Over the next few months, a small but expanding group of producers, led by Bob Allen, set the stage for an explosion of Canadian drama on TV. Within a couple of years, under the effervescent direction of Sydney Newman, who took over the CBC-TV drama department from Allen, there was a torrent of dramatic shows. An average year saw about two hundred CBC-produced half-hour, hour, and ninety-minute productions in the schedule, and none of them was in a continuing series format as most shows are today.

Newman had been destined for television since 1949 when, as an executive producer at the National Film Board, he had been sent to NBC New York to learn about the new medium. The NFB had hoped to become the television broadcaster of Canada since, Newman says, "We had the eyes and the CBC had only the ears." But the CBC won that political battle, and following a dispute with his NFB bosses, Newman moved to the CBC as a supervising producer for $7,000 a year, the only CBC-TV producer with any substantial television experience. Initially, he ran what were called "outside broadcasts," producing the first hockey game and first football game, as well as wrestling matches and parades. "But I got so goddamn bored, I decided to get out," he says. When the job as head of drama came open, Newman applied and got it.

At the beginning of television, most actors in the new medium were veterans of radio. They were unused to the complexities of live television, and some of them tended to miss cues and forget lines. The latter was a particular problem because, as Mavor Moore says, "If you dry up on live television, you're sunk." One of the most embarrassing moments of forgetfulness happened to announcer Joel Aldred. "He was the only person, I think, who ever went dry on his own name," says Larry Mann. "They were doing 'General Motors Presents,' and Aldred as the announcer looked into the camera and said, 'Good evening. My name is . . . ah . . . ah . . .' He blew his own name! Somebody whispered from the side, 'Joel Aldred!' " "His brains were all in his voice," says Moore.

Moore himself admits to a "quick forgettery" and would invent dialogue until his lines came back to him. When he forgot his lines in a cocktail party scene in one TV play, he ad libbed, "I don't know about the rest of you, but I've had too much champagne," whereupon he walked off the set, consulted his script, and came back in with a line about having had to go to the bathroom. Actor Frances Hyland remembers a similar escape by another actor who simply forgot to leave the set. When he finally remembered he was not in the scene, he ad libbed, "I think I'll go and play tennis for a while."

Barry Morse, who was one of the biggest stars of early Canadian TV drama, recalls working on the Alfred Hitchcock TV series once with a blonde-bombshell Hollywood actress who, like Aldred, had trouble remembering even her own name in the nervousness of television. The show was being recorded, but after half a dozen takes on a scene, she still didn't have the line right. "We stopped," says Morse, "and the great Hitchcock came waddling over like an old porpoise, put his big fat arms around her, and said, 'Don't worry, darling. It's only TV.' "

Lally Cadeau was literally left speechless when she was doing a show with, she says, "a dreadful actor who was so bad I was fascinated. My mind went blank, I was so riveted by this awful performance. I had to call out, 'Line!' which I'd never done before."

One way the floor director had of prompting forgetful actors was to push a button that cut off all the microphones in the studio, at which point he'd yell the line to the actor and then release the button. "I dismantled it," Newman says. "I said the fuckers had to learn their lines."

Newman remembers one live show featuring Basil Rathbone. "Every fucking word of dialogue went out of his brain in the middle of the show," says Newman. Rathbone's co-stars, William Shatner and Patrick McNee, suddenly had to improvise. "In every scene, they had to help Rathbone by saying to him things like, 'If you were going to ask me about that, sir, my answer would be . . .' and then Patrick or Bill would give him his own line. It was a nightmare, but the funny thing is, the audience didn't have a clue."

Robert Goulet remembers that the actor who played the queen in *Camelot* forgot her line at one point. As she stood there hemming and hawing, he quickly said, "Possibly, Your Majesty, you mean that at this time in your life . . ." and then proceeded to paraphrase her lines and do his own. "You just can't dry up," he says. "You have to keep on going."

Leslie Nielsen remembers a scene, however, in which the star did not keep going when he forgot his lines. Desperately searching for the right words, he ad libbed to his co-star, "Well, what do you have to say for yourself?" The startled response was "Nothing. I think I'll go to sleep." Whereupon the director cut to another studio for an announcer to read a commercial. The announcer, however, was not expecting such an early cue and was caught on camera reading a book. He hastily began his commercial, but in the background, cutting through what they thought was an idle studio, were half a dozen men dressed in Alpine outfits, walking to their positions for the next scene and arguing about where they should go. As the announcer was delivering his commercial message, the audience also heard, "I thought we were supposed to be over there? No, no . . . it's the other way."

Lloyd Bochner once starred in a live TV drama with the American actors Eva Marie Saint and Tony Randall. In one scene Saint was sitting in an airplane beside Randall when he suddenly forgot his lines. The director cut to Saint, who looked very puzzled, and then cut back to Randall, hoping he'd remembered the line by now. He hadn't, but he invented one that turned out to be unfortunate. As the plane supposedly soared through the skies, he rose from his seat, said to Saint, "Ah . . . this is my stop where I get off," and walked up the aisle and disappeared.

Don Harron recalls an actor who, whenever he forgot his lines, would continue to move about, silently mouthing words until the lines came back to him, driving the sound technician crazy and leaving the audience at home thinking something had gone wrong with the sound. "I once dried up completely when I was in the Broadway drama *Separate Tables*," says Harron. "I saw Marilyn Monroe in the audience, and I just forgot everything."

Sometimes it wasn't someone forgetting lines that caused the problem, but someone adding lines. Barry Morse was once in a drama in which an older actor played the bit role of a butler with a brief message for Morse, the master of the house. Instead of delivering the message, the butler said, "May I have a word with your Grace?" "Now that wasn't in the script," says Morse, "so I slowly and quizzically said, 'Yes.' " "I wish to give you my notice, sir," the butler intoned. When Morse ad libbed, "This is so sad and so sudden," the butler replied, "I came here first in your grandfather's day . . ." and went on for ten minutes about the house's history, his in-laws, and the chambermaid. He actually cried at one point before finally delivering his brief message and walking away. Then Morse got back to the script and the show continued. The audience, however, hadn't noticed anything amiss.

Cameras sometimes failed in the middle of a live production, necessitating hasty improvisation. On one occasion Morse saw a camera go out and quickly spotted another on the set some distance away. It was activated by the control room, and Morse, ad libbing as he went, led his mystified fellow actors to the other end of the studio to the working camera and they continued the scene.

Once, Lloyd Bochner was starring in "The Queen of Spades" for the CBC. His co-star, Mary Savage, had "died" and was lying in a coffin. "The scene went well," says Bochner, "but for some reason, Mary thought the camera was off her, and she sat up in the coffin on camera, got out, and walked off in plain view of the watching audience."

Bochner's worst moment came onstage in a drama, written by Morley Callaghan and produced by Mavor Moore, in which Bochner was the villain. There was a confrontation among himself, fellow actor

Don Harron, and heroine Diane Foster. At the climactic moment, Bochner was supposed to grab Foster's blouse and rip it off. It was a trick breakaway blouse, but on this occasion, Bochner accidentally reached in too far, grabbing the straps to her bra and slip as well as the blouse, and yanked everything off. She stood there stark-naked from the waist up in front of the audience. "I was aghast," he says. "Diane was at the point of fainting. She was shaking and could hardly stand. Don Harron, with what he claimed was presence of mind but which I knew to be pure lechery, leapt in front of her and took her in his arms." The curtain came down, and as they got offstage actor Alfie Scopp, who had been watching from the wings, came up to Bochner and, pretending they had earlier made a bet, said in front of Foster, "You son of a gun. You did it. Here's the five dollars." "Diane," Bochner says, "was ready to kill me."

Bochner was ready to kill a CBC propsman after doing a live scene in which Bochner and Barry Morse were supposedly sitting in an outside café on the Champs Élysées. They were drinking flat ginger ale the CBC had substituted for wine. The wine bottle of ginger ale, however, had been sitting open for a while on a props shelf and had attracted a lot of insects. "When the waiter poured it, I saw there was a quarter-inch of fruit flies on my wine and Barry's," says Bochner. "As he raised it to his lips, I said *sotto voce*, 'Don't drink it, Barry,' but he didn't hear me and tossed it back in one gulp. The look on his face as he swallowed the fruit flies was something to behold."

Morse had a much more unnerving on-camera fright during a CBC version of *Macbeth*. In one scene he had a particularly energetic sword fight with another actor. Morse had a saw-edge sword, and as the scene ended, he brought his sword against his opponent's neck. He got carried away, however, and pressed the sword too vigorously. "Suddenly, I could see blood coming out," says Morse. "I could hear the director shouting through the earphones of the cameraman, 'Oh God, there's real blood. Oh Jesus, hold it!' I'm standing there with all this blood dripping down from the poor boy. We're on live, and I have to rush out and get ready for the next scene, and the poor boy is now lying on the floor and there is blood all over my hand." The scene went to black, the actor was carted off to hospital for several stitches in his neck, and Morse carried on with the next scene.

Leslie Nielsen recalls an equally violent, although less bloody, moment in a space fantasy he once did. He was a commander on Mars, battling with two crew members. One started firing at Nielsen and then fell dead when he accidentally shot himself with his last bullet. Then the second crew member threatened Nielsen with his gun. "I've got my gun too," Nielsen said, reaching into his holster only to find it empty. Since this was live TV, and Nielsen was supposed to shoot and kill the other crew member, he didn't know what to do. Thinking quickly, he ran at his adversary and strangled him. The other actor was momentarily astonished at all this, not knowing what Nielsen was up to, but then fell to the ground. "The producer said the audience wouldn't know the difference, and it looked all right," Nielsen says.

Larry Mann was once in an airplane scene looking out a window when suddenly he and the audience saw two stagehands holding a ladder and having a cigarette. "They seemed to be walking by on the clouds and had stopped to have a smoke," Mann says. "They were on for a few seconds before the camera pulled off them."

Another unexpected moment for Mann occurred when he was dressing for a black-tie dinner in a scene and reached into a closet to get his formal jacket. While he and his co-star continued to chat, he put it on, only to discover it was a tweed sports coat and not the black formal jacket. He looked into the mirror and ad libbed, "Did you switch cleaners, because I don't like the way they do our stuff there." She couldn't think of anything to say and poured herself a drink. He went back to the closet not knowing how to get out of the scene. "I reached into the closet and there was a nervous little stagehand hiding there who had hung up the wrong jacket for me and now gave me the tux," says Mann. "I put it on, and we went on with the scene."

Leslie Nielsen recalls acting in dramas at NBC that forced performers to make clothing switches just behind the scenery in a matter of seconds. The network had glass booths above the sets so advertisers could watch the production. They not only had a view of the set but of the performers changing clothes as well. Nielsen remembers a show with Viveca Lindfors when she had to make a fast, total change of clothes: "She looks up in the middle of changing and here's a booth with twenty men all gaping at her almost stark-naked as she changes."

Advertisers

In the early years of television, advertisers not only wanted to see the production in the studio, but were far more involved in the programs they sponsored than they are today. In radio days advertisers often actually controlled programs. The CBC rejected that approach, although advertising agencies still had considerable influence. In some cases advertisers acted as censors seeking to eliminate controversial issues and any program theme they thought might be detrimental to their products. Their intrusions were sometimes minor, but still irritating, such as when a margarine company sponsor told "Pick the Stars" host Dick MacDougal not to wish contestants good luck because that was the name of a competitor's brand. A similar incident involved comedian Libby Morris, who was kicked off "Holiday Ranch" because the sponsor, Aylmer Foods, thought viewers would associate her name with the company's rival, canned-food maker Libby. On a program called "Here's Duffy," a reference to drinking coffee was removed at the request of the sponsor, a tea company.

Barry Morse remembers an ad agency representative for the Aluminum Company of America stopping production in mid-rehearsal and forcing a script change when one character spoke of drinking from a pewter beer mug. "They couldn't stand the mention of another metal," Morse says.

Morse got into trouble with General Motors in a show where he portrayed a beachcomber who at one point picked his nose. "They suggested if I kept doing this on the show, I might not be engaged in future productions quite so much," he says. "They just didn't think the image went with shiny new cars. I said there were three other places where I can do it, and I did."

"We always talked nasty about the sponsor," says Sydney Newman. "He was never someone you liked. Sometimes they came sweeping into the control room like big shots. They'd get scripts in advance of rehearsals, and it was always, 'We don't like this' or 'Why don't you consider this.' You couldn't say 'my God.' You couldn't say 'bloody.' Open-mouth kissing was out. Every week I had this."

CBC management's preoccupation with swearing never abated. Correspondent Stanley Burke created an uproar in the mid-1960s for taking the Lord's name in vain when he was involved in a news special from the United Nations. "Christ Almighty, don't throw cues at me!" he shouted at the beginning of a program on Cuba when the cameras mistakenly opened on him at the UN instead of Knowlton Nash in Washington. Headlines blazed with protest at Burke's profanity. Shortly after, a management memo went out stating that "Christ" and words such as "damn," "hell," "blast," or "my God" should certainly not be used. But by the early 1970s, attitudes to swearing had changed. In an executive discussion of swear words used in a prime-time drama, the producer was arguing for more language freedom. TV managing director Norn Garriock settled the argument by slamming the table with his fist and saying, "Okay, that's it! I've decided. We'll leave in three fucks and four shits, and all the rest have to come out."

Some producers occasionally sought to evade management's scrutiny of their programs if they thought the CBC might try to change it drastically. In some cases the management would be shown the script just a few hours before the program aired, so the only alternatives would be a reluctant approval or an order to yank the program off the air altogether and risk causing a big public scene. West Coast broadcaster Jack Webster says he remembers one time when, in order to avoid problems, the producer handed in a phony script for management's approval. "Daryl Duke was a great producer," says Webster. "For his show 'Crawling Arnold,' he'd have two scripts. He would show one to management and one to the performers. That way, management didn't know what was coming at them."

In the early years of television, sponsors as well as management watched closely for swearing and other perceived transgressions in scripts, such as those for the prestigious Sunday prime-time drama series "General Motors Presents." GM and its ad agency representatives tried to avoid all controversy by cutting out swear words, keeping watch on morality and brutality, and an eye open for what it saw as socialism. At one point the programmers labelled the show "General Motors Prevents" in light of the cuts, and GM actually withdrew its sponsorship of one play because it didn't like the theme. Sometimes the advertisers focused not on the show but on the commercials. Don Harron remembers sitting in a booth with two ad men who talked all the way through the show, pausing only to watch the commercials in reverential silence. Their sole comment to Harron after the program ended was "The Jell-O looked great tonight."

Writer Arthur Hailey's highly successful drama "Flight into Danger" aroused GM's apprehensions because the plot involved a pilot who got food poisoning from eating tainted salmon. "GM at that time was negotiating a huge sale to the salmon fishing industry out on the B.C. coast," says former advertising executive Ted Hough. "They just didn't want to upset the salmon industry by suggesting that there was tainted salmon available in Canada. There was quite a long struggle over that one." In the end the tainted salmon stayed in the script.

"Flight into Danger" was one of the great success stories of early Canadian TV, and it propelled its author into a career on the international best-seller lists with novels on planes, automobiles, and hotels. At the time he wrote it, Hailey was writing and editing stories for *Bus and Truck* magazine in Toronto after an unsuccessful career as a short-story writer in England. He was paid six hundred dollars for his script. "He wrote it in white heat over twenty-four hours after flying to Montreal and being served [on the plane] a dinner choice of meat or fish," says Sydney Newman. "He wondered what would happen if the fish were poisoned, and he rented a typewriter at his hotel and wrote the play."

Occasionally advertisers received complaints from their customers because of their sponsorships. One play on "General Motors Presents" depicted an RCMP officer as a brute. Four days after airing the play, GM received a formal letter from the RCMP declaring the show was a slur against the force. "The next time we place an order for cars, we will think as to who we will buy them from," Newman remembers the letter stating.

Advertisers had as many problems with live commercials, as much as producers and performers had in doing live drama. Hough remembers, "We would have models who were called 'upholstery strokers' because they would stroke the car's upholstery and sit behind the wheel in the commercials. One sat behind the wheel of a Buick, and the commercial went well, but she wouldn't get out of the car. Finally, someone went over after it ended and found she had gone to the bathroom all over the upholstery from nerves and had been too embarrassed to move." Another time, one of the "strokers" accidentally brushed against the horn, and it shorted out and kept blaring all through the live commercial. A stagehand had forgotten to disconnect the battery.

When he directed "Showtime," Norman Jewison got into trouble with General Electric for making some productions too sexy or impudent. They also objected to his hiring of writer Reuben Ship, who had been blacklisted in the United States as a suspected Communist. "Somebody got up in the House of Commons and said, 'Jewison is hiring Commies to write his shows.' And I had to go down and see the ad agency people. Everybody was upset because they thought the CBC was riddled with Commies. We had our own inquisition here."

Shortly after this episode, Jewison began to feel unappreciated by the CBC. "People in the arts have to be patted on the head once in a while," he says, and no pats were coming his way. When Mike Dann, the CBS program director, saw some of his work, he hired Jewison in 1958 for $25,000 a year, twice what CBC was paying him, and told him to inject some life into the show "Hit Parade." "I was really in search of a larger audience," says Jewison, "and besides, you really had to go away to be appreciated. When the Belafonte show won some Emmys, all of a sudden the Canadian papers said how talented I was."

Sidney Furie, a young, up-and-coming writer, was exasperated by one ad agency's efforts to prevent the airing of a romantic comedy he had written in which a boy from a poor family elopes to Buffalo with an heiress in the face of opposition from her family. Ad executive Hugh Horler told Newman to delay the show, and he did. It was rescheduled twice, and each time Horler refused to let it be aired. "You've got to give me a reason," Newman finally said. "I can't keep delaying it." It turned out, says Newman, that GM's vice-president of advertising was in a boardroom competition with another senior GM executive whose daughter had done exactly what was portrayed in Furie's play. Newman recalls Horler telling him that if the play went on, there would be a boardroom fight because the executive whose daughter had run away would think the advertising vice-president had put on the play deliberately to embarrass him. Newman reluctantly agreed not to put it on. Furie was so angry, Newman says, he quit the CBC and went to England, where he became a top film director.

Hollywood Calls

Furie and Jewison were part of the flood of talent that poured out of Canada after cutting their teeth on Canadian television in the 1950s and 1960s. Arthur Hiller, one of the early CBC star directors, got into an argument with the CBC over a $300 raise he wanted added to his $7,000 salary. "The CBC wouldn't give it to him, and he went to New York and got a job right away," says Newman. "We lost Arthur Hiller and all his talents, which brought him such acclaim in the U.S., for a measly $300." Lloyd Bochner wanted to stay in Canada, but he also wanted some financial security from the CBC and asked for a contract for so many shows per year, instead of being hired on a show-by-show basis. But the answer was no. He remembers being told by TV head Fergus Mutrie, "We've never done that." The result was that when Hollywood came calling, Bochner went.

This creative hemorrhage led, in time, to an end of the bright early years of Canadian television. Producers and directors who left included Jewison, Hiller, George McCowan, Harvey Hart, Norman Sedawie, Mark Warren, Bill Davis, Ted Kotcheff, Allan Blye, Bernie Orenstein, Saul Ilson, Chris Beard, Stan Harris, Bob Arnott, John Aylesworth, Frank Peppiatt, and a host of others who found success in Hollywood, New York, and London. "They left because of a bigger stage," says Blye, who wrote and produced major American network shows. "I loved working in Toronto, but you want to find out how far you can go."

Composer Jimmy Dale went to Hollywood for that and for the money. "I remember pulling down about $3,000-plus a week for a time in 1970, which was pretty fair for 1970," he says. "We had two Rolls-Royces, one white and one black. One with the licence plate 'Bloor' and the other licence plate said 'Yonge' because we felt like Canadians."

A parade of Canadian TV stars was also drawn south, including Robert Goulet, Lloyd Bochner, Lorne Greene, William Shatner, Larry Mann, Barry Morse, Rich Little, Paul Anka, Alan Young, and Austin Willis. In part they were lured by the money, which, to start, was often four or five times what they earned at the CBC, but in addition, says Bochner, "The Americans had a greater choice of scripts. They had far more writers." They also left because of what the performers perceived as a lack of appreciation in Canada and an absence of any Canadian star system. "You can be a full-time garbage collector in Toronto and you'll be accepted as such," says Mann. "Nobody says, 'If you were any good, you'd be collecting garbage in New York.' Only in show business is this said. No matter how good you are, none of it counts because you're based in Canada."

"Canada," says Sydney Newman, in noting a lack of appreciation for Canadian creative talent, "is really a sow that eats its own farrow." Juliette says, "I don't think the CBC ever really wanted anyone to have the kind of power a real star has because then they couldn't control you."

Frances Hyland, who chose not to move to the United States, nevertheless sometimes wonders whether she should have. "The only thing that worries me as a Canadian actor," she once mused, "and it's a constant and serious worry, is that at my age I have no savings, nothing to fall back on. If I lose my health or my ability to work, I think to myself, 'My God, is it going to be one room in Parkdale?' Sometimes that does make me wish I had gone abroad and into more commercial work with decent financial rewards."

Jewison estimates that by the beginning of the 1960s, up to 40 per cent of the key CBC creative talent had moved out of the country. At one point on "The Sonny and Cher Show" in the United States, almost everybody except the stars were Canadian, among them writers Allan Blye, Mark Shekter, Bob Arnott, Billy Van, and composer Jimmy Dale. Canadians also dominated backstage in "The Andy Williams Show," "The Smothers Brothers," and others. Norman Campbell stayed in Canada but visited the United States to direct episodes of "All In The Family" and "The Mary Tyler Moore Show."

What upset many actors who didn't move to the United States was that, compared to those who did go, they felt they were being treated as second-class citizens. "There simply was no Canadian star system," says Hyland. "There was a lot of fear in the CBC bureaucracy that we'd get ideas above our station. When they brought in actors from the States, they were treated very much like stars, but not us. They wanted to maintain control over us, and we were considered small fry. But I stayed in Canada because I learned more about my craft here than I would elsewhere."

"The star system didn't exist in Canada," says Bochner. "I think it was part of the Canadian self-effacing attitude, and as was said to me so often and to others, 'If you're so good, why are you still here?' "

Mann says that while he felt CBC executives expressed little appreciation or interest in him, this was not the case in Hollywood. On his first Hollywood show, he got a message on the set to see his ultimate boss, movie mogul Darryl Zanuck, who told him how impressed he was with his performance. "It's terrific and I love it," the Hollywood legend said. Mann started to cry and said, "I worked in Canada at the CBC and I won three best actor awards and not one executive said a bloody thing to me." Mann today says, "It was an eye-opener for me. Zanuck thought what I was doing was important."

Those writers, directors, and actors who went to Hollywood, New York, and London not only played on a larger stage but came to know the oddities and foibles of some American stars.

Allan Blye was, for a time, close to Elvis Presley, whose innocence of the real world Blye found fascinating. "He had no touch with reality," says Blye. "I once asked him, 'Do you know how much money you make?' He said, 'I have no idea. I was once told I make $30,000 to $40,000 a day. All I know is that I can buy anything I want.' You'd better not say to him, 'Gee, that's a nice looking car,' because he'd buy it for you. He just had no contact with reality."

When Blye once talked a reluctant Presley into walking across the street from his office to get a hamburger when they were working late one night, he didn't realize it wouldn't be a simple act. "He had his six or eight bodyguards – 'buddies' he called them – walk with us, and it's ten o'clock at night, but suddenly there's a traffic jam. Guys are blowing their horns at us, people are abandoning their cars in the middle of the street and surrounding us and following us into the restaurant. People kept coming over to the table, and while we were eating, the guys at the restaurant put up a sign in the window saying, 'Elvis is eating here.' "

Sometimes late at night, Presley would arrive at Blye's home on his motorcycle dressed in a black jacket, black helmet, and goggles. "We'd drink Scotch, get loaded, and then his buddies would come over in a truck and take him and his motorcycle home."

The leather-lunged Foster Hewitt first screamed, "He shoots! He scores!" into a microphone in 1923. For half a century, his Saturday night hockey broadcasts were a nationwide shared experience. *(National Archives of Canada, MISA 15142)*

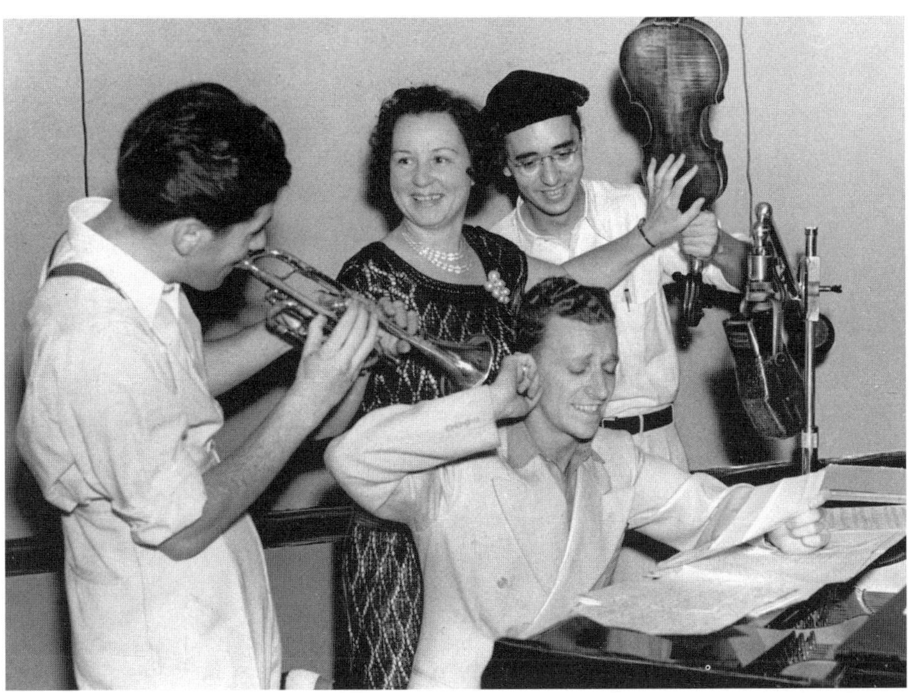

Two million Canadians tuned in to "The Happy Gang" at the height of its popularity. The original Gangsters are, left to right, trumpeter Bob Farnon, organist Kathleen Stokes, violinist Blain Mathe, and leader and pianist Bert Pearl. *(Courtesy of the CBC)*

Left, Bert Pearl in his heyday as Canada's first entertainment superstar and, right, forty years later, covering his bitterness at the crash of his career with a brave smile. *(Courtesy of the CBC)*

Left, Don Harron in the 1950s as a star of CBC-TV dramas and, right, forty years later, as the character Charlie Farquharson. *(National Archives of Canada [left] MISA 16142; [right] MISA 15660)*

The CBC's Matthew Halton was Canada's best-known war correspondent. His colourful reports captured the sounds and emotions of battle as no one else's did. *(National Archives of Canada, MISA 15870)*

Brilliant and demanding, Andrew Allan, centre, gave Canadians a golden age of CBC Radio drama by exploiting the talents of writers and performers such as Lister Sinclair, left, and Alice Hill, right. *(National Archives of Canada, MISA 16081)*

A trio of radio stars in Andrew Allan's "Stage" series who later gained international celebrity status. Left to right, John Colicos, Barry Morse, and Douglas Rain. *(National Archives of Canada, MISA 16152)*

John Drainie, regarded by Andrew Allan as the greatest radio actor ever developed in Canada. *(National Archives of Canada, MISA 16156)*

As Rawhide, Max Ferguson, left, was the most controversial program host ever on the CBC, and his irreverent sidekick, Allan McFee, right, was the greatest practical joker in CBC history. *(National Archives of Canada, [left] MISA 16160; [right] MISA 16151)*

In the glory days of early CBC-TV drama, no one shone more brightly than Lloyd Bochner, left, who later went to Hollywood, and Toby Robins, centre, who later went to London's West End. Here they are seen with the Hollywood actor Mona Freeman. *(National Archives of Canada MISA 16138)*

Lorne Greene, known as the Voice of Doom for his CBC wartime radio newscasts, later starred in "Bonanza" as the world's best-known cowboy rancher, Ben Cartwright. Between these roles, he performed in several CBC-TV Shakespearean dramas. *(National Archives of Canada, MISA 7685)*

Baritone Robert Goulet, star of Canada's pioneer TV music program "Showtime," and one of the "Showtime" dancers. Goulet went on to international stardom with the musical *Camelot*. *(National Archives of Canada, MISA 16149)*

Senior producer Mavor Moore's creative genius and irrepressible enthusiasm helped bring television progamming to the CBC in 1952. *(National Archives of Canada, MISA 16153)*

"Don Messer's Jubilee," with its exuberant and unashamedly corny country music, became a smash hit on Canadian TV. It made household names of its stars: left to right, fiddler Don Messer and singers Catherine McKinnon, Charlie Chamberlain, and Marg Osburne. *(Courtesy of the CBC)*

Norman Jewison originally wanted to be an actor, but his gentle authority and creative effervescence led him to become the most successful of all CBC producer-directors. After the CBC, he went on to Hollywood fame, winning an Academy Award. *(National Archives of Canada, MISA 14660)*

Director Sidney Newman, who shouted, "Cue the elephant!" during a test-run live TV show at the Canadian National Exhibition just before television began. The elephant wouldn't perform, but Newman still went on to run CBC-TV drama, BBC drama, and later headed the National Film Board. *(National Archives of Canada, MISA 14669)*

Presley told Blye he was embarrassed about his movie career and said, "I never again want to play a fucking gum-chewing singing mechanic." "He'd done something like that in virtually every movie he ever did," says Blye.

When Blye was pitching a comedy show idea about human-sized animals to a couple of American network bigwigs in Hollywood, he got some unanticipated help from his partner and from comedian Steve Martin. Blye was sitting at a table in a bistro making his pitch when his partner, dressed as a six-foot-six dog, and Martin, dressed as a gigantic feathered woodpecker, went by their table and sat at the bar. They thought their entrance would stir a commotion and excite the network officials, who would immediately see the merit of Blye's proposal. However, the bartender looked at the giant woodpecker and the huge dog and, without smiling, said, "What'll you have?" They both ordered Scotch and were ignored by the bartender and the network types as well as others in the restaurant. "Eventually, disillusioned, they walked out and back to the office," says Blye, "but later we did sell the show idea to the network."

Barry Morse

A critic once compared Barry Morse to the television test pattern – Morse was starring in so many shows in the early years of Canadian TV it seemed like he was on TV just as often. He and Lloyd Bochner were the leading male actors of the era, but Morse was the unchallenged veteran of television. He'd been on television as early as 1936, when the BBC was experimenting with TV.

A cockney from the London slums with an accent thicker than Ben Wicks's, the truculent young Morse skipped school much of the time and roamed the city, getting his education in the streets, libraries, art galleries, and museums instead of school. Still, he managed to win a scholarship to the Royal Academy of Dramatic Arts and soon found his way to the London stage and BBC Radio, as well as the new medium of television, although "the telly" was not well regarded in those days. A prominent West End actor met him in the late 1930s and asked what he was doing. "I'm at the BBC, sir," Morse brightly said. "Ah, the wireless." "No," said Morse, "sort of the wireless with pictures." "You're a bloody fool wasting your time on that twaddle" was the thespian's response. "Don't you understand it's just a fad like the yo-yo. They'll have forgotten about it by Christmas."

The cameras were so primitive in those prehistoric years of television, Morse says, that in order to get enough contrast on the screen "we had to be made up the colour of an orange. The exception was our eyelids and our lips, which were made up in navy blue."

Usually the actors played to only one camera and not infrequently it would go wrong. "Since we had only the one camera," Morse remembers, "they would put up a slide saying, 'Technical Difficulties. Please Wait.' And we'd just wait there until the camera was fixed and then carry on with the play."

Morse came to Canada in 1951, the year prior to TV's arrival in Canada, and he worked in many of Andrew Allan's radio dramas before becoming one of the most recognized faces on Canadian TV. He became one of the most recognized faces in the world not long after with the American network show "The Fugitive," in part a modern remake of *Les Misérables*. Morse as Gerrard, who spent more than four years as the detective chasing the wanted man, David Janssen, was a TV version of Victor Hugo's Javert. The final episode had the biggest audience in history for an entertainment show to that time, topped later by the last episode of "Dallas." To this day the series is repeated in a number of countries, but because the networks did not give performers long-term residuals in those days, Morse gets not a cent from the reruns.

The recognizability of his face once led him into a conversation on a London double-decker bus with a six-year-old boy who knew the face, if not the name. Puzzled at seeing him in person, the boy said, "Are you off the telly?" "Yes, that's right, son," said Morse. "How'd you get out?" "Well," Morse replied, "you see, it's Saturday, and they always let us out on Saturdays so we can have a day off." The boy then asked, "How'd you get so big?" Morse told him, "When they let us out we're always the same size as everybody else. You watch on Monday and you'll see I'll be small again." That seemed to satisfy the youngster, who went back to his mother.

Morse's own children, however, seldom saw him on TV because his programs were on after their bedtime. "His kids complained they never saw him on TV, but he told us they watched 'Howdy Doody,'" says Alfie Scopp. "He asked if he could play a role, and so we put him in with a chorus of kids. The camera panned across the kids' faces and suddenly there was Morse's big old face smiling and singing, 'It's Howdy Doody time,' and then his kids really believed he was on TV."

Morse and Lloyd Bochner were friendly rivals in the galaxy of Canadian TV stars, but their pay was a modest thousand dollars a show during most of the early TV years. After Bochner had done Hamlet, Morse was to play Macbeth, but Morse wanted a dollar more than Bochner. He also wanted the extra dollar to maintain the principle that there was room for negotiation in contracts for stars. When drama head Sydney Newman offered to give him a dollar, Morse refused, insisting it be written into the contract. "Finally, they assured Barry that he was getting a dollar more than I was," says Bochner. "Then, quite confidentially, they revealed to me that, in fact, I was getting a dollar more than Barry."

Lloyd Bochner

Bochner had first demanded a better fee a couple of decades earlier when he was earning five dollars per role as a teenaged actor in a radio show about the RCMP. At the start of one show, he was asked if he would rattle a harness, chains, and bells, and he did. After the show, he asked his boss, advertising agency head Harry "Red" Foster, for an extra five dollars for doing the sound effects. "Kid, what is this?" Foster asked. "You're asking me for an extra five dollars for rattling these chains? Kid, if you insist on this, you'll never work in this town again." Bochner did insist, got the extra five dollars, and became one of the busiest actors in Canada.

He had started acting at age ten in a play directed by Andrew Allan. In high school he performed with Don Harron, and Lorne Greene had been his summer camp counsellor. "He had a big influence on my life, and we remained friends all through his time in Canada and Hollywood," says Bochner. Another influence was Frank Shuster, Bochner's summer camp head of drama.

After wartime navy service and CBC Radio work, Bochner toyed with the idea of working with Mavor Moore at the United Nations. But when

Moore went back to Canada to help run CBC-TV as chief producer, he persuaded Bochner to return too. Soon afterwards Bochner began commuting between Toronto and New York before being wooed to Hollywood.

Frances Hyland

Other than Barry Morse, the earliest Canadian star on TV was Saskatchewan-born Frances Hyland, who was acting in BBC television dramas in the late 1940s. After university, she, like Morse, learned her craft at London's Royal Academy of Dramatic Arts and got her first stage break at age nineteen when she was cast as Stella in *A Streetcar Named Desire*. The streetcar conductor in the same production was a young, aspiring Canadian actor named Don Harron. He'd just arrived in London and had auditioned for the part after the producer asked him, "Are you American?" Harron said, "No. A Canadian." "What the fuck's the difference? You're hired," said the producer.

Like Morse when he did the early television in England, Hyland faced "huge banks of orange lights" when she performed on the BBC. "You wore this bright-orange make-up about an inch and as half thick – suffocating."

Hyland says she was "kidnapped" by director Tyrone Guthrie to return to Canada for the Stratford Festival to play opposite James Mason in *Measure for Measure*. From then on she was based in Canada, although she travelled to New York, London, and elsewhere for stage and TV roles. Like her fellow stars in the 1950s and 1960s, she was doing four or more TV shows a month. She performed with everyone from William Shatner to Anthony Perkins and Orson Welles. "Welles was frightening at first with his great entourage," she says. "That offended me, but then I realized he was very shy and needed a lot of people to shore him up."

One actor who didn't frighten her was Richard Burton. "I was desperately in love with Richard for a long time, and we had a wonderful affair," she says. "I was just a baby, but Richard laid seige to me, which didn't take long. During our affair we often went to Welsh pubs and met Dylan Thomas, the poet and legendary drunk. But, oh, what a conversationalist. You'd be spellbound for hours." Hyland adds that Burton "was a man of big, poetic imagination and he spoke magically. He was lovable and he also was very irresponsible. Ask his wife, Sybil! Ask me! But he was a charmer with his Welsh passion and energy."

At one point she asked Burton about the adulation he was receiving for his acting and remembers him telling her, "Everywhere you go, there's someone shoving a chair under your bum, and if you take out a cigarette, there are eighty-four people jumping up to light it and tell you how wonderful you are. And you know it's not true." To Hyland, Burton seemed a lot like his grandfather, who, Burton told her, had made a bet in a pub that he could race his wheelchair down a mountain at top speed. He did, but he died in the process.

Hyland later married director George McCowan. After she amicably divorced him, she never remarried, although she has said, "I certainly didn't remain celibate, and I had a very good time indeed with some nice and not-so-nice gentlemen." But she can become introspective at times. "I've spent forty-five years pretending to be somebody else in a life full of other personalities," she once said. "I don't think I've bothered to find out who I am."

A self-described "tough old broad," Hyland rejected living in the United States because, she says, "I didn't want to be an American. I'm a Canadian, and I liked that and am proud of that."

William Shatner

A fellow actor who took the opposite attitude from Hyland is William Shatner of "Star Trek" fame, who originally was an actor in the classics aired in the 1950s by CBC. Aside from roles in Shakespearean plays, he also starred in 1953 in a CBC children's series called "Space Command." His co-star in the series was James Doohan, who later co-starred with him as Scotty in "Star Trek." Future CTV president Murray Chercover directed "Space Command," a chore that, according to producer Ross McLean, brought Chercover to "the point of nervous collapse." He was, says McLean, "violently ill" with nerves before every show.

At the CBC and in Hollywood, Shatner was not universally applauded by his colleagues. "He is probably one of the most disliked people you've ever met," said Bruno Gerussi, who performed frequently with Shatner in the early Canadian TV days. He recalled discussing Shatner with "Star Trek" co-star Leonard Nimoy, Mr. Spock in the hit series. "He is not one of my favourite people and I've known him for a long time," Gerussi told Nimoy, who, normally reluctant to criticize anybody, then launched into a tirade about Shatner.

Hollywood star Doug McClure once did an ill-fated TV series with Shatner, and when Gerussi asked him what it was like for him during the shooting of the series, McClure said, "I get up, shave and shower, and drive to work down the freeway and say to myself, 'Oh Jesus, another six pages of Bill Shatner.' "

The "Star Trek" star is also the butt of innumerable jokes about his toupees. "He must have eighteen rugs," said Gerussi. When he was in Vancouver on a film shoot, Shatner worked for a couple of days with the "Beachcomber" Mountie Jackson Davies, who had a part in the film. "Jackson had heard my stories about Shatner," Gerussi said, "and on meeting him, Jackson, who's tall and bald, said, 'Bruno sends his best.' Then he looked at his hair and said, 'Nice rug!' Shatner never spoke to him again for the rest of the shoot."

Shatner had been one of the pioneering actors on Andrew Allan's "Stage" series, and Barry Morse remembers performing with him in *The Man Who Came to Dinner*. "In the show young Bill was given to mumbling rather a lot," says Morse. "I sometimes couldn't even hear him, and I used to say, 'What's that you say, son?' or 'Can't hear you, boy!' And he'd have to repeat it. He wanted to sound like Marlon Brando."

Morse says Shatner always treated him courteously, "but what I hear from elsewhere is rather a pity because he's been extraordinarily lucky. He's become a little too impressed with his own standing." Frances Hyland, who has performed with Shatner, says, "He was vainer than he had a right to be. He's charming in 'Star Trek,' but he's not really in the top rank of acting."

Shatner may not be in the top rank of actors, but he certainly has been among the top rank of TV stars because of the immense international popularity of the "Star Trek" series.

Lorne Greene

The most successful Canadian TV star was Lorne Greene, who went from being a CBC Radio news anchor to a Shakespearean actor and, finally, to Ben Cartwright in "Bonanza," the world's most famous rancher. The secret of his success, whether he was playing Brutus, Beethoven, Cartwright, or was the voice of the CBC "National News," was his majestic authority, which came partly from his voice and partly from his assured manner. It also came from his towering, white-haired physical presence that focused attention wherever he went. "He was the only man I've known whose voice exactly reflected his physical appearance," says Greene's longtime friend and colleague Leslie Nielsen.

Charmed by his deep, sonorous voice, Canadians hung on to every word Greene spoke on the "National News." This made it all the more embarrassing when, during one wartime newscast, Greene misspoke himself in an item on a big prairie grain crop, saying, "Western farmers are expecting their biggest crap in years."

Since most of the news was bad in the early years of the war, Greene was nicknamed the Voice of Doom. When the war news turned better, the CBC felt Greene's baritone was too gloomy and replaced him with Earl Cameron, someone, said CBC boss Ernie Bushnell, "whose tones and overtones were not quite so disturbing." Greene became, however, the first voice of news on Canadian television when on September 8, 1952, he appeared on the opening night of CBC-TV in Toronto, hosting "Newsmagazine."

Shortly after he was fired from CBC Radio news, he was also dismissed as narrator for the National Film Board's "Canada Carries On" series. "Lorne's voice was reminding everybody of the dark days of the war," says Sydney Newman, who was in charge of the series at the time. "So I called him in and said, 'Lorne, I'm not going to use you all the time in the future.' He just went white. Then I started using Lorne only occasionally and hired others to do the narration, like Fred Davis."

When the war ended, Greene was anchoring the news on a local Toronto radio station, CKEY, running a school for future broadcasters, and beginning serious acting. He'd won a scholarship to the Neighborhood Playhouse in New York, and his ambition switched from news to drama. On CBC-TV and at the Stratford Festival, he played Julius Caesar, Othello, and other classical parts. "He was very easy to work with, and he became passionately involved in his acting," says Lister Sinclair.

"Lorne had no idea of becoming a cowboy," says Lloyd Bochner. "He was a very serious actor." Mavor Moore agrees, saying, "Lorne could never have imagined himself in 'Bonanza.' Lorne was a very complex man, much more complex than most people think. He was always torn between a social conscience and making money."

He began acting in a serious way in a TV version of *Othello*, directed by David Green. As he searched for someone to play Othello, Green told his friend Barry Morse, "There are no voices like Othello's. The only voice who sounds like he could be Othello is that guy who is a news announcer – Lorne Greene." "Well," said Morse, "he is, in fact, an actor, so why don't you ask him?" Greene got the role, and his acting career was launched.

His breakthrough in the United States came by a fluke. He'd gone to New York with the idea of manufacturing a stopwatch for television that would show time remaining rather than time elapsed. While he was there, he had a call from Fletcher Markle, who had worked with Andrew Allan both in Vancouver and Toronto and had also worked in early CBC-TV dramas. Markle needed to replace an ailing leading actor in a Westinghouse Studio One TV drama he was producing. Greene stepped in, and after the program was aired, he was asked if he would appear in a Broadway show called *Prescott Proposals* with Katherine Cornell. He did, more television shows followed, and a Hollywood screen test led him into international celebrity with the role of Ben Cartwright on "Bonanza."

Despite his fame, Greene often returned to Canada, and in Hollywood his friends were mostly old colleagues from his Canadian TV and stage days: Leslie Nielsen, Larry Mann, Monty Hall, Austin Willis, and Kate Reid.

Kate Reid

If Lorne Greene was the elder statesman of Canadian performers, his friend Kate Reid was the doyenne of the actresses who dominated Canadian TV and stage into the 1980s. In television's early years, she was in starring roles every couple of weeks. "She was the greatest of actresses," said Bruno Gerussi, a close friend and colleague. "She had a quality that was gripping . . . a presence. All great actors have that. You don't see their techniques; they become the person they're performing."

Reid, in spite of her talent, was nervous and insecure, particularly when she was auditioning. "At a first reading, she was like a blithering idiot, but the minute she got in front of a camera or a microphone, she was terrific," said Gerussi. "She seemed to work best amidst chaos. If she didn't have chaos around her, she'd create it. She needed it and thrived on it."

What she also seemed to depend on was alcohol. "I don't know why Kate needed to drink," says Frances Hyland. "Perhaps she was in intense psychic pain. But drunk or sober, she was a very great actress."

Hyland and Reid played together in many shows and became good friends, although alcohol sometimes intruded. "We fought a lot, especially when she got very drunk and I would have to sustain a long scene. For the audience it didn't matter because she was so compelling, but once we had a serious rift over that, and didn't really see or talk to each other very much for some years. But she was an extraordinary person." "Kate was an immensely gifted person, but the latter third of her working life was blurred by drinking," says Barry Morse.

"It was heartbreaking to see her getting ready in the make-up room early in the morning," says Elaine Saunders. "She smoked and drank herself to death. We'd start off at five o'clock in the morning, and you could hear Kate coughing and throwing up in the bathroom. I thought, 'Oh God, Kate, that's sad.' "

In her later years, Reid's sight failed, and sometimes she didn't recognize friends. Saunders once met her in her apartment lobby and said, "Hi, Kate." Reid looked at her and said, "Do I know you?" "It was so distressing. She either couldn't see me or she was drunk," says Saunders. At a testimonial for Lorne Greene, Reid gave an emotional tribute to her longtime friend and came off the stage to embrace him. But with her sight largely gone, she put her arms around the announcer, Joel Aldred, instead of Greene as people whispered, "No, no. Not him! This one!"

"She was a major talent," says Lloyd Bochner, who had gone to the University of Toronto with her and acted with her in a number of CBC dramas. "She was undisciplined, but despite the booze," said Gerussi, "she still had that remarkable presence on camera – a charisma and a fierceness about her work that shone through to show her captivating greatness."

Leslie Nielsen

One graduate of Lorne Greene's Academy of Radio Arts in Toronto who rivalled Greene's own celebrity was Leslie Nielsen, now one of Hollywood's leading comedy actors. At the school and in his early years of performing on the CBC, however, he was terrified of comedy, preferring Shakespearean plays and other classical dramas. "Actually, I always wanted to do comedy," he says, "but I never made the effort because I was a coward. I didn't have the courage. I was a closet comedian. I was too self-conscious and lacking in confidence." One other problem for Nielsen's dramatic career, however, was that he is decidedly bowlegged. "It's very difficult to play a bowlegged Hamlet without getting laughed at," he says. Now that he is regarded as a great comic performer, he returns on occasion to serious drama, performing in a one-man show about the famed American lawyer Clarence Darrow in the fall of 1996 and hoping to play Willy Loman in *Death of a Salesman*.

Before going to Greene's academy in 1946, Nielsen had been a wartime RCAF air gunner and had worked at a Calgary radio station. He would listen to Greene anchoring the news and "the hair would stand up on my arms as his voice was so magnificent. When I met him, Lorne looked exactly the way he sounded, the patriarch. I could never have imagined him riding the range, herding cattle as he did in 'Bonanza.' But he became a friend who was always there, always gentle, always friendly. At the academy, though, he could be stern. But what a wonderful experience it was with people like Andrew Allan, Lister Sinclair, Mavor Moore, Esse Ljungh, and, of course, Lorne Greene, who all taught there."

Nielsen wanted to learn acting because he thought it would be valuable training for what he felt was going to be his career in radio production. Winning a scholarship to the Neighborhood Playhouse in New York put him on the stage, however, instead of behind the scenes. Nielsen competed for the scholarship with Fred Davis, finally winning when Mavor Moore, who taught drama at the school, recommended Nielsen over Davis. Nielsen says, "Fred was the role model of our class. He was always so impeccably dressed, and everything he did he did so well that we all wanted to emulate him. I, at least, put him on a pedestal, and he was someone I wanted to imitate. It's amazing that I was chosen instead of him."

Commuting between Toronto and New York, Nielsen starred in both classic and contemporary dramas, becoming one of the busiest performers on television, until Hollywood finally hired him to play a comedy role in the 1980 movie *Airplane!* and then, later, to star in the *Naked Gun* film series and the hit movie *Spy Hard*.

Nielsen not only makes his career in comedy, but in his private life as well, particularly with his "farting machine." For twenty-five years, his constant companion has been a small handheld device that, when squeezed, lets out the resonating, rich sounds of heavily breaking wind. His longtime friend Robert Goulet first introduced him to the farting machine, and he was fascinated. A short time later, a golfing partner gave him his own, a little gadget made out of a bicycle inner tube and a jar cap. "I became a basket case of laughter with it," Nielsen says. "I always have it with me. I never before realized the potential for having such enormous fun."

"He sleeps with the damn thing," says Goulet. Goulet and Nielsen occasionally trade their devices back and forth, and when Goulet once lost his, Nielsen supplied him with one of his spares. To truly mortify people when using the gadget in a crowded room, says Nielsen, "You have to have some body movement, some wiggling of legs and hips that get in rhythm with the sound of breaking wind. Actually, in the north, up in Fort Norman, that used to be the way we said goodnight, although, of course, then we did it naturally."

When he was doing a radio interview with Don Harron once, he let go with several loud and embarrassing sounds and several "excuse me's." "I was determined to ignore it," says Harron. "But finally I couldn't, and he demonstrated how the thing worked." Then I said to him, 'Leslie, are you part of that movement, the FFF, The Fight to Free the Fart?' Actually, I didn't think it was that funny."

But for Nielsen, the farting machine is irresistible, and he always takes one with him, to friends' homes, to the golf course, where he uses it especially when someone is putting, to cocktail parties, and even to royal palaces. Prince Rainier of Monaco was at first astounded and then enchanted with Nielsen's very unregal toy. He used it while playing golf with the prince as they chatted on a green. "We were on the fourth hole, and as we talked, I let go one and then let go another," says Nielsen. The prince looked over, startled, and after a third noisy one, he started to laugh. Later his security guard told me, 'Leslie, I've never seen the prince laugh so much. Twenty-five years, he hasn't laughed like that. He wants one.'"

Nielsen happily gave the prince one of the several "wind breakers" he keeps and says, "I can see the prince now, walking the hallowed halls of the oldest kingdom in Europe, happily squeezing the thing, upsetting his guards and startling his guests. Flatulence in the palace of opulence."

Elevators are Nielsen's favourite place to use his noise-making toy. Once while in Las Vegas at the Desert Inn, he got on an elevator with a friend, and two couples came in behind them. Squeezing his little gadget and twitching in rhythm with the sound, he asked his friend, "Is this an express elevator? I sure hope it is because I don't know if I'll make it!" He began to shift uneasily, emitting more rude noises and moaning about his urgent needs. Suddenly, the elevator got stuck a foot or two above a floor. Nielsen's captive audience became really alarmed as he shifted noisily back and forth, muttering, "For God's sake, I've got to go!" while making high-decibel farting noises.

"Finally," Nielsen remembers, "one of the guys in the elevator couldn't stand it anymore and with a stricken look on his face said, 'I'll get the damn door open.' He just tore the doors apart. Then he and the others jumped down the foot or two and ran off."

Goulet remembers another elevator escapade in London, where he and Nielsen were in a slow hotel elevator and were joined by what Goulet describes as "a very Milquetoast guy carrying his bumbershoot." Two more people got on at another floor, and Nielsen decided to victimize Mr. Milquetoast, who was standing between Goulet and Nielsen. Goulet says, "Leslie let go with his fart machine. It was quite loud in that small elevator. I turned and looked disapprovingly at the little guy, and Leslie looked at him, too, and frowned. The other people looked at us and then looked at the guy. Then Leslie let loose another one. The guy was getting red in the face as we kept looking at him and shaking our heads in polite disgust. He looked straight ahead and didn't do a damned thing. When we got to the ground, he rushed out as we tut-tutted behind him."

The trip to London was the climax of a glorious drinking tour of Ireland that Goulet and Nielsen had taken. "We were both drinking enthusiastically then," Goulet says. "And we went on a twelve-day tour of Ireland drinking the place dry." "That was a wonderful time," says Nielsen. "Halfway through we were joined by a friend, a mad Armenian. We were enjoying ourselves so much with a drink here and a drink there, what we should have done, like mountaineers, was to tie ropes around our waists so if anybody fell, we would know."

Although his early career was in serious drama, Nielsen had loved telling jokes since he was a child, partly, or perhaps largely, as a way of gaining approbation. He recalls with pride an incident as a youngster that spurred his father to uproarious laughter. They were eating a leftover chicken dinner, and "my father was chewing the bones, crushing them up like he was a tiger and laughing. I said, 'It's all a fake. It's all done with mirrors.' My father started to laugh. It was the funniest thing he'd heard, at least that day. Not only did he laugh, but I had done it – not my two brothers. That laughter represented a form of acceptance as well as love and approval. So this was a way to get affection and love through laughter. When people are laughing, they don't beat up on you. You're secure and safe. It's when they stop laughing that it's dangerous."

In his beginning years, drama was a shield for him. "It was like being a ventriloquist, but in comedy, you're out there on your own," he says. "You're always pointing out to centre field, saying you're about to hit a home run, and if you don't hear them laughing, you didn't do it. Comedy is a serious business."

Nielsen looks back wonderingly on his early years of classical drama, his fears about performing live on radio and television, his secret desire to do comedy, and now his worldwide acclaim as a comedy performer. "At this stage of the game in my career, to end up doing what I love to do at my age is just the greatest streak of luck in the world," he says.

The moment producer Sydney Newman shouted, "Cue the elephant!" at the dawn of Canadian television, a showbiz revolution had began. It was live, exciting, and more fun than television would ever again be. With the pioneering era over, television rapidly became the most powerful vehicle of entertainment and information ever known, and the best-known Canadian star it ever produced was Juliette.

4

Juliette and Friends

"It hurt me when they called me a bitch," says Canada's first lady of television, Juliette. "But sure, I was demanding. I was called the Iron Butterfly long before Margaret Thatcher came along."

Those who called her a bitch were mostly producers, executives, and sometimes columnists who wanted to transform the singer into something she wasn't. "They wanted to change me or the kind of songs I sang," she says. "They wanted me to dance around with male dancers. They wanted to do long-distance shots, but you lose eye contact with the audience if you do that, and they wanted to do up-your-nostrils extreme close-up shots. I've got a nose that has a bump on it, and it wasn't a perfect nose for television. I wanted straight-on shots. If I saw the camera was moving, I moved with it. I wouldn't let them get away with it. I just kept moving whenever the camera moved. Oh, there were a lot of quiet little wars going on. And you know that you're the only one on camera and you're going to get blamed for everything. But you need to be demanding. You also need to be coddled, but you don't get that at the CBC. I was demanding, but I wasn't mean to people."

"Juliette had this reputation of being such a dreadful bitch, a horrible person to work with," says Mary DePoe, who was part of Juliette's production staff. "But she wasn't. She just knew what she wanted.

Sometimes she would yell, but she wasn't horrible to work with. She didn't deserve the bitch reputation."

Critics made fun of Juliette's perpetual broad smile, panned her voice, and ridiculed her bouncy personality. "They used to say I had wall-to-wall teeth," she says. "They called me Florence Welk. I guess I was criticized the most of anyone on Canadian television for my hair, my smile, my teeth, for my happy attitude. They just didn't think I was real. They thought it was phony and maybe hokey. But it wasn't. It was just the way I am, and people liked it."

People not only liked it, they made Juliette the biggest, most glamorous star Canadian television has ever produced. To this day, nearly three decades after being unceremoniously dumped from the Saturday night slot she occupied for ten years, Juliette still is greeted by stares, autograph-seekers, and, when she makes a rare public appearance, with standing ovations.

Juliette has been singing all her life. At age seven, she was doing amateur shows in Winnipeg, dressed as a boy and singing, on bended knee, "Buddy Can You Spare a Dime?" At the end of the song, she would triumphantly pull off her cap, letting her blonde curls tumble down. Her family moved to Vancouver, and at age thirteen, she brought down the house at Vancouver's Orpheum Theatre singing "There'll Always Be an England." Pierre Berton, then writing for the University of British Columbia student newspaper, was in the audience, and, says Juliette, "He did a review predicting stardom for me." That led to her being hired, still barely just into her teens, as a feature singer with the Dal Richards Orchestra, which played on the Panorama Roof nightclub of the Hotel Vancouver. As Juliette left home for her opening performance, her mother admonished her, saying, "Are you going to work without washing your neck?" "She always said I only washed the bottom of my chin," Juliette remembers.

She rode her bicycle to work and took the elevator to her dressing room. It was here she had her first brush with sex. "When I was thirteen, the elevator boys were all dolled up in beautiful uniforms, and one of them had a real crush on me," she says. "He said, 'Someday, you're going to have my babies.' I said, 'Don't you talk dirty to me!' I was so embarrassed. I thought that was a terrible thing to say because there was only one way to make babies, and how dare he suggest that!"

Juliette did her first radio broadcast with the Dal Richards Orchestra from the Panorama Roof, and at age fifteen, she got her own CBC Radio program. In 1949 she performed in the CBC Radio musical "Oh Please, Louise," written by producer Norman Campbell. Even then, he says, "she was spunky and wanted things to be right."

In 1951, on the "Burns Chuckwagon" radio show, she became known as the Belle of the Chuckwagon. Three years later in Toronto, her début in television lit up the CBC's switchboards. She was stunned by television's impact. "People on the street would stop me, and a policeman talked to me," she says. "It was just instant. Everybody knew me so quickly."

She joined the Saturday night TV variety show hosted by the Irish leprechaun entertainer Billy O'Connor. It was here that the controversy about her began. "I was the buxom blonde, and Billy had a nice way of introducing me at the beginning of the show," she says. "It was a very friendly, intimate kind of thing. We were both very popular." But soon Juliette's popularity outran Billy's, and, she says, "He started insulting me a little bit on the air. Things like, 'Oh, you're getting a little bit heavy there, girl, aren't you?' "

"There were constant fights between Billy and Julie about songs," says Jim Guthro, who was a floor director for the show. "Many a time we went to air and we weren't quite sure she was going to sing the song we'd planned. Several times Billy and his group would start to play one song and Juliette would sing another. Billy couldn't read music very well, and sometimes he would start off in the wrong key. So we had some tense moments."

Guthro remembers Juliette fighting not only with O'Connor but with the producer as well. "He would start an argument with Juliette, and she'd say, 'No, I won't do that!' I'd tell the producer, 'She doesn't want to do this. It doesn't suit her. It's bad for her.' I had to be the heavy because he wouldn't come down from the control room and face her, so I was in the middle."

"O'Connor helped build an audience for Julie and lived to regret it," says veteran variety writer Alex Barris. "After a couple of years, the sponsors and the CBC sensed a public preference for Juliette, and she inherited the Saturday night show. She and Billy O'Connor have rarely seen each other since."

"She came to the show as the girl singer from Vancouver," says variety department executive Len Starmer. "And then, bit by bit, it really became the Juliette show with Billy O'Connor. They were never each other's closest buddies, but I don't think she went out to knife Billy in any way."

"I wasn't going to be second banana for very long anyway because that's not my style," Juliette says.

With her own show, "Juliette," for which she inherited the huge audience that stayed tuned after Saturday night hockey, Juliette became a national icon. She was tough and demanding but at the same time generous and innocent, characteristics that were all encased in a showbiz veneer. The show had a shoestring budget but a million-dollar smile. There has been nobody since Juliette with quite the same impact that she had on Canadian television. She knew exactly what she wanted and what her audience wanted, and refused to change. That determination was at the root of her problems with producers. "I knew what the people liked, and I felt I had a product that was saleable," she says. "Quite a few people I worked with who went to the States feel they really learned something from me, because when they worked with stars, they knew they couldn't tell them what to do. No way, not with stars of that character."

Allan Blye is one of those people who worked on Juliette's show before going to Hollywood. He says, "Working with Juliette prepared me for working with the Smothers Brothers or Sonny and Cher. They knew what they were, and Julie knew who she was. Julie would say, 'Allan, I'm willing to let you colour me and shade me, but I can't lose who I am.' "

"You have to be demanding if you know you're out there with two or three million people watching you," says director Joan Tosoni.

"There is no question, Juliette was the boss of her shows, not the producer or the director," says musician and composer Jimmy Dale. Blye says, "She had the instinct, the killer instinct, that great producers have. No way was she a dumb blonde."

"She knew what she wanted, and she was usually right," says Carroll

Hyde, Juliette's script assistant. "If you screwed her up, she didn't want you on her crew, but at the same time, if you delivered for her, she was very generous. One thing we always avoided was profile shots because she didn't like her nose."

Juliette's conviction that she knew what was best for the show often led to sparks with producers and directors. "I told Julie once that she wore her bra around her testicles," says one of her producers, Paddy Sampson. "She had the peculiar, psychotic thing that there had to be someone on every show who took heat – the studio director, a cameraman, one of the backup singers, a member of the band. I've seen her kill guests. She just jumped on people. Somebody had to be a villain."

"Paddy and I were always at each other," admits Juliette. "Paddy hated me and I hated Paddy. He was the one who wanted to shoot from the ground up your nose. He was experimenting all the time, challenging himself. But not at my expense, thank you!"

"Julie only wanted to do what was safe," says Sampson. "She didn't trust any of us, simple as that." Starmer says, "Juliette was very suspicious of everyone in many ways. She had to have confidence in you before she'd listen to you."

"Paddy and Juliette would have the most horrible fights about the way he was shooting her," remembers Mary DePoe. "Paddy, because he was so short, always did up-the-nostrils shots. Paddy saw the world that way because he was so short. We came to the conclusion that very tall people and very short people do not make good directors because you get too much headroom from tall people and you get up-the-nostrils shots from short people. Juliette sometimes would get annoyed also at the lighting, and in rehearsals in the middle of a song she would sing in tune to the lighting man, 'Cliffie, get that light off my nose!' "

Sometimes she could be joshed out of her distress. Producer Ray McConnell recalls her being furious about the lighting for one program. "I got a candle and lit it," says McConnell, "and walked onto the set and said, 'Julie, I'm a little concerned about the lighting, too, but maybe you could help us by holding this candle during the number.' From that day on, we've been good friends."

When Lorraine Thomson became the choreographer of "Juliette," she ran into Juliette's resistance to doing anything different. Thomson's first day on the job was a rehearsal, and she suggested a small change in the presentation. "I remember saying, 'Juliette, could you move to stage right of the singing group and face camera one.' 'Excuse me!' Juliette said, and she called over producer Bob Jarvis and declared, '*She* doesn't tell me what to do. If there are changes you want me to consider, *you* tell me!' That was my introduction to Juliette, and I was very wary of her for three or four months until she learned to trust me and know that I wasn't going to do anything to make her look silly. We became very good friends, one of my best friends. But she always knew what was right for Juliette."

But Juliette was grateful when her crew gave her the lighting, camera angles, and support she needed to do her shows her way. At the end of each season, and sometimes halfway through as well, she'd thank her stagehands, cameramen, lighting experts, and others with a party, providing cases of beer, mounds of fried chicken, and pizza aplenty.

Probably the most hurtful comment Juliette ever received came from the head of the variety department in the early 1970s, Jim Guthro, who once sent a memo to her producer critiquing a daily afternoon TV show she was then doing. His complaint was that she should sing more songs on the programs or "do something different that's entertaining." Guthro told producer Don Brown, "I know it's difficult to teach an old dog new tricks, but you've got to try. You've got to get her into something else to offset the fact that she's not singing so much." He thought his "old dog" adage was just a colourful phrase to illustrate his point, but it seared Juliette. "Such a cruel thing to say," she says twenty-five years later. "You couldn't teach him any new tricks either, and he was an older dog than I was."

"Don't forget," she says, "I was a liberated woman, and I was surrounded by men in the studio, and here I am giving these orders – demanding these things."

"She's a very determined, hard, tough lady," said Bruno Gerussi, who knew Juliette in Vancouver half a century ago. "With the kind of macho bullshit that went on in those days, you had to be a strong, strong woman."

Juliette's make-up artist for many shows was Elaine Saunders, who echoes Gerussi's words. "You've got to be tough," she says. "Nice girls don't make it to the top. She's a fighter. I've seen her and others with their claws out, and they're fighting, and they'll win. What they're really saying is, 'Think my way or get the hell out of my way.' It's a genetic thing they have in their souls that makes them do it. By the time they've walked into the make-up room, I know they've crawled over a lot to get there."

"You don't get to be a star by being a Miss Milquetoast," Don Brown says. "She had to get her own way, and she had an uncanny way of knowing what's good for her."

With her fiercely competitive spirit, Juliette was ever aware of potential rivals. Brown recalls Juliette's producer, Bob Jarvis, once being asked, "What happens if Juliette gets sick?" Jarvis replied, "I mention [singer] Sylvia Murphy's name and Julie gets miraculously well."

Juliette, however, always did and still does encourage young singers, warning them to retain their individuality. "Juliette kind of took me under her wing," says Anne Murray. "About my make-up, telling me to 'stay the way you are.' She also said, 'Stick to your guns and principles,' and I've always done that."

Rita MacNeil was another up-and-coming singer Juliette advised to be wary of producers. "I knew by the way she looked that producers were going to try to change Rita," she says. "They're going to demand she lose weight, forgetting what made Rita such a big hit. She's got a very sweet face. Rita is very sensitive about her weight and I was too. And she's sensitive about the media and I was too. If they can't pick on your voice, they'll pick on your body."

Occasionally she would alarm a fellow performer when she would call them by a different name than they normally used. Catherine McKinnon remembers Juliette calling her Cathy instead of her full name. "Doing my first 'Juliette' show I was really scared, overwhelmed," says McKinnon. "When she called me Cathy, I thought, 'Nobody calls me Cathy. Nobody does!' I wasn't going to take this. All through the rehearsal she called me Cathy. Juliette and I had the same manager, so I told him, 'If she calls me Cathy one more time, I'm going to walk off the show.' He spoke to Juliette and her response was, 'Feisty girl. I like that!' She never called me Cathy again, and from then on, I liked her."

Juliette's feud with trumpeter Bobby Gimby was deeper and more lasting than most of her confrontations, exacerbated by the same kind of first-name incident as McKinnon describes. At one rehearsal for her show, Juliette introduced him as Bob Gimby, and he blew his stack. "She knows damn well I'm known as Bobby, but she does it deliberately," he told producer Bob Jarvis. "My billing is Bobby Gimby, not Bob." After that she always called him Bobby, but there was great tension between them. Alex Barris says, "Gimby's wife at the time kept egging him on by saying 'They don't treat you right. They don't treat you like a star.' And he'd go up against Juliette, but she wasn't having any of it."

The Juliette–Gimby feud erupted once while they and their producers were watching a replay of their latest program. Barris, a writer on the show, whispered something to Juliette, and she burst out laughing. "It was right in the middle of Gimby's number," Barris remembers, "and Gimby exploded. 'That's it! That's it! I can't stand this. My one spot in the show and she's talking all the way through it!'

"Suddenly the light went on," says Barris, "and they were yelling and screaming. She finally had it with him and said, 'Oh, fuck off!' He froze, walked out of the studio, and we never saw him again."

Juliette's language at times could be salty, and she joked about sex. Director Joan Tosoni recalls what it was like during band rehearsals. "The band members would pay attention to me, and I'd blush and get all embarrassed," says Tosoni. "I was a shy person. I remember Julie once laughing and saying in front of everybody, 'Look at her, blushing like that. Sure she's so innocent, but she's slept with everyone in the band.' I blushed and blushed and blushed and thought, 'If you only knew. I'm not getting anything, Julie.' "

When Juliette and several other singers from the salad days of variety programming in the 1950s and 1960s got together for a retrospective program, she couldn't resist a gentle poke at one of them, Joan Fairfax. Barris remembers that after Fairfax finished a number, Juliette told her, "Oh, Joan, you still sing like a virgin."

But, for all the showbiz brassiness, Juliette was and is a straight-laced, old-fashioned girl. She was leery of cleavage shots and suggestive lyrics. "There's a façade there," says Ray McConnell, "with all that coarse, earthy language, there's a very big prude there. The real Julie is a frightened little girl in a way."

Barris recalls, "She was singing a romantic duet with George Murray once and insisted that after singing the song she had to say, 'We were only kidding.' She added that she had her husband's permission to do the duet. She felt her fans knew she was married and wouldn't approve of her flirting with George."

Bob Crane, the star of "Hogan's Heroes," was smitten by Juliette when he met her at the CBC studios. "He followed her everywhere like a puppy," says Mary DePoe. "We all thought it was kind of interesting, but she kept saying, 'No, no. My Tony's waiting.' "

In another highly romantic duet, she was gazing deeply into the eyes of matinée idol Robert Goulet when her mind wandered from the lovingly haunting lyrics of "The Way We Were." "I hadn't seen him for a long time," she says, "and as I was looking into his eyes, he closed them, and I'm thinking, 'Oh my goodness, he's had an eye lift. Isn't that interesting.' There were tiny incisions above the lid, and I was flabbergasted because I didn't think he would do that. But I didn't skip a beat. I just kept on singing."

Lorraine Thomson had a similar experience with singer Wally Koster on the early TV show "Hit Parade." She was playing a Hawaiian girl doing the hula-hula while Koster was singing a romantic song to her. "I'm looking up at him while he's singing, and as I'm doing the hula-hula, my eyes are focused on the gold fillings in his teeth and I'm thinking, 'This man has an awful lot of fillings.' "

While the TV audience sees a performer dreamily lost in a love song, often, like Juliette or Thomson, she or he is thinking much more pragmatically. "You wonder where the camera's moving to," Juliette says, "where the lights are, and what is that guy doing moving off the set. You wonder, what do I do next? Where is the cue-card man for my farewell words?" Actor Cynthia Dale says, "Sometimes you're doing your laundry in your head. You're thinking, 'Maybe I ate too much garlic today to kiss this person' or 'He shouldn't have eaten that Caesar salad at lunch.' "

In the 1970s, Alex Trebek, now host of the American game show "Jeopardy!," was host of a noon-hour radio show that starred Juliette, and occasionally the cast and friends would gather at his downtown Toronto home for a party. "I went to Alex's powder room," Juliette remembers, "and I looked on the wall and thought, 'Oh, what a lovely picture of dancers.' There were about forty different couples dancing in this picture, or so I thought. As I looked closer, I saw they actually were all in different sexual positions. They weren't dancing at all. I was embarrassed. I thought, 'Oh my God, isn't this awful? Why would Alex have anything like this on the wall?' So I stole it. I took it off the wall and out of its frame and took it home. I've still got it. I never said anything to him but I'm going to send it back to him now with a letter of what I thought of him twenty-five years ago with all those nudes cavorting on his wall."

Juliette also twits Trebek for being excessively careful with his money. "Alex is very tight," she says. "He may tell a different story, but whenever we went out to lunch, Alex would say he wasn't hungry. But he always enjoyed a little bit of everybody else's lunch. We'd end up paying the bill, but Alex didn't have to because he didn't order."

Trebek does indeed have a different story. "Juliette was fun to work with, but she had a bit of a weight problem," he says. "After the show, we'd go to a restaurant nearby. We'd all order something and Juliette wouldn't order anything. But then she'd pick off everybody's plate, saying, 'Oh, that looks good, Alex, let me try that.' It was like somebody who says he doesn't smoke and then smokes yours."

Producer Ray McConnell at least partially supports Trebek's story, saying, "You'd be sitting in a restaurant and no matter what was ordered, she would want to try yours. She would delve right into the middle of your plate."

Her weight wasn't Juliette's only fixation. "She was a clean fanatic," says Elaine Saunders. "She would tell you, 'I always like people who wash their hands.' What she was telling you was 'Wash your hands!' On the afternoon show we did, she used to have a fan at the bottom of her feet to cool her thighs. We used to make jokes about this fan blowing up her skirt."

Whenever Juliette visited a friend for a few days, the friend would spend hours scrubbing the house to make sure it was clean. Once when she was spending a week with Lorraine Thomson, she remarked to Thomson after the first day, "You know, Lorraine, there was a lot of dust under your refrigerator. So I cleaned it out." "When she was travelling," says Ray McConnell, "the first thing Julie would do would be to go into her hotel-room bathroom and wash it out because she was such a bug on cleanliness."

Juliette was never a problem for the CBC make-up artists. "It was easy because she knew exactly what she wanted," says Elaine Saunders. "It was like paint by numbers." She would, however, spend a long time in the make-up room checking her make-up and clothes. "I took her to a public relations party once," says Don Brown, "and she said, 'I have to go to the ladies room. I'll just be a minute.' She was gone for a very long time, and finally she came out and said to me, 'Sorry I was so long. I met a friend in there. The mirror.' "

Juliette looks as glamorous off the screen as on. "I get all dolled up even if I'm going to the corner grocery," she says. When she steps outside her home, she steps onstage. "If you rapped on Juliette's front door and she opened it, she would look exactly as she did on television or she wouldn't open it," says Len Starmer. "I remember travelling with her on shows, and we would meet at 8:30 A.M., and I would say, 'God, you look lovely, Julie!' and she'd say, 'Yes, but this started at four o'clock in the morning.' "

She told actor Roy Wordsworth, "I know I'm a big Polish broad, but I don't want to look like one."

In the early days of television, almost all shows were live, which meant no retakes when something went amiss. Once when Juliette was doing a show from Winnipeg, something went wrong with her microphone stand. "As Juliette was singing," says Ray McConnell, "the mike started to slide down the stand. It kept going down and down, and she started to go down with it. It got right down almost to the floor. She was furious." On another show, as Juliette was walking down a staircase, she tripped and fell. "My heel caught. Thank God I didn't swear. The camera switched to someone else and the band started, and I came back laughing. But to this day, I cannot walk down a staircase on camera."

"She just hated stairs," says Mary DePoe. "It was awkward for her. She had these big gowns, she was tightly corseted, and she had to sing and smile and listen to the music, and it was live, and on top of all that she had to come down a staircase! Sometimes producers would purposely put a staircase in. Why should she have to put up with that? A lot of producers thought they were the stars and Juliette was just somebody there to make them look good."

Juliette's impact on Canadian audiences impressed American entertainers such as Arthur Godfrey, Perry Como, and Harry James, all of whom tried to lure her south of the border. After her shows with Godfrey and Como, each of them offered her several times what she was earning in Canada, but Juliette said no. "I would have earned a lot more money, but I had my own show on the CBC and would have been a second banana with them." James pursued her, in part because of her resemblance to his wife, the film star Betty Grable. She had a friend in the James band who warned her, "As the girl singer, you'd just be a fill in, and he treats them very roughly. You'd just be another band singer." Instead of singing for James, Juliette stayed in Canada and became the blonde queen of Canadian TV.

Although it was very modest compared to the money she could have been making in the United States, Juliette was impressed with the $125 a show she started out with on television and with her fast raises to $250 and $450 a show. At her peak she was earning more than $1,000 per show. "But still I was probably the lowest paid of all the other girl singers," she says. "Even so, it was great money for me, and I did public appearances, too, all over the country." In 1954, the first full year after she came to Toronto, she was earning about $35,000 from her TV shows and public appearances. "Somebody at the CBC told me, 'You're earning almost more than the prime minister,' and I said, 'Well, he's underpaid, because I'm sure not overpaid.' "

Although it wasn't widespread, there were some undercover kickback deals among CBC programmers in those days. Juliette was approached repeatedly but rejected every proposition. The first time, she was approached by a producer who proposed she be listed as a researcher and writer on her program and be paid an extra $50, which she would then give back to the producer. "Who pays the income tax on that?" asked the ever-practical Juliette. "You do" was the answer. "No thanks," she said.

"Naturally the star was making more than the producer, and there was a little bit of resentment there," she says. "Actually, it was kind of a common thing among some producers, and some were notorious. They told you exactly what they wanted. But that never sat right with me because I could just think of the tax bill, plus ethically, I didn't like the feeling of it."

In some cases agents would buy expensive gifts for producers who gave roles to their clients. "There were several occasions when people were caught doing things they weren't supposed to," says Paddy Sampson. "Quite a few of them were slapped on the wrists or moved. Some got into real trouble. And I know of one instance where a star 'shopped' a fellow performer who was giving kickbacks and then took over his job."

As the reigning monarch of Canadian TV, Juliette was ill-prepared for the axe when it fell on her in 1966. Her show was abruptly cancelled by program executive Doug Nixon, who felt a younger face on the screen would be more attractive to advertisers. "I should have had an idea," she says, "when I saw the producer and my replacement sitting in the corner of the Celebrity Club having cocktails, and he was nibbling on her ear – this gorgeous, exotic-looking woman. It should have given me a hint, but I guess I was quite stupid."

She did get a warning, however, from a friend who was the secretary of one of the CBC executives. Juliette was told that he would fire her over lunch. "So I dolled myself up, with my blonde hair, a glamorous dress, and my beautiful blonde mink coat, and sailed into the restaurant, sat down, and smiled. They told me, 'Don't worry, dear, you're going to be doing four specials a year.' They always say that. They tell you you're going to do four or more and you're lucky to do one."

Shortly after the lunch, Juliette ran into Betty Kennedy, who had just finished taping a "Front Page Challenge" program. Juliette says, "I had just lost my show, and we were talking about how I was feeling terribly upset because it was a big shock to me and I was very traumatized. And Betty just very casually said to me, 'Well, you know, you should go into real estate. Everyone's doing that now.' I was mortified. I thought to myself, 'Betty, I'm a star. A star doesn't sell real estate.' "

In spite of her bravado, Juliette was devastated by the loss of her show, so much so that she lost her voice. "I guess it was all that fear and lack of confidence and hurt about losing the show. I went to a hypnotherapist. I was so upset and felt myself a failure. But I just poured it all out and cried it all out, and then the throat came back again."

After the cancellation, she starred in a radio series, did an afternoon television series, and continued to make personal appearances across the country. But her career was never the same again. However, it gave her a deeper relationship with her husband, clarinet player Tony Cavazzi. Gentle and soft-spoken, Cavazzi was the only man in her life. She had "set my cap for him" when she first saw him looking for a band job in Vancouver at the end of the Second World War. "He had a gorgeous body, very slim, lovely buns, and a tight, tight Navy suit. A beautiful guy," she says. She pursued him for three years, quitting one job to work at the club where he played, following him to restaurants, and inviting him home for dinner. "Finally," she says, "I said, 'Look, we've been going together for three years. I think it's about time you married me.' "

"Tony was her life," says Mary DePoe. "He was wonderful and didn't mind all the snide comments he got about not being a very good musician or being the make-up case carrier. Tony was her backbone."

For thirty-seven years, Cavazzi was Juliette's hidden strength, looking after their finances and always being quietly there for her when she came home. Alzheimer's disease struck him in his mid-sixties, and it was a living hell for Juliette for three years until his death. "He started forgetting me and not knowing me at all," she says. "The hardest part of the disease is when they fade away from you. I just could not come to grips with that. A terrible personal change came. He was punching me about quite badly. We all became the enemy. A nurse friend said every time she opened the door in the morning she didn't know whether she'd find me dead on the floor. But having to take him to a care facility that has locked doors and bars, that's very hard. He didn't deserve that kind of an end. He was too nice a human being.

"I thought I deserved it, that I had brought this disease on him. Maybe my career was too much for him, too much stress. I hated losing him. I really did."

In the years since Cavazzi's death, Juliette has gone on dates, but there has been no romance. "My doctor told me, 'Julie, get a man in your life. Get married.' But I'm not interested in getting married again. Tony has been the only man in my life. When a gentleman calls up for a date, I always say, 'Look, I don't fool around. I don't hop into bed and I don't intend to be kissing you.' I set the ground rules that I'm not dessert. I told my doctor I didn't think the anointed penis was the answer to women's problems, that it cures absolutely everything. Men do have that impression, but I'm doing just fine."

The proudest moment of Juliette's life came when she was awarded the Order of Canada in 1975, ten years after her father had died. "As I walked down to get my Order, I thought, 'Daddy, can you believe this?' I hadn't even finished high school, and my father was devastated. But he was thrilled that a girl of Ukrainian background could be on television. My parents couldn't read or write English, but you'd never know it. My mother would fake it in a restaurant, listening to what everybody else was ordering. She'd always have the menu in front of her and make like she's reading it."

Juliette was born Juliette Sysak in Winnipeg. Her mother was from eastern Poland and her father from the Ukraine. When she first started at the CBC, she was told, " 'The CBC is not looking for ethnic names, so we'll just call you Juliette.' "At least I was using one of my own names," she says.

Another bit of advice she got early in her career was to lie about her age. When she came to Toronto and got an agent, he told her to cut five years off her age. "I was in my middle twenties then," she says. "So they cut five years off my age, and that age was in all my papers, everything, including passports. I've lied so often I sometimes don't know how old I am."

The fibbing caught up with her when Juliette turned sixty-five and did not receive her pension cheques. When she protested, the government told her she had five more years to go. "I have not!" she thundered. But then she remembered her career-long lie about her age and quickly said, "Oh, my mother must have made that mistake." "I put the blame on my poor mother, but I got the pension," she says. "Now, they're clawing it back."

Juliette always ended her programs by saying, "Goodnight, Mom." She started it when her mother was hospitalized and then stopped when she got better. "But people liked it and wanted me to leave it in," she says. "So I started saying it again. I guess each mother felt it was her daughter sending a message to her. Some critics thought it was hokey and a gimmick, but it wasn't."

"I think I had a good voice, not a terrific voice," she says. "The looks weren't terrific either, but they were very photogenic. But personality was, I think, the thing that did it for me. The smile was always good and spontaneous, and I like to laugh. And I love that camera. I was totally in love with the camera and the audience beyond."

Juliette, a nice Ukrainian girl from Winnipeg, did it her way to become the most glamorous star Canadian TV has ever produced. She was an inspiration for a trio of Maritime vocalists who swept into our living rooms after her: Anne Murray, Catherine McKinnon, and Rita MacNeil. Juliette's advice to all of them was "Don't let them push you around." All three followed her counsel, and none more so than the girl from Springhill, Nova Scotia.

Anne Murray

Anne Murray has been singing as long as she can remember. When Murray was nine, her aunt heard her singing "Come Down from Your Ivory Tower" and said, "My she has a lovely voice." "I later found out she was tone-deaf," says Murray. "But I just opened my mouth and sang at school concerts, churches, curling clubs, and the local theatre. The first time I got paid, I was singing at the Colonial Inn in Amherst, Nova Scotia, when I was eighteen. I wasn't supposed to be there because they served booze and I was underage."

She sang at the University of New Brunswick, where she was nicknamed Mur, and then auditioned in Halifax for CBC's "Singalong Jubilee," flying from Fredericton at her own expense. Sitting on a stool, wearing a little porkpie hat, plunking a guitar and singing "Oh Mary, Don't You Weep, Don't You Mourn," Murray knew she was the best of all the would-be singers at the audition. She was thanked, flew back home, and two months later got a rejection letter. "I was flabbergasted, absolutely shocked," she says, "because I thought I was a shoo-in. I thought, 'Well, that's that!'" Two years later, in 1964, she got a call from "Singalong Jubilee" host Bill Langstroth that changed her life, professionally and personally. He wanted her to audition again. "Over my dead body!" she said, still smarting because "my pride had been hurt by the earlier turn down." Langstroth persisted, telling her the audition was only a formality and that she really had the job. The producer of the show, Manny Pittson, was uneasy about hiring her, however, because, she says, "He didn't want some uppity, smart broad, a college graduate, coming in. But still, I was better than any other regulars on the show."

There was also hesitation at CBC headquarters in Toronto. When Langstroth called variety department head Len Starmer saying he wanted to hire Murray, Starmer was reluctant to give her a contract until he saw her on camera. When he did, he liked her style and says, "She seemed to meld in beautifully with the 'Jubilee' singers. I thought her voice was interesting, but I don't recall thinking, 'Wow! There's a voice!' " Murray got her thirteen-week contract and combined singing in the "Jubilee" chorus and doing solos with a teaching job in Summerside, Prince Edward Island. She soon gave up teaching, however, in part because she was making $4,450 a year as a gym teacher and $15,000 singing.

Not only was she on her way professionally, she was also on her way romantically. "I thought she was as cute as a bug. Man, her looks!" says Langstroth, Murray's tall, mischievous husband, who at the time looked like a young Gregory Peck. It was not love at first sight for Murray, however. "Bullshit! Get out of here!" she laughs when Langstroth recalls how awestruck he was at their first meeting. "I thought he was an asshole," she says. "I was so quiet and laid-back, and he was just overwhelming. He just took me aback with his energy. But I changed my mind later. Once we were working together, I realized he was very serious about what he did."

Eventually they began living together and then in 1975, giving themselves three days' notice, got married. Murray, who never thought much about clothes, forgot to buy anything special for the ceremony, which was held at her Toronto home. "I was in bare feet when we got married," she says. "It was great." It wasn't great, however, for their wedding photographer. Murray's brother, Bruce, had put candles everywhere and as the couple said their "I do's" in an alcove, the photographer backed into a group of candles and caught fire. "He had on a polyester suit and, boy, did he ever go up in flames," Murray says. "We had to break off the ceremony and push him out of the house and roll him around in the backyard to put out the flames. It was quite a wedding. I went to work at the studio the next day."

Being married in bare feet was typical of Murray, who spent much of her time shoeless. "I never put on shoes unless I absolutely had to," she says. "I didn't wear shoes on 'Singalong.' It was a gesture of revolt, of defiance, and typical of flower children at the time. When I think back now, I'm surprised I didn't get some disease or get a nail through my foot. I used to walk the streets barefoot. My father thought I was crazy. I don't do it now, though."

"She just loved being a barefoot tomboy," says her onetime script assistant Carroll Hyde.

Murray moved onto the American record charts in 1970 with what became her signature song, "Snowbird," appeared on "The Merv Griffin Show," and became a regular on Glen Campbell's programs. And then, she says, "The CBC grabbed me. They wanted me for everything." For $20,000 they signed her to a one-year contract, for appearances on "The Tommy Hunter Show," "Singalong Jubilee," and specials. "She did two Hunter shows, but didn't want to do any more because she didn't like the producer," says Jim Guthro. "He would have her doing Broadway stuff, and she didn't want to sing that. She was tricky to work with. If you tried to overproduce her, ask her to change her hairdo or her clothes, she'd get very defensive. She also didn't like string sections and brass. She was just a country girl, just plain folks."

"I had the feeling that the people on 'The Tommy Hunter Show' never wanted me there," Murray says. "Tommy was always great, but the producer was a bit of a lech, and I didn't feel comfortable there." Murray also felt uncomfortable about Toronto itself. "There was a feeling of inferiority on my part, or superiority on the part of Torontonians. I had a feeling that everybody in Toronto looked down their noses at us in the Maritimes. That's the reason why they don't like Toronto anywhere in Canada." When a group of CBC stars from Toronto were touring the Maritimes once, they met Murray's mother at a dinner in Moncton. "They were in shock at this gracious, beautiful woman," she says. "I think they expected a fishwife."

"In those early days," Murray says, "people were constantly trying to change me into a glamour baby. I remember having to wear white boots on 'Wayne and Shuster.' I didn't like them. They made me look like Nancy Sinatra, and I didn't want to look like her. I wanted my hair short, but everyone wanted me to have long hair. I fought twenty-five years for my short hair. But in time, I smartened up and realized I at least had to put on nice clothes." Over the years Murray has moderated her "down home" look, thanks largely to her former manager, the late Leonard Rambeau. She says, "He let me stay in control, and yet he guided me. If he felt strongly about something, I always went with him. And if I felt very strongly about something, he would go with me."

"I was cautious about everything at the beginning," Murray says. "I got over my shyness, but I still don't like cocktail parties. Early on, everybody wanted a piece of me. They were just grabbing at me on the one hand and looking down their noses at me on the other. I thought, 'Get me the hell out of here.' I was much better off in the United States because there they don't care where you're from."

She became an American favourite and a Las Vegas star in the 1970s. Elvis Presley loved her singing, and she performed at a Los Angeles party for John Lennon, Alice Cooper, Harry Nelson, and Mickey Dolenz of The Monkees. "They were all drunk, and I was the entertainment, served up as a sort of musical dessert," she says. She worked with, among other stars, Perry Como, Johnny Cash, and one of her favourites, Glen Campbell. "Glen never felt totally comfortable in my presence, so he would always have ten or twelve people around him," she says. "One time Jimmy Webb, the songwriter, and I were giving him shit about this. He said Jimmy and I intimidated him because we were both educated and could carry on conversations, and he felt inferior because he was just a country boy. We said, 'Get out of here!' and we talked to him for hours. He was just afraid of himself, but he's a very smart guy. We told him, 'Look, you have so much to offer. It's got nothing to do with the way you talk.'"

"Nice" is the word most of her colleagues use to describe Murray, although they all note her sauciness and humour. Steve Hyde remembers leading her backstage on a TV show "when she suddenly grabbed the cheeks of my ass. I jumped and she said, 'God, you're getting old, Hyde. Ten years ago you would have wriggled.'"

"I don't know anybody who's as loved as Anne Murray, from the most junior kid on the studio floor to the top executives," says Hyde. "Anne never pretends to be anything she's not. On and off camera, she's simply

Anne Murray, the kid from Nova Scotia. She knows everybody's name on the floor and she'll talk to each of them."

She once brought her children to a TV taping, and they asked to be in one of the skits. Problems delayed the shooting, and after midnight, one of the youngsters said, "Mommie, I'm tired. I want to go home." Hyde remembers Murray replying, "See all these people working around here? They've been here for nearly eighteen hours. You've been here five. You wanted to be here, so act like a professional." Murray herself copes with the heavy workload by taking quick naps. "I can fall asleep on a clothesline," she says.

Being professional not only means long hours, as she advised her youngsters, but also swift recovery when things go wrong on live performances. One of Murray's most embarrassing moments was when her pants fell down in the middle of a song. "I had on these gorgeous sequin breakaway pants, and at the appropriate moment, I would rip them off and be standing there in a short hot-pant type of thing," she remembers. "But somebody forgot to fasten the long pants properly, and suddenly they fell down around my ankles. I couldn't move. I was in shock. 'This was supposed to happen later in the show,' I ad libbed. I turned around and looked at my backup singer. 'Debbie, for God's sake, come here!' I said. "She ripped the pants off and I started in again."

During another show before several thousand people in Toronto, Murray was interrupted by a man shouting loudly, "Show us your tits!" "I made the mistake of saying, 'Pardon?' so he said it again. He said it about six times. Finally I said, 'If somebody doesn't get rid of that guy, I'm coming down there and will do it myself!' Eventually, somebody dragged him out."

Excessively ardent fans can be a continuing problem for superstars, and Murray has been dogged for years by a Saskatchewan farmer who is convinced she is in love with him and who has served time in jail for harassing her. "I've had several like that," she says. "There was a guy who used to send me flowers all the time, and then he heard someone in his office say that I was sleeping with somebody. He wrote me, asking, 'Is this true?' He thought I'd deserted him for this other person, and all of a sudden he hated me. There was another guy who came right to our front door and asked for his daughters. 'I want my daughters back and I know you have them,' he said. That was scary. I called the police."

Her recognizability prevents her from going out on her own most of the time. "I don't ever go any place alone," she says. "I feel uncomfortable if I do. I need somebody who can take me away if I get caught."

Being an international star does not always mean universal recognition, however. Peter Gzowski remembers being astonished when he mentioned to author Mordecai Richler that Bruce Murray was going to be on his program. "Bruce, you know, is Anne Murray's brother," he told Richler. "Who's Anne Murray?" Richler asked.

Murray has never been obsessively ambitious. "I don't think she ever had a great dream about being a celebrity," says Joan Tosoni, a comment that reinforces Murray's own remark to a prospective agent in Toronto: "You know, I ain't hurtin' to be a star."

"Anne has a strong personality and she knows exactly who she is," says Tosoni. "She'll sit back and swear a bit and get a little raunchy. But she spends a lot of time with her family, and there is a bit of Cape Breton still in her. She loves to play tennis and golf and is a real jock." Her style has led to gossip about lesbianism. Tosoni remembers that when she was directing a show with Murray and k.d. lang, lang wanted to do a duet with Murray on "Love Song." When Murray was told she said, "Great." "This was before k.d. came out, although everybody pretty much knew that k.d. was a lesbian," says Tosoni. (In fact, lang had said she had a crush on Murray and wanted to flirt with her.) "Anyway, when I was told by Anne's manager, Leonard Rambeau, I was a bit silent and then said, 'I'll be frank with you, Leonard. Have you thought about Anne Murray and k.d. lang singing together, "I want to sing you a love song?"' He then went to Anne."

"Joan just wants to know if it's a concern for you," he told Murray. "Well, Leonard," she said, "people are gonna think what they're gonna think. Basically, k.d. likes the song. I like the song. I think we'll do a great job." "And they did," says Tosoni. "Anne knows exactly who she is, so she's not going to freak out about what other people think of her."

Road shows have occasionally presented Murray with the problem of keeping her musicians on the relatively straight and narrow. "Some of the guys in my early groups were into drugs and booze until I finally woke up to what was going on," she says. "We used to go through the Chicago airport with these guys and I'd be scared to death. If we were there for more than an hour, almost all of them would get pissed. You never knew when you got to the boarding gate who was going to be in what kind of shape. It was horrible!"

In Canada, while touring military bases, Murray ran into an adventure of another kind with her travelling companions. She was at a Summerside, Prince Edward Island, base with a number of stars from Toronto, some of whom got overly amorous. "They were a bad bunch. The horniest of guys," she says. "We were sleeping four beds to each barracks, and one night I could hear this familiar voice over in a corner giving a big come on to a Miss Canada contestant who was travelling with us. They thought I was asleep, and went right to it."

No matter how far she's travelled from home, Murray's thoughts always return to the Maritimes. "I think those days in Halifax, those 'Singalong Jubilee' days, were some of the best that I ever had," she says. "I was learning so much, and it was so much fun." She was also excited to meet her first genuine star in those early days – Catherine McKinnon. "I was in the dressing room all by myself and she came in," Murray says. "She was a star and I was only starting out. Everything about her just oozed being a star. She had the Gucci bag and shoes and had just flown in from England. I was so shy and nervous, and she was just the perfect star."

Catherine McKinnon

Catherine McKinnon has wanted to be a star since she was five years old and sang "All I Want for Christmas Is My Two Front Teeth" at a Christmas concert. "I used to sing in my high chair," she says. "I was always going to be a singer. It was something I loved." At age four, she heard a recording by Bing Crosby and asked her mother to take her to meet him. "She tried to explain that he was on a record," she says. "I was enraged and said, 'You're just saying that because you don't want to take me.'"

McKinnon was an Army brat, moving from base to base, wherever her father was posted with the medical corps. She did her first radio singing in Saint John, New Brunswick, and, later, in London, Ontario, on CFPL, she moved from the chorus to a solo performance with disastrous results. "I opened my mouth and nothing came out," she says. "I was nine, and absolutely nothing came out. I can remember perspiring and being so totally terrified. It was the only time I ever had stage fright. I just stood there and started to shake."

She got over her nerves, however, and three years later was auditioning for a Detroit radio station. "We would like to have her as a soloist," a station official said, but her parents felt that, at age twelve, she was too young and said no. "You've ruined my life!" she wailed. "You've destroyed me. You only get one chance and this was it. Don't you know what you've done to me?"

Soon afterwards the family moved to Halifax, where McKinnon entered music festivals. Later she auditioned for "Singalong Jubilee" in front of the show's host, Bill Langstroth. The original host was supposed to have been the popular American folk singer Pete Seeger, who had done a pilot for the show, but he ran into trouble with McCarthyists in the U.S. Congress. "He wanted desperately to do the show," says Langstroth, but thought that if he left the States they might not let him back in again. Langstroth got the job instead, and a year or so later, Catherine McKinnon joined the show. Shortly after that she also began appearing on Don Messer's program. She had become a full-fledged star by the time Anne Murray joined "Singalong." "But there wasn't any vying for position on the show," says McKinnon. "We were all sort of the same. There was no rivalry or anything. Annie was a lot of fun with her crazy jokes."

After zooming to stardom, CTV featured her in "The Catherine McKinnon Show," a weekly prime-time program she hated doing. "I didn't have any input," she says. "I felt very uncomfortable and insecure. I said I didn't want to go on, but nobody would listen. I was becoming increasingly frustrated. There's always a fight to retain your identity against the producer's desire. Why do they constantly want to change you? It's very bizarre. It makes no sense." She enjoyed guesting on big-time TV shows, however, working with everyone from Bob Hope to Bob Newhart; from Tommy Common to Tommy Hunter. It wasn't easy for her to stand beside Hunter. "I'm five foot one and he's six foot four, so when I stood beside him I was always looking up," she says. "My head just about hit his navel."

During a performance at the Charlottetown Festival in 1966, she fell in love with Don Harron. Both were stars in their own right, but when they first met neither had heard of the other. Harron had been in London, New York, and Hollywood for much of the previous decade, while McKinnon had been totally focused on her singing. Harron was abashed at McKinnon's popularity, and after they married he found that people who knew who she was often had a hard time remembering his name. "It's so ironic," he says. "I've been in the business sixty years and yet I get called Don McKinnon all the time and What's-his-name with Catherine McKinnon. In Halifax we got into a cab once and the driver said, 'Oh, celebrities.' I said, 'Yeah, who?' and he said, 'Catherine McKinnon.' I said, 'Who else?' and he said, 'Oh yeah, Don Farquharson.' "

Today they often work together in shows, but McKinnon thinks stardom isn't what it used to be. "To be on television today doesn't really matter so much," she says. "What happened to those of us on television in the early years could never happen today because there are so many channels to choose from. How can you shine as one person? Now, it just can't be done."

A fellow Maritime singer who does shine in contemporary TV, however, is Rita MacNeil, who is the antithesis of the svelte, glamorous star.

Rita MacNeil

She is everything a TV star is not supposed to be: short, fat, middle-aged, shy, thin-skinned, and harelipped. And yet more than any glamorous TV personality in recent years, Rita MacNeil has captured the hearts of Canadian viewers. What would be handicaps for anyone else have made her endearing. "They've given her a deep kindness, a sensitivity that shows in her eyes and in her smile," says Elaine Saunders. It shows in her songs, as well, which are hauntingly poignant, sung from a wounded soul. "God knows," says Saunders, "she's really paid her dues."

Life began for MacNeil in Pond Inlet, a tiny Cape Breton hamlet where her roots remain deeply imbedded. She was one of eight children in a poor family. Like Juliette, Anne Murray, and Catherine McKinnon, she sang as child, but mostly only to her mother because she was too bashful even to sing for a music teacher. In the security of her home, she used a broomstick as a microphone. Later, when she confronted a real microphone and a real audience at a Kiwanis music festival, she froze halfway through her song. But she has a tenacious streak , and at age seventeen, she went to Toronto, married, and began singing at feminist rallies and concerts.

Unlike Juliette, Murray, and McKinnon, MacNeil's rise to musical stardom was agonizingly slow. When her marriage ended, she worked as a cleaning lady for a while and then, economically and emotionally bruised, she went back to Cape Breton. She began singing again, but she was still so nervous that she would often throw up just before a performance. Fighting back her fears and nerves, she went on the road singing in grungy bars across the Maritimes and then across the country, slowly getting better known until she finally got her big break as a headliner at Expo 86 in Vancouver. After that, what had been a slow climb became a fast track to stardom in England and Australia as well as Canada.

For all her success, however, MacNeil remains terrorized by her insecurities. Her weight is the most obvious one, and she suffers the gibes of the Royal Canadian Air Farce and assaults from more biting critics. When she sang the national anthem at a World Series game in Toronto, a columnist from Philadelphia called her a "corpulent anthemist" and rudely suggested she should have been taken out onto the field to sing by a forklift truck. When reporter Eric Malling asked her during a TV interview why she didn't lose weight, she said, "The weight is my problem. I'm the one carrying it."

"If she were thin," says Saunders, "she'd just be another down-east singer who's really good. But her weight has given her something that's connected her with all the audience, and they just love her. Another thing is that, as almost everybody knows, she's gay, and that's been something for her to deal with too."

MacNeil once wrote a two-page letter to Juliette seeking her advice. "Don't let them change you" was Juliette's reply. "Don't let them do anything. Don't let them trim you down. Don't let them take away your signature hat or your style. There always are people who want to do different things to you. They can't leave well enough alone."

"It's kind of sad for Rita because to try to make that wonderful woman into a female version of Ed Sullivan is so wrong," says Catherine McKinnon. "She's so painfully shy. I remember Anne Murray once saying, 'You know, I've given birth to two children, and even when they were babies they were never as vulnerable and shy as Rita is.'"

"Yes, she is very shy and very sweet," says Murray. "She's like dealing with Mother Theresa."

Don't get MacNeil wrong, however, for she also can be tough. "Oh, I can get angry," she says. "I have all the emotions that everybody has."

"Rita's nobody's fool and very street-smart," says Saunders. "If she ever dismissed you, you would know you've been dismissed. But she can sometimes cry, too, and before a show she'll be very nervous."

With her crystal-clear voice that expresses her pain, faith, and defiant hopes, MacNeil has achieved the dreams she'd harboured as a child clinging to a broomstick and singing to her mother. She did it, she says, by living by her own precepts. "Never let the hard times take away your soul," she sings in one of her favourite songs, and it's been the theme of her life. "Keep your feet on the ground," she says. "In gentleness lies your strength, and keep a bit of humility in your pocket. It will come in handy."

It may not work for everybody, but it has for Rita MacNeil.

5

Comedy's Battling Boys

"Migawd, the yelling we did – there was blood on the floor," says Frank Shuster of his relationship with his lifelong partner in comedy, Johnny Wayne. "We fought and we fought, but we were fighting to improve what we were doing. We never had a feud, although sometimes the fights were a little ugly, but from them came something better."

Out of the flames of their battles, Wayne and Shuster – "the boys" to their colleagues even into their seventies – created a brand of literate slapstick humour that captivated Canadians for more than half a century and made them international stars.

Their partnership lasted longer than any other comedy duo anywhere, beginning when they were in high school and continuing until Wayne's death at age seventy-two in 1990. Today their partnership has been extended beyond the grave by newly packaged reruns of their shows, which still light up the screens of the nation.

In truth, most of the yelling over the decades was done by Wayne. "He was more emotional than I was," says Shuster. They never resorted to fisticuffs, but sometimes it came close. Former script assistant Jill Burns remembers sitting in an editing room with them once while they were arguing. At one point Shuster's fist began flying towards Wayne. "I pushed my chair back to the wall to get out of the way," Burns says, "but Frank stopped before anything happened. Johnny was absolutely startled."

While their legendary battles on the set and in the editing room never did come to blows, their verbal warfare left indelible impressions on their colleagues. "The crews didn't like Johnny because he could be a nasty guy on the floor," says Steve Hyde, a floor director for many Wayne and Shuster shows. "Johnny really was two people. On the floor he was a son of a bitch, but outside he was one of the nicest guys you could meet."

That split personality is noted by several of Wayne's colleagues. "Johnny was like Jekyll and Hyde," says Elaine Saunders, make-up artist on "The Wayne and Shuster Show." "He was so kind about many things, and yet such a brat and nasty in other ways. Frank took it all. Frank's not a fighter. Johnny was the fighter." "Johnny came from the school where the person who talks the loudest and the longest wins the argument," says Roy Wordsworth, who was part of the show's family of actors.

They would argue about jokes, about timing, about each other's performance, about the lighting, about the editing. "Johnny would crap all over Frank, but Frank would take it because he knew it didn't mean anything," says variety writer Alex Barris. "One rehearsal they got into an argument on the set, so the director called a break. During the break they needed Johnny to stand in a spot on the set to line up a shot, so the director had him paged. A voice went out on the loudspeaker, 'John Wayne wanted on the set. John Wayne wanted on the set.' Out he walked on his little bowlegs and went to the centre of the set where the microphone was. And he said, 'This is Johnny Wayne, not John Wayne. Johnny Wayne. John Wayne is fortunate enough to have a whole horse as a partner.' "

"Frank is the ultimate gentleman, charming, subtle, and self-effacing," says director Joan Tosoni, a onetime script assistant on the show. "So people got a lot more irritated and hurt about how Johnny treated Frank than Frank did because Frank was used to it. But people would say, 'Oh my God, how can he take that?' "

One day he didn't, according to Steve Hyde. "Johnny was giving him a really bad time, and Frank turned to him and said, 'I don't need this!' " recalls Hyde. "He walked out of the studio, got into his car, and drove home. Johnny was stunned. He called him, apologized, and asked him to come back. For the rest of that show, Johnny was laid-back. The next show he was at it again."

Hyde remembers a sketch that called for the two to get into a vegetable-throwing fight. "The gag line was that everybody had to throw fruit and vegetables at Johnny and Frank," he says. "They gave them to the crew, and there wasn't one piece that went near Frank. Johnny was angry, but he didn't understand what was happening. 'No, no,' he said. 'You have to throw them at both of us.' The crew said, 'Oh,' and immediately threw them all at Johnny again. Johnny said, 'No, no. This isn't working,' and called a break. But the crew loved it, whacking him with lettuce, oranges, and tomatoes and saying, 'Give me another one, another one.' "

Shuster wasn't a total angel, however. He was demanding, too, and, as former script assistant Carroll Hyde says, "I often thought Frank made a lot of the spitballs that Johnny fired."

Lighting directors and other technical staff frequently wailed, "What do I have to do to get off this show?" Norman Campbell, who heard that cry, says, "Johnny was a wonderful guy, but when he got into the studio he became mad. In one of the shows, he lit into my lighting director and gave him hell. I told Johnny, 'I don't ever want to hear you do that again. You can give me hell, but don't talk to the lighting director.' He was very shocked, and the next day apologized to the lighting director. And he behaved for half a day at least."

When he started working on the show, Steve Hyde was warned, "Oh God, they're awful! They'll drive you crazy, especially Johnny." "I watched Johnny crucify lighting, crucify props," he says. "I said to him, 'If you shout at my guys one more time on the floor, I'll close your show down. You can scream at me and I'll let my guys know what you want.' " Wayne agreed reluctantly, but kept the peace only a short time.

"I was frightened of them," admits Juliette, who sometimes appeared on their show, as they did on hers. "They were always yelling at each other, and they were always calling the producer this and that. I was quite vocal on my show, but not that loud."

Wayne was obsessed with the TV monitors on the floor. He would watch the sketches intently, examining every action in the skits. "It was amazing," says Roy Wordsworth. "He watched everything – the costumes, the make-up, the lighting. Johnny was a perfectionist, and he would go over the stuff over and over again. Perfection is what the arguments were all about."

"He wanted to perfect perfection," says Hyde. "Frank would do a bit and Johnny would say, 'Jesus Christ, Frank, when did you ever become a comedian? How were you able to make a living in this fucking business?' Frank would say, 'Well, gee, Johnny, I thought it was okay.' 'Okay?' was the response. 'We're going to do it again.' "

Their battles on the set spilled into the editing room. They would fight over whether to cut out one frame or two – a difference of one thirtieth of a second. "I'd want to go a touch tighter to get the show jumping a bit more," says Shuster. " 'Over my dead body,' John would say. 'Just take one frame out, not two. Let them sit back and savour it.' "

Joan Tosoni sat through many an editing session with them and recalls "lots of fights back and forth about what shots should be used. Johnny would win most of the arguments. 'No, no. You've got to do this!' he would shout. 'No, no. How about this?' " And once I heard him say, "Yeah, yeah. Use a two-shot of me here!"

At one all-night editing session, a frustrated Wayne screamed at Shuster, "This is insanity! It's three o'clock in the morning. Why am I in this stupid editing room editing this crazy show? Why do I need this argument with you? I could be in Italy. I could be on a wine-tasting tour of France. I could be in Japan. I haven't seen Japan yet." Shuster replied, "All right, leave then." A chastened Wayne muttered, "Oh, where would I go?"

One editor had his own technique to end their arguments. Jill Burns remembers the editor telling her, "Whenever they start yelling too long, I put on my earphones. They think I'm listening to something on the show and they stop fighting so I can hear. In fact, I'm listening to nothing, but it usually ends the arguing for a while."

"John was a control freak and that was the problem," says Norman Jewison. "But if you let him control things that weren't important, it worked out okay."

"Johnny hated the way he looked, so he always wanted a certain shot of his face," says Mary DePoe. "They wanted lots of close-ups, but you could never have just a close-up of Johnny and not a close-up of Frank. You had to treat them equally."

Battles seem to be the custom for comedy duos. Abbott and Costello hated each other; Laurel and Hardy clashed; Martin and Lewis warred; the Smothers Brothers came to blows; and even Sonny and Cher were locked in combat. The worst confrontation Allan Blye encountered after leaving CBC for Hollywood was on "The Smothers Brothers Show." "I'm talking left hook and right cross," he says. "I'm talking about 'Get out of my way, I'm going to kill that son of bitch.'" For Wayne and Shuster, as Steve Hyde says, "Once they were back in the office, you never heard Johnny put Frank down or any really loud battles."

Despite all their arguments, Wayne knew he needed Shuster and vice versa. In their private lives, both were cultivated, highly intelligent men who thought comedy was a serious business. Part of the reason for the longevity of their partnership was that they kept their personal and professional lives apart. At one point early on, Wayne said to Shuster, "You know, I'm going to have a party next week, but I'm not going to invite you because we're always together and we'll start in about the business. So, to hell with it." "You know, you're right," said Shuster.

"That was very shrewd," says Shuster today, "and we made a pact not to see each other socially."

"We always used to wonder how this marriage could ever last because Johnny would fly off the handle and insult everybody," says Lorraine Thomson, a dancer on Wayne and Shuster shows. "Johnny was the sparkplug, and boy did he spark! Frank would go about patting people on the back and telling them not to worry."

"Their arguments were public, and that's what made people uncomfortable," says Joan Tosoni. "Johnny did not realize how obnoxious he seemed in other people's eyes. Johnny was a very charming man as well. He was very knowledgeable. He loved languages. He read a lot, loved to travel. I got to see a side of Johnny that was quite cultured and contemplative. Frank always had that exterior, whereas Johnny seemed like a little bulldog so much of the time."

"They were both extremely literate guys, and they both knew a great deal about painting and sculpture," says Mavor Moore. "When I worked with them, it was a daily battle. Not in private, but in rehearsal, Johnny would dress Frank down unmercifully. Frank was a model of patience and quiet determination. I think Frank realized Johnny was the genius of the pair, but Frank was probably the better actor."

Towards the end of each day of shooting, after all the time-consuming, adrenalin-draining arguments, there would be a rush to get as much done as possible. Wayne would bounce about flapping his hands and repeatedly saying, "Come on. Let's go! Let's go! Time! Time!"

"There was always panic at the end of the day," says Tosoni. "The crew wouldn't work overtime because they were pissed off with all the yelling and stress."

"The technicians always shut down at six or the end of the scheduled shooting, no matter what," says Roy Wordsworth. "There was always a panic because the lights would go out at the end of the day. So the last fifteen minutes were hell. We were always behind, and where you had been doing six or seven takes during the day, in the last fifteen minutes suddenly everything was in one take." And when the day's shooting or rehearsing was over, the cast and technicians would look over to Shuster. They were waiting to hear if he called Wayne by his real first name, Lou. "If he said, 'See you tomorrow, Lou,' then we knew that everything was forgiven whatever the arguments, whatever the pressures," says Wordsworth.

Lou Weingarten, who became Johnny Wayne, and Frank Shuster began their partnership in 1931 in the second year of high school at Toronto's Harbord Collegiate. The duo entertained their schoolmates with skits and Gilbert and Sullivan operettas at the school's "Oola Boola" drama club and, says Shuster, "We worked out a nice relationship. If you had two guys who had a great deal of ego, you'd be dead. Johnny had a major ego. And I understood I couldn't be like him. He'd argue about something and I'd keep quiet and eventually I'd sneak something in. Sometimes I'd get my own way, sometimes I wouldn't. He painted in broad strokes, and I was like a minimalist. I would try to be subtle."

Wayne came from a moderately well-to-do family that ran a sporting goods business, while Shuster's father kept the wolf from the door, but just barely, as a movie operator. "There was no money to spend, and I'd go to university with a briefcase full of salmon sandwiches. I'd have ten cents for milk or coffee since I'd leave at eight in the morning and come back at midnight because of all our extracurricular work."

The Shusters were a creative family. Shuster's cousin Joe was a cartoonist who, with a friend, originated the Superman cartoon character. "Joe was a quiet, mousy boy, a real Clark Kent who used to do weights so he could be stronger," says Shuster. "He sent me a sketch of Superman on a small piece of paper and said, 'What do you think of this idea?' 'Pretty good,' I said."

After entertaining classmates at high school and the University of Toronto, Wayne and Shuster's first commercial radio series came in 1941 – a household hints show on CFRB Toronto called "The Javex Wife Preservers," for which they were each paid $12.50 a week. Later they did a show called "Co-eds and Cut-ups." Before going into the army, they did their first work for the CBC in sketches for the Buckingham Cigarette show, "Blended Rhythm."

They went overseas in 1943 with "The Army Show," entertaining troops in England and on the continent after the Normandy invasion. One of the highlights was a sketch in which Wayne would go into the audience, pick up items, and ask Shuster, dressed as a swami, what he had in his hands. Once while Shuster was doing a magic chant and Wayne was saying, "Oh, swami, what have I got in my hand?" the sound of an oncoming buzz bomb suddenly stopped, and there was an eerie silence as everyone waited for the bomb to land. "You can't get off the stage. You can't hide," says Shuster. "If you die, you die." In the middle of the silence, Wayne repeated, "Oh, swami, what do I have in my hand?" "All of a sudden, whap!" remembers Shuster. "It landed about a quarter of a mile away with a big explosion. I said, 'You have in your hand – a buzz bomb!' " "Right," said Wayne. The troops cheered wildly both for relief at escaping the bomb and at the duo's "carry-on" spirit. It was their closest call, although they were sniped at and strafed near the front lines in Europe.

Another less dangerous but equally nervy wartime experience for Wayne and Shuster came during a 1943 radio program with comedian Jack Benny. The number-one American comedy star agreed to appear on their Canadian Army radio show. As they were rehearsing, Benny suggested a small script change to a sketch in which Benny pleads with recruiting sergeants Wayne and Shuster to get into the army. He wanted to explain why he wished to enlist. But Wayne and Shuster said, "Oh no, our script is fine as it is." "Imagine," says Shuster today, "we said no. These two kids starting out in the business, telling Jack Benny no! Twenty-five years later I'm sleeping and it's five o'clock in the morning and I wake up and say, 'Oh my God, he was right!' "

From the start they had been known as Shuster and Wayne. But after the war, they changed to Wayne and Shuster when Toronto advertising executive Bill Byles suggested it sounded better that way. "We were both getting the same money so it didn't matter to me," says Shuster, and the first Wayne and Shuster comedy show aired on CBC Radio in 1946. It was a breakthrough at the corporation, for the CBC had never used performers' names in a network show title before.

They had, by now, been comedy partners for fifteen years, and their reputation was spreading fast. "The first time I ever worked with them I was sixteen years old, working in a Mother Goose pantomime at the Royal Alexandra Theatre in Toronto. When we were rehearsing onstage, they came down the aisle and we just stopped," says Lorraine Thomson. "They had such a presence."

Their presence was felt in the United States as well, when they were hired to do a summer network series replacing William Bendix and "The Life of Riley." In 1950 in New York, they uneasily tiptoed into television on "Toni Twin Time" with host Jack Lemmon, the future Hollywood star. He was, says Shuster, "a very callow and scared youth who was terrible in the show, although he is a good actor." The advertising agency running the show asked them to take it over, but they refused because they preferred being in Toronto and were apprehensive about television. Shuster was especially spooked by TV after watching Milton Berle in rehearsal for one of his shows in New York. Berle was known as Mr. Television for his enormous popularity, but he was known in the business as a demanding monster. "The pressures were unbelievable," says Shuster. "He knew where the lighting should be, he knew the music, and if it wasn't right, he'd run around. I thought, 'Oh my God, I don't want to be in a business like that.' "

When television came to Canada two years later, they rejected it, despite the pleading of senior producer Mavor Moore. "Look," said

Wayne, "you guys don't know anything about television. We don't either. Why don't we wait until we both know something about it?"

They did agree to make an appearance on one CBC-TV program in Montreal in the fall of 1952, but it would be two more years before they took the plunge into television with a regular show. It was the beginning of an illustrious television career that saw their shows become a prime-time smash hit in Canada, as their radio shows already were. The shows were broadcast in fourteen countries, and Wayne and Shuster became favourites on the Ed Sullivan Sunday night show, appearing on the program sixty-seven times over twelve years.

In comedy, as in so many things, the devil is in the details, and Wayne and Shuster were forever chasing down the details to make their shows better and, in the process, driving directors, technicians, executives, and even performers crazy. If in a sketch someone would enter carrying a tray, they would shout, "Stop! The tray's too big. It works better with a smaller tray." A time-consuming search would then ensue to find a smaller tray. Len Lauk, then a CBC executive, recalls what he refers to as "the Wayne and Shuster fifty-dollar banana." One sketch called for a fruit bowl filled with oranges, pears, apples, and some grapes. Wayne saw it and said, "Stop! No. We've got to have a banana in there." "Someone jumped into a taxicab," says Lauk, "roared off to a fruit store, bought a banana, and triumphantly brought it back to the studio, where Johnny happily put it in the fruit bowl. Then the shooting got underway again. The cost of the banana and the cabs was fifty dollars, to say nothing of the delay in production."

Production was delayed another time when Wayne, playing in a Superman skit, lost his Clark Kent glasses when he was making the quick change from Superman into the mild-mannered newspaperman. Comedian Dave Broadfoot was in the show and says Wayne had stuck the glasses in his Superman leotard. "When it came time to put on the glasses, he realized they had slipped down to his crotch," says Broadfoot, "and he couldn't get them out from between his legs. Shuster then cracked, 'God, he's got seeing-eye genitalia!' The cast broke up and the taping stopped."

Given their demands for perfection, scripts were often being rewritten right up to airtime. "The nice thing about Wayne and Shuster," says Roy Wordsworth, "was that you got your script in the mail but you didn't bother to learn it because by the time you got to the studio there were a whole bunch of rewrites. Johnny spilled over with ideas. He couldn't stop inventing stuff, and he'd be rewriting right up until the last take. A lot of good actors couldn't do the show because they couldn't take the pressure."

Additional pressure for actors on the show came from the duo's sometimes conflicting direction. "Frank would say, 'Do it this way,' and Johnny would say, 'No, no. Not like that, like this!' " says Wordsworth. "So you had to walk a fine line, but we were used to it. And Johnny would have the last say."

"Johnny wrote better than I did," says Shuster. "We used to alternate on the typewriter, one typing and the other pacing or lying down on the sofa. In the quest for the perfect quip, we'd battle each other right up until show time.

"We were very serious, damn serious, and we'd sit there sweating and fighting over lines, and when we started to laugh hysterically, we always quit because we knew the following day we'd come back and say, 'What's funny about that?' Comedy is very fragile. The words are important. There is rhythm, and we don't want anybody changing lines. It's written in stone."

In later years Wayne thought a computer would help their writing, and he started to mock Shuster's trusty old Underwood typewriter. "Frank, this is no longer the age of the dinosaur," said Wayne. "You must move with progress to create funny." Shuster quivered with rage, saying, "You know what's funny? A pencil is funny. I'm ready to go back to the pencil!"

"I don't know anything about this computer stuff," Shuster now says. "Johnny was more interested, but I always ran away. I always say I'm not ready for power steering."

"They needed each other to write," says Wordsworth. "But Frank was a much better actor by far. Frank played parts, but Johnny always played Johnny. He never wanted to lose himself."

"They had an absolute infallible idea about what was funny," says

Lorraine Thomson. "And what they thought was funny was a kind of cross between a more erudite British sense of humour and the more American vaudevillian sense of humour. They treated their audience with respect."

"There is absolutely no doubt that the art of comedy is the most difficult in the entertainment industry, more so than drama by a country mile," says former variety department executive Len Starmer. "And everyone thinks they know what is a good joke." Joan Tosoni remembers a variety department secretary who, while typing comedy scripts, would simply leave out jokes she didn't like. "I said to her one day that several parts of the script were missing," says Tosoni, "and she said, 'Well, they were sexist jokes and they shouldn't be on the air.' She had simply censored all the stuff she didn't like."

But Wayne and Shuster's biggest problem was with directors. Wayne would eat directors alive with his demands and criticism. "Look what the schmuck is doing to us!" he shouted from the set once while denouncing director Bill Davis. When Stan Jacobson replaced Davis, it was the same story. "They'd be totally insulting about everything he was doing," says Mary DePoe. "You felt very sorry for the director," adds Wordsworth. The nightmare for the director would end only when he did what Wayne and Shuster wanted. The last director was Trevor Evans, who always delivered what they asked for. "He would suggest things," says Wordsworth, "and if they said no, he would do it their way."

Evans, however, was subtly able to get his own way once in a while. Former floor director Steve Hyde recalls that sometimes after a sketch had been shot the way he felt it should be, Evans would ask, "What did you think, Johnny?" Inevitably the answer would be "I didn't like it." "Well, tell me what you want." Then, Hyde says, "Trevor would go upstairs to the control room and do exactly what he'd done before, and afterwards Johnny would say, 'You see, much better.' "

One director, Don Hudson, told Starmer, "I love those guys, but you can't really direct Johnny and Frank."

"They wanted to call all the shots," says Starmer. "It was impossible to be a director. And they were right for the sketches. Directors would come in and say, 'I need to have some authority in the sketches.' I would say, 'Well, you won't have it. The boys know best what they want. You're not going to have any real authority. You're going to take pictures according to Wayne and Shuster.' "

Starmer, who took over as executive producer of the Wayne and Shuster shows in the early 1970s, gave "the boys" more freedom, letting them put in their own laugh tracks and do their own editing. "Hallelujah!" said Wayne. "Hey, I'll do it for free."

"These guys were amazing," says Wordsworth. "They were in their seventies, and they would go into the studio at seven-thirty in the morning for make-up and costumes. They'd be on their feet all day not only performing but directing, overseeing the production, sets, costumes, casting, and everything as well as being the stars. We'd break for lunch, and usually during lunch they'd be checking up on costumes or make-up and then they'd work till six or sometimes seven-thirty. The pressures and the energy they had were amazing. Then they often did all-night editing sessions."

Occasionally, off the set, they would take time out to encourage one of the actors or production staff, in startling contrast to their argumentative intensity on the set. "They would never criticize anyone on a personal level," says Mary DePoe. "And if you weren't well, Johnny was the first one there to see how you were."

"In a sense, it was a family at 'Wayne and Shuster,' " says Wordsworth, the youngest cast member who, ironically, usually played old men in the sketches. "They were very loyal to us and we were very loyal to them. When Carol Robinson had cancer they were really protective of her, making sure she was in the show but that her role would not be too demanding. They would have her sitting instead of running about."

Joan Tosoni remembers Wayne encouraging her after one particularly long day, saying, "Stick with me kid and you'll be wearing diamond socks. I'll teach you about this business and you're going to go places."

Wayne and Shuster themselves went places and most spectacularly on to American television screens through "The Ed Sullivan Show." "Sullivan was a strange and wonderful man," says Shuster. "He thought we were wonderful. His wife, Sylvia, was crazy about us, and I always suspected that was why we worked with him so much."

As host of the program that owned Sunday night television, Sullivan would showcase the best of ballet dancers, opera singers, magicians, rock and roll musicians, pop singers, actors, animal acts, and comedians. He was a genius at spotting talent and awful as the host. He was awkward, nervous, couldn't remember names, couldn't pronounce two-syllable words, and made convoluted introductions. On one occasion he introduced a group of paraplegics in the audience, asking them to "stand and take a bow." Another time he introduced the great blind guitarist José Feliciano by saying, "Not only is José blind, he's Puerto Rican."

"Ed Sullivan fooled everybody," Shuster says. "People thought he was an inarticulate bumbler, but he had an instinct for picking talent. He loved comedy, and he'd always surprise you." Wayne and Shuster's relationship with Sullivan began with a 7:30 A.M. phone call from a New York agent who said, "Ed Sullivan wants to see you. Get the hell down here as fast as you can." When they met in Sullivan's apartment, he said, "I like what you fellows do. It's very good. We want you on the show."

The two knew Sullivan's reputation for brutally slashing the length of acts on his show and so Shuster said, "Mr. Sullivan, we do long sketches." "I know you do, and I'm not pleased about that," he said. "But I know that you're different, fresh. So I say to you, do it your way. I will not touch you guys." For $7,500 a show and a one-year contract, they began their twelve-year run as the most successful comedy act Sullivan ever showcased. Sullivan gave them *carte blanche*. He told his staff, "If Wayne and Shuster want twenty elephants, they got it. Just do what they want." Addressing Shuster as "Francis," he warned him not to change. "Don't listen to anybody, Francis," he said. "There are no geniuses in this business." "Mr. Sullivan," Shuster replied, "what if you don't like what we're doing? What happens then?" "If you feel in your heart that I'm wrong, forget it," he said.

It was an astonishing commitment to Wayne and Shuster by a man known among his colleagues as the Butcher for his habit of cutting the length of skits. He did this to the stand-up routine of Canadian comic Dave Broadfoot, unnerving Broadfoot. "He was changing everything. It was a nightmare," says Broadfoot. "He was saying, 'You can't say this, you can't say that,' and it's getting closer and closer to the start of the show." In the end, Broadfoot ignored Sullivan's instructions, did his original material, and Sullivan said not a word.

In another instance, Sullivan demanded a two-minute cut in an acrobatic act featuring eight monkeys. "It took me years to train these monkeys," their keeper cried. "How can I get them to cut two minutes now?" The problem was solved by starting the monkey act behind the curtain two minutes before Sullivan's introduction.

With Sullivan's promise of no cuts, Wayne and Shuster were the envy of all the stars who appeared on the show. On their first Sullivan show, a Julius Caesar skit ran fourteen minutes, and on the second show, their sketch lasted sixteen minutes. Meanwhile, says Shuster, "people are being cut left and right and are asking, Who the hell are these guys to come in and take over so much time?"

Only three times in a dozen years did Sullivan question their sketches, and in two cases he backed off. "Boys, I'm very disappointed in that sketch," he said after one rehearsal. Wayne replied, "Ed, we've been working with you a long time, and we only come in with the very best things we've got." "He nodded," says Shuster, "didn't say a word, and walked away because he had made a pledge to us."

Another time Sullivan questioned them about a Scarlet Pimpernell skit. "You know that scene in the cells in the Bastille," he said to them. "Is it important?" "That's very important, Mr. Sullivan." Shuster said. "Oh, all right, you son of a bitch," Sullivan grimaced.

The one time "the boys" agreed to cut a line was when Sullivan objected to a comment by Wayne in a sketch on Russian hockey. Acting as the Russian coach, Wayne claimed hockey had been invented by the Russians and that baseball had been too. Shuster said, "What about Abner Doubleday?" And Wayne replied, "What about the lynchings in the South?" Sullivan was fearful of offending the network stations in the South, and Wayne and Shuster agreed to take out the line.

Sullivan called Wayne and Shuster "my Canadian egghead comics" because of their more educated comedy pieces, such as their popular Julius Caesar sketch. In it, when Wayne at a Roman bar orders a "martinus," the bartender says, "You mean a martini." Wayne replies, "If I want two, I'll ask for them."

One of Sullivan's favourite sketches was the Seige of Troy. They built a fourteen-foot-high horse, which Shuster says in the sketch was "the greatest weapon in the history of war." Suddenly a group of protesters arrives shouting, "Ban the horse! Ban the horse!" Wayne says, "Don't worry. It's just a bunch of crazies who believe in only one God. They're just this far away from atheism." Actually the whole sketch was written because they desperately wanted to use the line "Is there a doctor in the horse?"

One joy for them in doing the Sullivan show was the chance to meet some of the world's greatest performers. Shuster remembers singing "Mimi" to Maurice Chevalier, the international French star. At the end of the show as they headed to their dressing room, Chevalier put his arms around them and said, "You know, we foreigners are so lucky that Americans love us."

Just before going on another Sullivan show, Wayne and Shuster were chatting with trumpeter Louis Armstrong when "Satchmo" looked around at the other guests, including Duke Ellington and Paul Anka, and said, "Louie is here. The Duke is here. Paul Anka is here. Wayne and Shuster are here. All the top shit is here."

While in New York they would go to parties with show-business celebrities. At one Wayne met his idol, Groucho Marx, whose approach to comedy inspired Wayne's own. "You guys are doing very good work," Groucho said and, turning to Wayne, added, "And you, young man, I know where you get your style from." "Sir," said Wayne, "I only steal from the very best."

Although they were hailed as superstars of comedy, Wayne and Shuster were dazzled at finding themselves in the company of other international stars, and never considered themselves in that league. Among others, they partied with Elizabeth Taylor, Eddie Fisher, Cary Grant, Walter Winchell, Kitty Carlyle, Moss Hart, and Bennett Cerf. "It was fun," says Shuster. "It was like a vacation going to New York. I was working hard, but it was fun being with the magic that surrounded us."

Although they were ardently wooed, they were never seriously tempted to go to the United States permanently. Shuster considered Sullivan "like an older brother" and says, "Sullivan loved us because we stayed in Canada. He said, 'Don't come here.'" They were urged to come to the States first in 1951 and again, more forcefully, after their reputation soared because of the Sullivan show. "We just didn't want to go," says

Shuster. "They told us we could earn a lot more money in the U.S. But we said we were concerned about family and lifestyle, our self-comfort and well-being."

The Broadway producer of *A Funny Thing Happened on the Way to the Forum* called Shuster to persuade them to star in the show. Roy Wordsworth remembers Shuster saying, "Yeah, we wouldn't mind doing it, but we'd have to be replaced after the first two weeks because we'd have to get back to Canada to do our show." "Can you imagine that?" exclaims Wordsworth. "Most people would kill to get that chance, but their priority was to stay in Canada."

One New York agent pleaded with them, "You've got to come down. Your career will flourish here." When Shuster gave a final no, the disgusted agent told them with a sad shake of his head, "You know, Frank, there's more to life than happiness."

"Their decision to stay in Canada probably gave all of us who have followed them in comedy the confidence to also stay here," says Royal Canadian Air Farce comedian Roger Abbott.

Wayne and Shuster were given the star treatment everywhere they went in the United States and England, but despite their loyalty to Canada they were never treated like stars at the CBC because there was no star system. The different treatment they received outside Canada was vividly demonstrated when they flew out to Hollywood to do "The Rosemary Clooney Show." The show paid for their wives to go first-class, a chauffeured limousine met them at the airport, their wives were taken shopping, and they had a star on their dressing-room door. They flew back to Canada to start work on their next CBC show and were not allowed on the CBC parking lot because they didn't have a pass. At the time, only senior executives were given passes. In later years, however, the CBC gave in and provided them with parking spaces.

Even some fans rated the Canadian shows inferior to their appearances with Ed Sullivan. Says Shuster, "We'd hear from people who'd say, 'How come you guys are so much funnier on the Sullivan show than you are on the CBC?' We'd say, 'We're not funnier. We're doing exactly the same thing.' But the aura of being on 'Sullivan' with all the stars made it seem better to some."

They didn't behave like stars in their private lives, either. Far from indulging to excess in the legendary wine, women, and drugs of showbiz, they were squares – "civilians," as Shuster says. Both were happily married, and their lifelong wives, Bea Wayne and Ruth Shuster, created a rock of comfort and stability for them. "They were extraordinary in guiding their men, in soothing them, in cooling them, and in telling them when they we're going too far," says Mavor Moore. "The times when Ruth had to rebuild Frank's ego after one of the schmozzles, it was really marvellous. These two women never received the credit they deserved."

When Bea died of cancer in 1980, although Wayne tried to hide his grief, he never recovered from the loss. "When Bea was dying, we had to do a show," says Roy Wordsworth. "Normally you'd think we would postpone it. But he did it, and it was agony to see him going out every day and pulling himself up to do the show, to be funny. When he finished, he'd go to his dressing room and listen to classical music."

Wayne and Shuster had been "the boys" for so long with their enthusiasm and indefatigable twelve- to sixteen-hour workdays that they seemed ageless. But now it was different. Wayne's spark was still there in the studio, as he clowned, did pratfalls, fought over jokes and lighting and shots, but once he stepped outside, the spark went out. Within a few years, he also fell victim to cancer. "He would come into the office determined not to let this get to him," says Len Starmer. "Oh God, all I wanted to do was just cuddle him."

The day before he died in 1990, Starmer and Shuster visited Wayne at his Toronto lakefront apartment. Drifting in and out of a coma, he opened his eyes to see them and said, "Oh, Frank. Oh, Len." And then he drifted away again.

"He was lying there and holding my hand so tightly, I knew he was saying goodbye," says Shuster. "What can you say? What can you do? We had worked together for a whole lifetime. But I could still feel his strength – a young man's strength. He seemed to be saying, 'Okay, I'm going. We did all right. Wish me well.' "

After Wayne's death, Shuster immersed himself in producing a "Wayne and Shuster" retrospective series, packaging old shows with new introductions. He found that even in death Wayne's spirit was sitting on his shoulder telling him what to do. "I think of what he would say," says Shuster. "I realize he might object to this or that, and I say, maybe if I did it this way, he might agree. It's as though he were still alive today and we're still fighting over funny lines. I constantly find myself turning to talk to him, listen to him, argue with him. I can hear Johnny protesting, 'Frank, you shouldn't have made that cut. That was bad judgement.' When I'm writing, I have him over my shoulder saying, 'You're not going to say that, are you?' And I say, 'Wait a minute. I'm fixing it.' But altogether, I'm winning a lot more arguments today than I used to."

The new series has given Shuster a new life. He spent months in the studio, in darkened editing rooms and in writing the introductions. It may not be his last hurrah, but at age seventy-eight, it's close to it. "It's getting near to the finish, I guess," he says. "But it's nice to work. I want to work to the very last day."

As he finished preparing the twenty-two-episode retrospective series, the CBC took away his office and ended his contract after he'd worked there for more than half a century. "I thought this job would be a steady thing," he says. "But," he adds, "it's been fun, wonderful all the way. Sometimes you sit back and say, 'Hey, I did something nice.' It's not earth-shattering, but it's very satisfying.

"You like to hear people laugh. It makes you feel good because it makes them feel good. Laughing is very important. It really is."

6

"Front Page Challenge"

"Front Page Challenge" marched triumphantly onto the nation's screens in 1957 and ended thirty-eight years later slinking off amid recriminations and rancour.

No Canadian network weekly TV program has lasted so long or seen such a panorama of high-profile guests, iconoclastic panellists, and rampaging egos as those who strode before the cameras of this grand old lady of all Canadian TV shows. Beginning as a summer replacement, it received applause from its audience and yearly obituary notices from its critics before finally being killed with a management indifference that bordered on brutality.

Stars and VIPs paraded before the cameras, from the stripper Sally Rand to the first lady Eleanor Roosevelt, from Indira Gandhi to Mickey Mantle, from Boris Karloff to Malcolm X, and every Canadian prime minister between 1957 and 1995 except Brian Mulroney. It seemed that for Canadians, no one was a true star or VIP until he or she appeared on "Front Page Challenge." "At last," said rock musician Burton Cummings on his guest appearance on the show, "at last, my mother will think of me as a star." Luminaries from Hollywood or the political world were sometimes drunk, occasionally belligerent, and often nervous, but still they came into our living rooms for nearly four decades through the cameras of "Front Page Challenge."

It was a star-driven show whose producers wisely let Pierre Berton, Toby Robins, Betty Kennedy, Gordon Sinclair, Allan Fotheringham, and Jack Webster go their own maverick ways under Fred Davis's quietly smooth emceeing. They did, that is, until its last dyspeptic years, when producers and management, in a search for issues and headline publicity, changed its approach from one of providing entertaining information to that of pursuing significant social issues. Even the handsome financial rewards of about $2,500 a show did not ease the professional agony of the panellist stars who felt bruised and downgraded by the shift in focus from them to what Allan Fotheringham called "nobodies with an issue, [such as] a one-legged lesbian black wife who was beaten in Nanaimo."

When network vice-president Ivan Fecan decided to have "Front Page Challenge" produced in Vancouver, instead of Toronto and various regional locales, he hired as producer Cameron Bell, a hard-nosed Vancouver television news veteran, and told him to "put some edge in it." That order precipitated a confrontation that led at times to shouts, insults, and frosty tension. Bell thought Berton, Kennedy, Fotheringham, and Webster had lost much of their wallop. He says the show needed to be "more sharply focused on contemporary, relevant issues, which would more likely make news. . . . There was a fundamental philosophical difference between the cast and the mandate to give the show some edge . . . I was persuaded that we could not run a show on celebrities alone."

Bell and Helen Slinger, his deputy, who like him was a tough news veteran, felt they were on a Fecan-inspired mission to revive the ratings with hot, contemporary issues, while the panel, led by Berton, felt the program's personalities and informative entertainment were responsible for its longevity and popularity. "Our unhappiness, I think, showed," says Berton. "They were bugging us all the time. They would stop the tape – with the audience there – and harangue us. They were trying to tell us what questions to ask. We revolted. So they were always upset."

At one point Berton ordered Slinger never to come onto the studio floor to talk to the panel. "Cam, keep her off the floor," Berton asked the new producer. "We don't like her. We don't want her. We don't want anything to do with that woman. You're going to lose all of us. Just get her out of here." "We never saw her on the floor again," Berton says.

"They thought we'd become prima donnas – big shots from Toronto," says Fotheringham. Bell cautiously says, "They all had personal professional personae. They are where they are today as a result of carefully currying those personae." What Bell and Slinger wanted to do, says Kennedy, was "to have complete control . . . take it away from the panel. I think that is what it was all about."

Berton remembers Fecan telling him, "Each year I tried to kill that program, but each year the ratings were so good, I couldn't." But what Fecan and his predecessors did do, in the process of trying to strengthen the overall schedule, was to juggle its time slot around until viewers hardly knew when it was on. It was also taken off mandatory carriage by all affiliates, which reduced its audience, and over the years the number of shows produced each season was decreased from thirty-six to twenty-six to eighteen.

By the spring of 1995, the ratings were in the 500,000 to 700,000 range and the CBC swung the axe. Phyllis Platt, who succeeded Fecan, was the executioner. To try to minimize publicity, Platt killed "Front Page Challenge" in a series of panicky phone calls to the stars made just before a weekend. Berton never did hear the news directly. Instead he learned from an associate that the show had been cancelled. Fotheringham, Webster, and Davis were informed just before the announcement; Kennedy's husband heard the news on the radio and told her before Platt managed to contact her. "The way this was handled was despicable and bush league," Fotheringham says. The panel angrily rejected a farewell lunch suggested by the CBC. "I'm not having any goddamn lunch," Fotheringham said.

"Front Page Challenge" was over.

For most of its life, "Front Page Challenge" was produced in downtown Toronto at the CBC's old, ugly, and tattered Yonge Street studio, which had been converted from a 1920s automobile show room. The half-hour program was originally a summer replacement show, the brainchild of twenty-nine-year-old comedy writer John Aylesworth – a simple concept of having a panel guess the identity of a hidden guest and then interview that guest. Before beginning on June 24, 1957, its first panellists did dry runs in the basement recreation room of producer Harvey Hart. The irascible radio commentator Gordon Sinclair, the lustrous actress Toby Robins, columnist and TV personality Alex Barris, and writer Scott Young were led through that first show by the longtime voice of Paramount Newsreel, Win Barron. The opening program featured Montreal Mayor Jean Drapeau, a midwife at the birth of the Dionne Quintuplets, and a survivor of the 1936 Moose River, Nova Scotia, mine disaster.

"The thing died, although the corpse will be kept around for weeks yet, perhaps for autopsy purposes," reviewed the *Toronto Star*. It was judged a success by the CBC, however, and began a regular season run in the fall, with Pierre Berton replacing Barris, and Fred Davis replacing Barron, who, while charming in private, clearly felt uncomfortable on a live show and was terrible as host. There would also be a different guest questioner each week.

There has never been a show quite like "Front Page Challenge," with its mix of information and entertainment, its journalistic star inquisitors grilling the glitterati of show business, politics, and breaking news. After appearing on one show, Mike Wallace, then just beginning his career as a TV hot-seat interviewer, tried to sell the idea to the American networks, but failed. Comedian Ernie Kovacs did a version of "Front Page" in the States, but dropped it after two or three weeks. Another effort to emulate the show was made in Britain, but it didn't get off the ground. In Canada, however, the show was a hit, and it made household names of its panel celebrities.

Pierre Berton

When "Front Page Challenge" died, of the original team in its first full season of 1957 only Pierre Berton and Fred Davis, both aged seventy-four, were left. Both had made appearances on the summer replacement show, but didn't join as full-fledged members until the fall season began. Almost from the beginning, Berton was the team leader. From his on-air know-it-all certainties, his loud-voiced inquisitorial style learned from Mike Wallace and Gordon Sinclair, his encyclopedic knowledge of everything from Hollywood to politics, his towering physical presence, and his showbiz flair, you would expect Pierre Frances de Marigny Berton to be an extroverted egomaniac. But that's not the real Pierre Berton.

When they first began working together on the show, Fred Davis thought, "Gee, this guy Berton is such a cold fish. He inhibits me. I can't get next to him. Maybe I've offended him," adding, "Even to this day, sometimes he'll open up and sometimes he doesn't see you." Davis once sought advice on how to deal with Berton from his longtime colleague Barbara Moon. "He's inordinately shy," she said. "He's not a slap-you-on-the-back type." Davis said, "He still is shy, but he covers it up with bravado and all his success."

"Fred Davis thought I was a son of a bitch when we first knew each other," says Berton, who, to those outside his circle of intimates, can appear haughty. "Betty Kennedy threw a farewell dinner when 'Front Page' was cancelled," says Allan Fotheringham. "And I took a young lady, who was seated beside Pierre. Later she told me, 'That's the most arrogant man I've ever met. He said hardly a word to me all dinner.' I get this from a lot of people, especially at a party. 'That tall, imperious look . . . that arrogant bastard.' Actually, I think he is quite shy."

"Pierre *is* very shy," says Kennedy. "He doesn't have that war chest of small talk. He's not very good with strangers at cocktail parties. He often comes off aloof, and he may pass you without saying hello. Half the time he doesn't see you because he's very short-sighted."

"Pierre is one of those introverted extroverts," says Lorraine Thomson, the show's program co-ordinator for almost two decades. "He's a shy egomaniac. He stands off to one side at most parties, seemingly reluctant to take part in conversations. A lot of people take this shyness as arrogance."

Berton accepts the criticism. "I am very shy. Not professionally, but socially shy. Big guys are shy and I'm six foot three. I can't be jocular with people I don't know. I don't know why. At cocktail parties, I try to be nice to people who know me, but I can't open up to them." But, professionally, Berton does open up, and he admits to liking, even loving, the spotlight. "I'm a ham," he says. "There's no use pretending that you're not a ham if you're in show business." Even as a star, however, he always gave himself reminders: "Sit up straight, stupid!" he'd scrawl on notepaper in front of him on the set. "Another problem I have in television is not to look bored, because a lot of it is boring, you know."

He may worry about boredom and shyness, but they're not the first words that generally leap to mind for Berton's longtime friends. "When Pierre came to *Maclean's*, we were all anxious to meet him," says writer June Callwood. "He was this big kid from the West, and we were astonished at his size. The man has a kind of physical gaucheness. He's apt to make gestures that look awkward. I always think of him as a marvellous big kid.

"We were all introduced to Pierre at a party at Ralph Allen's, our editor. We drank our heads off, and he was drinking like everyone else. He recited 'The Shooting of Dan McGrew,' and at the end, when Dan falls with a shot by the lady known as Lou, Pierre took a full-length fall right across the room and filled up the whole living-room floor. This was our introduction to Pierre, so we never thought of him as shy."

CBC Radio host Vickie Gabereau, whose father was a good friend of Berton, remembers as a teenager when Berton came back from Toronto to Vancouver to visit her father. "He would come in like a colossus," she says. "It was fantastic. They were just terrors. Pierre would come thumping into the house. They used to do close-order drill in the living room. They stayed up all night. They screamed. They yelled. They sang. They jumped on the furniture. My girlfriend came over and she said, 'I can't believe it's Pierre Berton.' "

This romping gusto is a side of Berton seen only by his closest friends. "You can't help respect his intelligence and versatility, but Mr. Warmth he ain't," says Alex Barris. "He's concerned with issues, but not the people involved in them."

"Pierre was probably the most unpopular with the crews because they found him very snobby, very aloof," says Steve Hyde, a onetime floor director on the show. "He was all for the working man, but he didn't want to rub shoulders with them. None of us were ever invited to Pierre's house. I only saw him when he came in and when he was performing. On the road, you never saw him. He went into his hotel and that was it."

While at times Berton rues his shyness-induced arrogance, he also defends it. "It's time some Canadians were arrogant," he says. "We need more arrogance." Contributing to his air of arrogance is the forceful certainty he displays at times. "Pierre has never said, 'On the other hand' in his life," says Allan Fotheringham. Berton says, "My wife always says, 'You say things so strongly everybody believes them.'" But as he himself admits, "Certitude has its pitfalls."

Fred Davis recalled one such pitfall when Berton was dead wrong at the top of his voice. "We were in Halifax, and the panel had read in the local papers that they were shooting a movie down in Lunenburg, starring Patricia Neal and Darren McGavin," Davis said. "Pierre and the others talked about it in the green room and figured we might have one of the stars on the show. On the air, we began with a Hollywood actress, and, knowing the movie was being shot, Pierre blurted out, 'I'd know that voice anywhere. It's Patricia Neal!' Well, it wasn't. It was Joan Fontaine, who we'd brought up from Los Angeles. Only Pierre could jump in with both feet like that."

When Berton was doing interviews for the CBC current affairs TV program "Close-Up" in the mid-1950s, he was equally certain of his judgements. He remembers, "The producer, Ross McLean, once said to me, 'I've got a great woman for you to interview in New York. She's a singer and she's on her way up. She's going to be a big star.' 'Who is she?' I asked. 'Her name is Barbra Streisand,' said Ross. 'I've never heard of her, which means the audience has never heard of her. She's just a singer and I'm not going to do it, Ross.' So, I didn't interview her."

At age seventeen, Berton worked in a Klondike gold mine earning $4.50 a day that went towards his university tuition fees. The experience reinforced his socialistic sympathies. "My mother was the daughter of the first Marxist socialist in Canada," Berton says. "A Marxist to his fingertips, my grandfather. Mother took me to my first CCF meeting when I was fourteen.... When I first came to Toronto, I helped edit the CCF newspaper secretly. I was working for *Maclean's* and didn't tell anybody. I got out because it was too conservative for me.... But I never flirted with communism. I couldn't stand their jargon and their shrillness."

Although now a millionaire, Berton retains his left-wing views. "I think I'm more radical now than I used to be," he says. His old friend Lister Sinclair says, "Pierre is essentially a poor guy who happens eventually to have a lot of money. In attitude and sympathies, Pierre is always on the side of the victims."

Before going to the University of British Columbia, Berton spent nearly four wartime years in the army, rising from a private to a captain in intelligence. He never got to the front lines, which Gabereau says was lucky. "Even though he was feeling like he missed the boat, my father always said it was a good thing he never went because he was in the infantry and would have been in the trenches, and he would have been a 'Let's go over the top, boys!' type. Because he's tall and had red hair, he would have had a bullet in his head in two seconds."

With his exuberance, relentless curiosity, and flair for writing, Berton was a natural for journalism, and at UBC he became the university correspondent for the *Vancouver Sun*. "He was like a refugee from *The Front Page* – the press card stuck in his hat," says Sinclair, who was a fellow student. After UBC, Berton joined the *Sun* full time, becoming a journalistic boy wonder, chasing fires, robberies, and murders. He was a favourite of editor Hal Straight, whose wild and hard-drinking ways typified the rollicking, ferociously competitive newspaper town that Vancouver had become. "I was his drinking pal," Berton says. "As soon as the noon edition was out, Straight and I would drive down to Stanley Park and drink a twenty-six-ounce bottle of rye sitting in his car. Then we'd go back and put out the next edition."

Berton went east in 1947, wooed by Scott Young, then an editor at *Maclean's*. "Young said to me," Berton recalls, "'I'm empowered to offer you either $4,000 or $4,500.' I said, 'I'll take the $4,500,' and off I went." At that point Berton intended to go to the United States to work for the *Saturday Evening Post* or *Life* magazine. "I wasn't much of a nationalist in those days," he says. "I became a nationalist by working on *Maclean's* magazine and rubbing shoulders with editors and writers like Arthur Irwin, Bruce Hutchison, and Ralph Allen, who brainwashed me very quickly."

He also succumbed to the lure of television, loving the combination of showmanship and news concocted by producer Ross McLean and knowing that television could help turn the books he intended to write into best-sellers. His initial television appearance was on a CBC program called "Court of Opinion," and, at first, he resolved never to go on television again. "It was a horrible experience," he says. "All these wires, and people waving at you. I couldn't even think. But the next morning, some cab driver said, 'Oh, I know you. I saw you on television last night.' And I thought, 'Oh boy. That's powerful. I'd better revise my feelings. TV sells books.' And that's why I really went into television. It sells books."

Berton had written radio plays for the CBC in Vancouver, given radio talks, and hosted a CBC show called "City Desk." "I was an eager young beaver," he says, but he found a new love in television. "He's an entertainer more than a journalist," says Jack Webster, another *Vancouver Sun* alumnus, agreeing with "Front Page Challenge" producer Ray McConnell, who adds, "Pierre is a performer first." "To the unwary onlooker, Pierre appears to be everything he isn't," says his longtime friend Larry Mann. Gabereau agrees, "To me, he's an absolute hero. I think he's completely underrated by a generation of people. They take him for granted."

While Gordon Sinclair had the reputation of being the terror of "Front Page Challenge," Berton, the shy ham, says he asked tougher questions. "Over the years I've developed a skin as thick as an elephant. You have to in our business. I don't care what they say. I was attacked viciously for asking rough questions on 'Front Page Challenge.' I was the villain. Gordon was never really the villain."

Gordon Sinclair

To his critics Gordon Sinclair was "this cantankerous old man," "a rude bully," "that bombastic, overstuffed, conceited nothing," "a loudmouth vulgarian," and "the anti-Christ." In truth, he was a cocky, opinionated braggart who could give sartorial and impudence lessons to Don Cherry. But he also was, in private, soft-hearted and sensitive, qualities he refused to reveal publicly for fear they would damage the ornery public image he had so painstakingly built up. This garish bundle of contradictions was quite simply the most unforgettable character in Canadian broadcasting.

On one of his commentaries on Toronto's CFRB, he reported the expulsion of prostitutes from London's posh Mayfair district and noted the plea of an English vicar who urged "every clergyman in England to take home one of these poor unfortunates . . . and let her live for a few months at least in a godlike setting." Sinclair paused, then added, "How about that folks? Take a whore home in the name of Jesus!"

In another broadcast he said that when he'd been a private in the army, he had been issued free condoms, "and the guy who gave them to me said if I didn't use them, my cock would drop off." No wonder that Pierre Juneau, then CRTC chairman, once told CFRB, "You must control this man."

Given Sinclair's avowed atheism, it is ironic that his first job in radio was to help Foster Hewitt cover a Baptist church service in Toronto in 1923 when they both were working for the Toronto *Daily Star*, which owned a radio station. The service was not broadcast, however, because Hewitt's batteries went dead, for which Hewitt blamed Sinclair.

Whether or not he was sabotaging God that time, Sinclair did frequently denounce the Almighty as a fraud. "On or off the air, he'd say God should be utterly ashamed of himself for allowing all the wars, the cruelty, and evil there is, for allowing children to starve to death in Africa or Asia," says Lorraine Thomson, a longtime friend and colleague. "He ridiculed people who believed in God and scoffed at all religions." Members of the "Front Page" band would mischievously taunt him by saying to him just before a show, "God be with you, Gordon" or "God bless, Gordon."

Because of Sinclair's attitude towards religion, the other panellists were nervous during one program that featured the widow of a missionary who had been killed in the Congo. "She seemed nervous and had a thin, wavering voice, but was as tough as nails," Fred Davis recalled. When Sinclair said off camera that he'd stay out of the questioning "because you know what I'm like with these religious stories," the widow responded, "Don't worry, Mr. Sinclair. I won't be too hard on you." Sinclair was similarly one-upped by a female version of himself, the vinegary B.C. publisher Margaret "Ma" Murray. He chided her, saying, "You're a good Mick, but you married a Protestant." "Yes," she replied, "I'm an optimist."

Sinclair strutted like a bantam cock, flaunted his Rolls-Royce, boasted that he was the richest journalist in Canada, with $1.5 million in the stock market, and he dressed in the loudest, most outlandish clothes. At the same time, he would take time to talk about investing to his cameramen and other technicians. "He was always giving financial advice to the guys," says floor director Steve Hyde. "He'd talk to us about mortgages, savings, and he'd answer all our questions. Gordon was a beautiful doll."

"A beautiful doll" was not what some of those he questioned felt about Sinclair, for he sometimes asked astonishingly personal and often outrageous questions. "Gordon had a quality that is extremely important in television, which is to have the public say, 'What is that crazy son of a bitch gonna do next?' " Berton says.

"Like him, hate him, enjoy him, you didn't want to miss him because he was always the topic of office conversation the next day," said Davis.

Producer Ray McConnell remembers one of Sinclair's not infrequent falls from taste. "We had Barbara Amiel [later a columnist and the wife of Conrad Black] on the show and Fred makes the introduction. Barbara, who is very well-endowed, walks across the set to her seat. The others are seated and I leave their mikes open for atmosphere. Suddenly, as Barbara strides across, I hear a voice softly muttering, 'Boom titty, boom titty, boom titty, boom, titty, titty.' It's Gordon and it's going on the air."

"The first time I met Gordon Sinclair, in 1947," Berton says, "he was wearing a mustard-coloured check jacket, green pants, a purple shirt, a bow tie made of calf skin, and a jolly little hat. Somebody said, 'Gordon, none of this goes together.' Gordon replied, 'That's my costume. I'm in show business.' That was Gordon, above all, a showman." Sometimes he would wear a kilt.

Sinclair was sensitive about going bald. "He had one hair on top, and it had to be just right," says McConnell. "He wanted to be reminded that he had at least one hair. "What hair Gordon had, he dyed, and he had his teeth fixed as well," said Davis. "He told me, 'I'm in show business, so why not?' "

How much Sinclair truly believed in what he did, and how much was simply to get attention, remains a question. "Gordon learned relatively early in life that the most important thing was to be noticed," says Alex Barris. "Even if people got mad at you at least they paid attention to you. And boy he sure got a lot of attention. Everything he did was aimed at that."

Even in his early career as a correspondent for the *Toronto Star*, his gee-whiz style of reporting marked him as belonging more to showbiz than to the news biz. "He was always the showman," Davis said, remembering the first time he saw Sinclair. "Back in the 1930s when I was in high school, Sinclair would come back from his tours of India and Africa and turn up in my school auditorium for a speech wearing his pith helmet, brandishing the spears given to him by natives, wearing short pants, his tropical khaki jacket. It was a wonderful show."

After twenty-one years at the *Star*, Sinclair was fired by a management exasperated by his antics, his irreverence, his guest appearances on radio, and his many speeches. He always maintained a frenetic pace as a workaholic. "I don't enjoy vacation time," he once said. "I hate it . . . and that's my major difficulty in my whole life." CFRB in Toronto approached Sinclair to do radio news, but he refused at first, "because," he said, "people wouldn't accept my style of news. I use slang, cuss words, sex. Some of my acquaintances are garbage men, harlots, newsboys, waitresses. I get drunk. I don't believe in goodness." He was hired anyway.

When television came calling for him in 1957, again Sinclair was reluctant. He'd had a taste of TV in 1938 at the Canadian National Exhibition in Toronto where Canadian General Electric had demonstrated a primitive version of television showing Sinclair interviewing boxer Jack Dempsey and singer Jessica Dragonette. In 1957 the caller was Harvey Hart, who was organizing "Front Page Challenge." He asked Sinclair to try out as a panellist. "No. I'm too old and bald and wrinkled," Sinclair responded. "What's more, I'm impolite. They'd kill me." But, on second thought, the lure of show business triumphed over Sinclair's apprehensions, and he auditioned along with other candidates in Harvey Hart's basement. He got the job.

Sinclair quickly overcame his fear of TV and revelled in the nationwide attention it brought him. "He just loved it," says Berton. "He loved being in the make-up room and chatting and going on the air. He loved being in the limelight." He also loved the image of being a cantankerous curmudgeon both on and off the air, and his temper not infrequently got the better of him. As Scott Young recounts, during the 1962 Cuban Missile Crisis Sinclair's CFRB program was broken into with a news bulletin, and when he came back on the air he bellowed, "What the hell is going on? Yankee propaganda. If those bastards ever break in on me again, I'm through. I'm through. I'd never come back. Goddamn fools!"

In his later years, Sinclair hated being called old, especially in public. He used to get enraged at Bruno Gerussi whenever Gerussi acted the part of an old man by imitating Sinclair in skits on CBC Radio. Sinclair also blew up at Jack Webster after Webster, on television, dismissed Gordon as "an old man who made his fame by standing in a desert in India with his foot on the head of a tiger he had just shot." Sinclair waited for the next time Webster was a guest panellist on "Front Page Challenge." "I was sitting in the little green room," says Webster, "and boy oh boy, Gordon steamed into the room, took one look at me, and said, 'You horrible son of a bitch! How dare you say things about me like that? How dare you suggest that I'm old because to be old is to be near death, and I'm not near dead! You are a loudmouth clod and stupid!' "

It was a clash between eastern and western curmudgeons, and this time Webster blinked first. "I was demolished," Webster says. "I apologized, and when he finished harrumphing at me, he said, 'All right. It's all over now. Forget it. Just don't do it again. We've got a show to do. Let's do it.' After the apology, we became friends. The real Gordon Sinclair was delightful and courteous."

Fred Davis also felt Sinclair's sting when, on one of the early shows, he apologized for something Sinclair had said. "He could hardly wait to get off the air," said Davis. " 'Don't you ever apologize for me!' Sinclair shouted at me. 'I know more about the libel laws than you'll ever know, you young whippersnapper.' What bothered me was that everybody else was around, and he was using some fairly free language and I guess my pride was hurt. I said, 'You can't talk to me that way in front of these people.' So we had a screaming match."

Davis added, "I had an interview show on the CBC with Anna Cameron called 'Open House,' and he called me a 'cream-puff interviewer.' I thought, 'Gee, he hates my guts.' . . . When we met next in the green room he didn't really apologize, but he said, 'I think I overreacted and I don't think what I said was called for. Let's shake hands and forget about it.' "

"One thing about Gordon is that he never held a grudge, and he had no sense of revenge," Berton says. "And Gordon was the making of 'Front

Page.' He taught me how to make a question interesting. The secret is not in the answer, but in the question."

Sinclair asked questions most people wanted to ask but wouldn't dare. He was forever asking guests how much money they earned, but what his critics called the rudest question ever asked on Canadian network television was his query to Olympic champion swimmer Elaine Tanner as to whether she swam when she was menstruating. Obviously embarrassed by the question, she said that she did. Phones rang off the hook with viewers protesting; more than two thousand letters poured into the CBC – all but twenty-one attacking Gordon – and it became an issue in the House of Commons. The CBC apologized to Tanner, and Gordon offered to resign. "There has never been an uproar quite like it," Davis remembered.

Curmudgeon he may have been, but it was an act that covered a soft centre. "While Gordon would often be bombastic and ask rude questions," Lorraine Thomson says, "he would be the only one of the panellists who would come to me after the show was over and ask, 'Did I hurt that person? Have I injured them? Are they okay? Will they be all right? You know, I'm not really a journalist. I'm an entertainer and this is show business.' "

Alex Barris says, "Gordon was a most exasperating newsman, terribly opinionated, sometimes shockingly inaccurate, often passionately devoted to the nuttiest of causes, illogically opposed to many reasonable ones. For instance, he violently opposed fluoridation of drinking water. 'Rat poison,' he called it. But there was not a mean bone in his body."

"Gordon hated to have stories told about him where he had done some act of kindness," Davis recalled, "because that wasn't compatible with the image he wanted to project." Betty Kennedy remembers Sinclair seeing a man coatless on the street outside CFRB on a bitterly cold winter day and Sinclair gruffly asking the man, "Why haven't you got a coat on?" "Because I don't own a coat," the man replied. "Here," said Sinclair, "take mine."

Sinclair could sink himself into morose self-pity at times, too. "He was very moody," says Kennedy. "I would go and see him and take him flowers, and he would say, 'I've had it. I'm finished. I'm done.'" She recalls visiting his home one day and finding him stretched out on the couch. "Just look at me," he said. "I'm old. I'm tired. I'm worn out. I'm not any good for anything. And look at my wife, Gladys, over there. She's old and she's cancerous and she's blind and she can hardly hear." At which point Gladys piped up, "I am not cancerous."

"He could really get down in the dumps," says Kennedy. "My guess is that he probably did have what today would be called clinical depression. He would be gone like that for three or four days until we'd persuade him to come back to work and tell him he was needed."

Politically, Sinclair shifted his attitude as the "Front Page" years rolled by. "Gordon was quite left when the show began," says Berton. "He became more right wing as the show moved on, and by the end he was well to the right."

While Sinclair bragged about how much money he had, he was outraged at the taxes he had to pay. "Gordon was hell to live with around income tax time. . . . He was impossible to talk to in April," says Berton. "You just stayed away from him. I mean, he was touchy and angry."

"This would last four to six weeks before he'd calm down," says Ray McConnell. "He'd say to me, 'I've just written this goddamn cheque for $37,000!'"

Kennedy remembers Sinclair bursting into right-wing anger during an Ottawa taping of "Front Page Challenge." "We had on a prominent NDP member of Parliament as a guest panellist, and after the show we were backstage and for some reason Gordon went on a rampage. 'You're the fella who would insist that in my house I would have to have so many other people living there because the house is too big for me!' he shouted. He worked himself up into a towering rage, and this poor man just sat there. He hadn't said any of those things at all. I don't know what provoked it. Then Gordon got up, laughed, and walked off."

He sometimes sought solace from his black days, his anger, or his tax pains in liquor. He'd been a hard-drinking reporter most of his life, and he often drank champagne before going on "Front Page Challenge." "Gordon loved a bottle of champagne, and if he had it just before going on the air he'd be sparkling," says Berton. "He'd arrive full of energy, but you had to get him right on the air. In a while, he would begin to get sleepy and fade about the second show, so we tried to make sure he'd drink his champagne just before he went on the air."

When he died in the spring of 1984 at age eighty-four, he had achieved, in Berton's words, "the status of lovable old coot, an eccentric uncle who's indulged by his family. . . . 'Front Page Challenge' was never quite the same without Gordon."

"I've often thought," says Kennedy, "that Gordon should be the centrepiece of a musical. I can see Gordon just strutting onstage. Here he comes, the cock of the walk."

Toby Robins

Toby Robins was quite simply the most beautiful woman ever to star on Canadian television. "Toby was lustrous!" says Pierre Berton. "She just glowed. She had that marvellous rich beauty, so that any woman standing next to her faded. There was an aura about Toby of the mysterious east. Toby was Jewish, and she had that classic 'Arabian Nights' look and she bubbled. She was very naive in many ways – an ingenue."

Larry Mann, who in the early years of "Front Page Challenge" was the audience warm-up man and sometime panellist, says, "Toby had an inner beauty as well. She outgraced Grace Kelly."

Not only did she charm, she studied for the show, too, poring over newspapers, researching in libraries, and examining magazines. As the only non-journalist among the "Front Page Challenge" panellists, she had to put in extra effort at research, especially since, as June Callwood and Pierre Berton say, before going on "Front Page Challenge" she had never read the entire front page of a newspaper in her life. But after she was hired, Jim Guthro says, "She read every newspaper in sight, the *New York Times*, the *Christian Science Monitor*, the *Toronto Star*, the *Globe*. She had almost a photographic memory, and she was a very intuitive person. She could guess stuff even quicker than Pierre could.

"Toby would read up on all the history of Canada and all the news stories, and she had a little book in which wrote everything down so that, to our surprise and sometimes consternation, she would get the guest," says Guthro.

The producers saw a Beauty and the Beast pairing between Robins and Gordon Sinclair. "Toby was manna from heaven," said Davis. "We had this marvellous juxtaposition of the irascible curmudgeon Gordon Sinclair and, sitting right beside him, the beautiful, vivacious Toby Robins. You couldn't get anything better than that for drama."

"Toby sparkled on television," Berton says. "She was a bona fide Canadian TV star. I think she was chosen as decoration on the panel, but she was much more than that as it turned out."

Robins's research didn't make her immune to mistakes, however. Her worst gaffe happened when film star Don Ameche disguised his voice so well, she blurted, "Are you Jane Russell?"

Robins got the job by exploiting her luck. As a child her family had talked about a distant relative who'd died in a fire at the Coconut Grove nightclub in Boston. By chance, the story in her "Front Page" audition was on that fire, and she guessed the story, impressing the producers. Robins couldn't believe her luck. It was luck and hard work that made her a TV success, although her first love was always the theatre. At age fifteen, she had been cast by director Mavor Moore in a Shakespearean play, and when she quit "Front Page Challenge" four years after she began, it was to concentrate on the stage. "The show," she said at the time, "was like a golden cage. It was marvellous and you were famous, but you were famous for the reasons I didn't want to be famous for. I felt it got in the way of the acting."

She left a lasting impression on the TV audience. As Barbara Frum, who watched Robins when she began, said, "The whole country was in love with her . . . Toby was a formative figure . . . I remember when she was pregnant and stayed [on the air] right through her ninth month. . . . To even be pregnant in public at that time was a disgrace, and people used to hide in their houses. They sure wouldn't go out in a gown and on television in their ninth month. It was unheard of." At the time, Robins's only comment was "When I started out to do the show I was pregnant, and I thought, 'Oh, well, it's a nice sitting-down job until I have the baby.' "

She also challenged tradition by changing her brunette hair to blonde for a while. "I was there one night," says June Callwood, "when Robins came in and put a stocking over her head and then put on a blonde wig. I watched in fascination. I thought I was daring to put on eyelashes."

"I've always wanted to be a blonde," Robins explained when a storm of controversy broke out over her wig. One Calgary viewer wrote, "If someone has to wear a blonde wig, try it on Gordon Sinclair." She got police protection when another irate fan threatened to kill her if she wore the wig anymore. Finally, she gave it up.

When she went back to full-time acting, she and her husband, producer Bill Freedman, moved to England, where they both worked in the London West End theatre district. She died of cancer in London in 1986.

"Toby was all light and joy," says Callwood. "She was smart, funny, kind, and so beautiful. She had that kind of beauty that just makes you stare. And she had a kind of honest sweetness. Oh gosh, she was such a nice woman."

Fred Davis

He looked like an easygoing, never-a-worry, never-a-care host, who effortlessly guided his scrappy, competitive panellists and guests through every "Front Page Challenge" half-hour. But nothing could be further from the truth. Whatever the audience saw on the outside, butterflies fluttered inside as Davis fussed about timing the show, letting everybody have a proper share of time, keeping things moving, and worrying about saying something that would mislead the panel in their search to identify the guest.

"I worried that I was not a newsman," Davis said, shortly before he died in the summer of 1996. "I had this terrible fear where I allowed a geographic thing to screw me up – to this day, I'm not sure where Asia Minor is. I just worried about doing something that would make me look stupid or would screw up the game."

"He was the sweetest man possible," says Lorraine Thomson. "He was witty, he was caring, but he was a worrier. If he had bitten his nails, they would have been down to the quick." Allan Fotheringham says, "Down in his gut, there was a lot of churning. He had the toughest job in the show."

Betty Kennedy agrees. "If you could think of anything that could go wrong, Fred would think of it. Of all of us, he was the biggest worrier. And yet he always came off as though he didn't have a care in the world, as though everything was as smooth as silk."

Not everything went smoothly, of course, and he was once was thrown by comedian-pianist Victor Borge. As a commercial ran just before the ending minute of the show, Borge asked Davis if there was any time for a final comment. "I figured he was hot on something," Davis said, so he got the director to drop the closing credits. "He's got forty seconds before we're off the air," Davis was told. When he was back on camera, Davis said, "Mr. Borge, was there something else that you wanted to say?" Borge replied tersely, "No." "I fell off the chair laughing," Davis recalled. "It was the greatest put on – a great inside joke."

Another nervous moment for Davis came while he was doing a TV commercial for a new car, and he couldn't see the script on the teleprompter because it was too far away. "I had given the year of the car and I made the dumb mistake of thinking back as I'm saying the next sentence. 'Did I say 1967 or '66?' Your mind should be going ahead, not going back, because you can't do anything about it because it's live. I got to the end of the sentence and my mind just went completely blank. Luckily I was beside the car, and I ad libbed a couple of things about the windshield until I finally got it all back. You feel that if you screw up badly, there goes your job."

But everyone agrees that Davis never screwed up. "Fred was a genius at what he did in that he made it look so casual and so easy," says Berton. "Fred was the man with an iron grip inside his suede glove," says Webster. "I never had a cross word with him in all the years I worked with him."

"Fred was a pro's pro," says Cameron Bell, the last producer of "Front Page Challenge." "It's those butterflies that kept him up there. They gave him the energy. He sweated his script, and his timing was exquisite." So was his appearance, to which he paid particular attention. "We were always waiting for him because he took longer than the rest of us to get ready," says Berton. "He was always late."

Somebody else who waited for Davis, according to June Callwood, a frequent "Front Page" guest questioner, was Prime Minister Lester Pearson. "One time Toby Robins and I were told there was no make-up person for the show, so we were busy doing our own make-up," she recalls. "The prime minister was going to leave the House of Commons to do the show, and we had to begin the minute he was there. Fred came in and said, 'I'm a professional and I'm going to have professional make-up.' Almost at that instant the make-up person showed up, and Fred sat there very calmly and kept the prime minister waiting while he got his make-up on. It's not critical of Fred, but I learned something from that. When a woman does something like that, she's said to be a bitch. When a man does it, he's a professional."

"Yeah," Davis said, "I make sure my tie is straight, my suit fits, my make-up is good. I don't want to inflict the Fred Davis face with the jowls and lines on the country."

Something else that looked good on Davis was the rich brown colour of his hair. "I've never had a brush cut and it's never been dyed," he said. "My barber gets this all the time: 'Sandy, would you give me that dye job you give Fred Davis because it looks so natural. I won't tell anybody.' Nope, I never did dye it. With all the trouble involved, why the hell would I bother?"

Davis's protectiveness of his image was tested one time when the "Front Page Challenge" panellists had just arrived in Vancouver from a tour of interior British Columbia and were using Kennedy's hotel room as a meeting place and dressing room before the show. The wardrobe girl asked, "Does anybody need any pressing?" Davis replied, "I've been sitting in these pants on a plane for three days so you could press them." "I go back to my room," said Davis, "take a shower, and there's a knock on the door. I wrap a towel around me and, dripping wet, answer the door. Just across the hall an old couple was going into their room and looked over at me half naked. And the wardrobe girl said, 'Oh, Fred, sorry to bother you, but you left your pants in Betty's room.' I prayed they didn't know who I was."

"Sweet" is a word that comes up most often among colleagues in describing Davis. "Fred was an absolute gentleman, a sweet, nice guy," says Alex Barris. His charm showed on the air, but what was not visible on television was his wicked wit.

"I think you might have cast Fred on the enigma side," says Berton. "Fred was not a man who revealed himself in public. One of the things that really didn't come across was that he was very, very funny. He had a crackling wit." Kennedy agrees. "He would tell you stories complete with dialect and characterization, and just be funny as a crutch." "I don't think anyone could laugh as much as we did with Fred in the green room," says Juliette, who worked many shows with Davis.

Davis loved doing dialects and once considered becoming an actor. He gave up the idea after reading a review of what turned out to be both his acting début and farewell performance. "About Fred Davis," it read, "when he walked across the stage he looked like a meter reader on his way to the cellar." A conversation with producer Mavor Moore gave him another reason to give up acting. "I'm really torn," Davis told Moore. "I'd like to be an announcer, but I'd also kind of like to be an actor." Moore advised, "If you're not sure, don't be an actor because you're going to starve."

So Davis made announcing his career and became a star, although not necessarily to his children. "When they were really small, they would see me on the air and they'd say, 'There's Fred Davis.' When I got home and walked through the door, I was Daddy. To them there were really two people. The guy that was Daddy and the guy on television, Fred Davis." Even some of his fans were not sure who he was. "People come up to me on the street and say, 'Hi, Lloyd,' and I've been mistaken for Knowlton Nash."

More than an actor or even announcer, Davis would have liked to have been a trumpeter. As a teenager in prewar Toronto, he played at nearby resorts and then got rid of his long hair and wide-shouldered zoot suit and took his trumpet into the Canadian Army Band. It bothered him that he saw no war action, however, especially when the band visited Canadian military hospitals in England. "Jeez, what are they going to think about us?" he wondered at the time. "I've got all my limbs, and these guys, these amputees, are being wheeled in, in traction. I'm not really a soldier. I'm a musician."

After the war he decided he wasn't going to be the world's greatest trumpeter, and besides he felt "there was more security in being an announcer." Davis's father also warned him against being a musician. "When you're fifty or sixty, do you still want to be playing a jazz trumpet in some dive somewhere?" his father asked him. The answer was no, so he enrolled in Lorne Greene's Academy of Radio Arts. Among his fellow students in 1946-47 was Leslie Nielsen. In fact, Davis remembered, "It was a toss-up between Les and myself as to who would win a two-year scholarship at the Neighborhood Playhouse in New York. Les got it and graduated into live television drama. Just think if it had been the other way around, I could have been in *Naked Gun*! But Les needed it more than I did. He didn't have a dime, and I was still jobbing the odd night with bands and able to make a few bucks." It was Mavor Moore who finally decided against Davis and for Leslie Nielsen. However, Davis did win the academy's announcer scholarship worth $100. "I bought a car radio with the money," he said.

After graduation Davis got a job as a radio announcer at CFRA in Ottawa and later worked with the National Film Board on documentaries. When "Front Page Challenge" went on the air in the summer of 1957, the host was Win Barron, the devilishly handsome, deep-voiced Paramount Newsreel narrator. He seemed ideal, but, as Davis said, "He was never able to relax, and when the red light went on he was like a piece of wood."

In late summer the CBC auditioned others to replace Barron. Davis tried out but was "very nervous and uptight." He remembered, "Then it was the same old thing. You know, 'Don't call us, we'll call you.' I sat by the phone all week and didn't get a call." No one called because an argument was raging between producer Jim Guthro, who wanted Davis as host, and CBC variety executive Bob McGall, who wanted Alex Barris. Barris, like Davis, had done a summer try-out. Finally, McGall agreed that Davis should get the job. In the following thirty-eight years, he never missed a show.

Like all panellists, Davis had been asked to run for political office, and like all his colleagues, he said no. "I felt as a professional moderator it would be wrong, plus the fact that I couldn't stand being in the political arena with the compromises and political correctness. That would drive me crazy. I've always believed I was middle of the road. But it seems to me over the years the whole world has shifted to the left, which I don't think is that great. So, by default, I've gone to the right. If everyone is screaming socialism, then we middle-roaders tend to lean more to the right."

Of Davis's conservatism, Lorraine Thomson says, "He was not as right wing as Genghis Khan, but he had very strong opinions. I was always sorry he didn't have the opportunity to ask questions occasionally of the guests because you would have seen a different side of Fred."

Another of Davis's hidden traits was his temper. "When he let go, and he very seldom did," says Allan Fotheringham, "but when Fred let go offstage, whoo, it was ballistic. It didn't last long, but he could dish it out."

"I only saw him get mad twice in fifteen years," says Steve Hyde. "Fred had to be perfect and always wanted to know which camera he was working to well ahead of airtime. Once, they were busy in the control room and didn't tell him. He got mad, threw down his pencil, and said, 'I won't do a fucking thing until someone tells me what my camera is.' Fred was Mr. Cool outside and Mr. Uptight inside."

"Fred had a volcano boiling inside him," says Ray McConnell. "But you wouldn't see any bursts of anger in public. You might have seen things slammed down sometimes. Fred hated to get up early in the morning, and there was a flash of anger once when we were in Yellowknife. We had to leave very early, and we were having coffee at the airport. Webster joined us and put down his horrible old tartan bag between the chairs. In came Fred. He had a face that said life is not worth living. He walked up, looked at Webster's bag, muttered, 'Jesus Christ!' and kicked the bag halfway across the coffee shop."

"Yes, I've been known to blow my cool on occasion off camera," Davis said. "I try to keep that part of my nature hidden because you never accomplish anything if you flare up at somebody. The older I get, I think I get a little more crotchety. I want things to go smoothly. Also, I don't want to sit at the back of the bus. I want to go first-class. I figure I've earned it. I want to be rested and prepared if I'm going to do a job, and if there are arrangements that don't work, I might give vent to my feelings. You can't be Mr. Nice Guy all the time."

But he was, almost all the time.

Betty Kennedy

Betty Kennedy was the nice girl on "Front Page Challenge," a dignified and refreshing change from the tough, rough powerhouse questioners like Berton, Sinclair, Fotheringham, and Webster. "When I think of Betty, I think of the three Cs – calm, cool, and collected," said Davis. "She's elegant, every woman's idea of a lady," says Berton. "She's good at being nice. The rest of us aren't." "I can't imagine people using swear words around her," says producer Don Brown.

All of this explains director Joan Tosoni's astonishment when, as "Front Page Challenge's" secretary, she opened the program's mail one day to find a large package addressed to Kennedy. "It was an eight-by-ten glossy photo of a glistening penis, fully erect," Tosoni says. "I went to Don Brown, the producer, and asked if he thought it should be passed on to Betty. He said, 'No, I think we'll leave that alone.' Maybe Betty would have liked it, framed it, and put it in her office. But actually, I couldn't fathom Betty Kennedy – of all people – getting this."

As dignified as she is, there's another side to Kennedy that's rarely seen by the audience. "She's got quite a temper if she wants to use it," says Berton. "I've seen it."

"Do I know Betty Kennedy?" says Fotheringham. "I'm not sure anybody does. Everyone thinks she's nice little Betty, but the other night she turned on some people and just ripped them up, down, and sideways. Betty is a surprising person in that, down behind those blissful good manners, there's a backbone of steel. When she gets mad, she can't be pushed around. She's a very tough lady underneath."

"She has claws – she's a very strong person," says Ray McConnell. "You see it in disagreements that might arise in meetings about the show. You see it in her being very conscious of her own turf and her own stature. Put yourself in the middle of those 'Front Page' personalities, Betty had to be made of pretty stern stuff to survive."

"When she had her baby or when her first husband was dying, she kept working. She never stopped for a moment," says Elaine Saunders. "She's a trouper, although she can be a very cold person and aloof. She's tough, as tough as Pamela Wallin or Hana Gartner. They're tough women. They're going to survive no matter what. They're tigers." Juliette says, "You don't get too close to Betty. She's very reserved. Regal or maybe snooty."

"I don't think I'm aloof," says Kennedy. "I think I'm a very agreeable person, but don't push me, don't make the mistake of thinking you can push me around. It will be a mistake, believe me!"

Kennedy remembers a man coming up to her after a meeting where she had spoken out sharply and telling her, "Oh, your claws were showing!" "I said, 'Yes, I have them. I don't use them often, but they're there.' Don't be misled, I will not stand for any kind of treatment that I don't think is right or just. No, as the man said, behind that innocent face, there are claws. There are. There are."

"The last thing in the world I would want to do on any show," says McConnell, "was run out of time before Betty had a chance, because I would have heard about it. She was always conscious that she should have her fair share of time. She felt she deserved as much time as the men, maybe altogether." She can be tenacious in her questioning and, said Davis, "Betty is a little more pedantic, asking these triple-barrelled questions which eat into the time of others."

As a guest questioner, Juliette was sometimes terrified to be on the show because of how seriously the panel prepared their questions. "They scared me," she says. "In the green room they're going over headlines and ideas and I'm sitting there wondering, 'Oh God, what am I doing here?' They took it so damn seriously. And on the air, you had to jump in because they didn't let go of their questioning. They were not generous at all – so very competitive. You were strictly on your own."

At one point there was talk of replacing Kennedy, says Don Brown. "Shortly after Jim Guthro took over as head of the variety department," says Brown, "he came to me and said, 'I want you to fire Betty Kennedy.' So I said, 'Sure, I'll fire her as soon as I find someone better to replace her.' And I never did."

"Betty is a superb newspaperwoman," says Berton. "People forget that. Latterly on 'Front Page,' she was getting all the answers. I used to get them all! What you have to know about Betty is that she's not Mrs. Milquetoast in any sense of the word. She can be tough, and she has a considerable ego, as you must in this business." "Betty is the only one who consistently won the games – more than Pierre," says producer Cameron Bell.

Betty Kennedy's quiet but persistent assertiveness showed early. When she was sixteen, she walked into the *Ottawa Citizen* newsroom and asked for a job. The newspaper had wanted to hire a boy, but she argued, "I can do anything a boy can do." She was hired to fetch coffee and corned-beef sandwiches, answer phones, and write obituaries. In those days she was called Gus because the paper already had a writer named Betty.

She moved on to radio and television journalism, along the way dabbling in modelling and fashion writing, and wound up as host of an hour-long daily commentary and interview show on CFRB in Toronto. The only instruction she received was "Just try not to get us sued." She was there for twenty-seven years "loving every minute of it." One of her colleagues was Gordon Sinclair. "A lot of people were really quite intimidated by Gordon, but I must say I never was," Kennedy says. "He reminded me too much of my own grandfather – quite gruff, but really very kind."

When Toby Robins quit "Front Page Challenge" after four years over a salary dispute and a yen to do more acting, the producers looked for a glamorous carbon copy. Fred Davis and his colleagues said, "No, no. A carbon copy will just remind people that we haven't got Toby Robins."

"Toby quit because she found out she wasn't getting as much money as the men," says June Callwood. "They told me I would get her slot, but I said, 'I want as much as the men too.' Toby and I were friends, and I didn't want to take less money than she wanted. I said, 'You have to give me the same as Pierre and Gordon.' They said, 'Well, no.' I don't know what Betty got but, she got the job. Maybe they gave in – or maybe she didn't know."

"It was very nerve-racking to do the show, and at first I was absolutely petrified," Kennedy recalls. "It took a long time before those nerves calmed down a bit."

She usually followed Sinclair's often incendiary questions and seemed to provide a softening to the program. Davis said, "She was always the lady, but in there, there was the aggressiveness that they all have. She had class and claws."

Allan Fotheringham

When Gordon Sinclair died, Ray McConnell's first choice for his replacement was Pierre Trudeau. "The message we got back from our first approach was 'He wants to know how much?'" says McConnell. "I gave him the fee, and it was a wonderful moment. You got the feeling he really would have loved to have done it." Fotheringham says, "They were quite serious about getting Trudeau, but he would have been disastrous because his every question would have been twenty minutes long. But still, it would have been a great publicity gimmick."

When Trudeau finally said no, McConnell's second choice was Jack Webster. "Jack was in a very touchy negotiation stance at the time with the Vancouver station where he worked," McConnell says. "It broke his heart, but he said, 'Ray, I can't even ask permission to do the show regularly. They don't mind an occasional guest spot, but not this.' "

McConnell says Barbara Frum was an option at one point. "I also was fascinated by Charlotte Gobeil. But hiring either of them would have put Pierre beside two females and that became unworkable."

Allan Fotheringham was the third choice. McConnell, who produced "Front Page" for nineteen years, says, "I wanted to borrow some of Fotheringham's legitimacy as a daily news columnist and he also had contact with a younger generation." So the irreplaceable Gordon Sinclair was replaced by Allan Fotheringham, the flame-spitting Southam columnist who had long yearned for the job.

"I had a secret to myself that when Gordon Sinclair died they'd ask me to take his place," says Fotheringham. "He died in the spring of 1984 and I didn't hear anything. Months and months went by. Then in the summer of 1984, Southam asked me to go to Washington as a correspondent. I was in the shower in my hotel in Washington and the phone rings and a voice says, 'This is Ray McConnell of "Front Page Challenge." ' I said, 'What took you so long?' "

Given his provocative journalistic style, it was expected that "Dr. Foth" would be a flash-and-burn inquisitor much like Sinclair. But it didn't work out that way. "No one is the same in print as they are in person," Fotheringham says. "I was expected to step into the shoes and kilt of Gordon. I was supposed to be a sour, biting guy, and I sort of overreacted and pulled back. No one could be Gordon, but Gordon."

"Foth told me a number of times that basically he was there to be the curmudgeon," says Cameron Bell. "His view of being a curmudgeon, I think, was to ask obnoxious questions. But they didn't really sound that way."

"He was smart enough to not even try to be Sinclair," said Fred

Davis. "And Foth in person doesn't come off as he does in print. He's a very good newsman and asks perceptive, probing questions, but he throws it away. He's not acerbic. He sits back and shoots from the hip when he can, but he shoots with a silencer. I suspect there was a kind of disappointment about Allan's initial performances. The country had an image of this dragon, which Allan is at a typewriter, but that's not his on-air personality."

"He will often say the most devastating things in such a sweet, calm voice," says Betty Kennedy. "I suspect he's also a lot shyer than he comes off and a great deal more vulnerable than he lets on. He always squires the most beautiful women – he wouldn't be complete without a beautiful girl on his arm, it doesn't matter what city you're in. But I think that there is an enormous vulnerability there. I think he is quite, quite vulnerable."

Foth claims he's grown mellow, kinder, and gentler as he's aged. "I'm not as angry as I used to be," he says. "You become softer, and you realize that you have made mistakes in being a little cruel and unfeeling about some people."

His impertinent approach in his early journalistic career brought him quick celebrity, although he now regrets attacking Pierre Berton in his *Vancouver Sun* column. "In my youthful arrogance," Foth says, "I said in a review on his book about religion, *The Comfortable Pew*, 'Come on, Berton, what is this junk?' I would get furious letters from Elsa Franklin, his flack and manager, and she'd be screaming and hollering. Only later did I get to know him and admire him."

Berton normally ignored such criticism, but he once threatened to sue Fotheringham for libel. "He said I got a fat fee for travelling around the country for Canada Day," says Berton. "I didn't, and I tore a strip off him. I saw him sitting in a bar in the Georgia Hotel in Vancouver having a beer. I said, 'You son of a bitch, I'm suing you for every nickel you've got!' He turned white. I had no intention of getting into a court case with him, but I thought I'd scare the hell out of him, and I think I succeeded." "I've been sued twenty-four times, so threats don't worry me," Fotheringham says.

"We all attacked our betters, or what we thought were our betters, in order that we might become the betters of the next generation," says Berton. "We all did it, every one of us. It's a cheap and lazy man's way of making your name, and I think most of us who have used it – and we all have – now wish we hadn't."

Fotheringham himself is philosophical about being attacked by young journalists today. "I understand now the place Berton was when I was a young pup," he says, "because they love to attack me now. It used to bother me, but not anymore. Who cares? Life is too short."

Fotheringham began his career in journalism by writing high-school news for the daily paper in Chilliwack, British Columbia. Later he wrote for the student paper at the University of British Columbia and after graduation became a sports writer and then columnist for the *Vancouver Sun* before winding up in Ottawa and then in Washington, D.C., as a Southam correspondent. In the mid-1970s, he began writing for *Maclean's* magazine and in 1984 started a syndicated column for *The Financial Post* and twenty-five other newspapers across the country.

Although he writes with seemingly deep-rooted cynicism, Fotheringham says he's basically an optimist. "Yes, I disguise it, but I am an optimist – a pessimist in the short run and an optimist in the long run. I do not think the world is going to hell in a handbasket. I do not think my kids will have a worse life than I have.

"I never go to the hospital. I am not a Christian Scientist, but I believe in mind over matter. I don't even have a doctor. If I get run down by a bus, break my leg, or get cancer, I'll go see a doctor. But, generally, I feel you can tough things out. I think strong people don't get sick."

Fotheringham's biggest fan is his mother. "I guess I'm a momma's boy," he says. "You ask my two sisters and my brother and they'll say, 'Oh, she always did like you best.'

"My mother would crawl on hands and knees across broken glass and barbed wire to see me on television," he laughs. His mother may love him on television, but Fotheringham is not entirely sure he's happy being there. He recalls co-anchoring a TV special on a First Minister's Conference and desperately grabbing anybody in sight to interview to fill in time. His companion, *Toronto Star* reporter Val Sears, looked glumly at him after their marathon talkfest and said, "This is not work for a grown man." Fotheringham is still not sure whether it is.

Jack Webster

"One question I've never put to myself is what made Jackie run," says Jack Webster, the last person to join the "Front Page Challenge" panel. The answer is guilt mixed with fear of being poor. "I suppose it was financial insecurity," he explains. "And I suppose it also was a personal tragedy when my wife had our baby before we were married, and the baby was adopted out before she really saw the baby. I suppose I suffered from a massive guilt complex and probably still do. But that's what made Jackie run."

The baby was born in 1936, and Webster immediately signed papers for her to be adopted since he was not yet married to his future wife, Margaret. She was seventeen and saw the baby for only five minutes. For the rest of her life, she felt the baby had been stolen from her. "In later years it became a fixation with her," Webster says. "She began to travel to Britain once a year looking for her daughter." In 1972 she hired a private detective agency that traced the daughter to the south of England where she was married with three children. Webster's wife demanded they go over to see her. "To hell with you," he told his wife. "We've been through this agony for twenty-five or thirty years. Just drop it." "But," he now says, "she was tougher than hell and blamed me considerably. So we went over to meet our daughter. When we met, it was tense to say the least. There were all kinds of tears." After their first meeting, he whisked his daughter to a Soho restaurant, where he had tipped in advance the waiter, maître d', doorman, and wine steward to get the best possible service. "It was a traumatic experience," he says, "but that's the way life bounces. It was the most exciting thing that ever happened in my life, but my conscience still kills me."

Another source of guilt for Webster was authorizing a lobotomy for his wife. "That's the thing I'll carry to my grave. I should have said no, but I didn't." Margaret's always delicate health had weakened over the years, and she suffered terribly from agoraphobia and "anxiety nerves." Her personality changed, and, Webster says, "You could not put back together the pieces of her brain."

Driven by these emotional shock waves, Webster developed a sabre-toothed public exterior to hide the tenderness inside. "Like many people who sound very gruff, there's a soft heart there in Jack," says Betty Kennedy. Fred Davis added, "He's the sort of fellow you want as a friend. He would always be there. Understanding and brusque and hearty and all heart." "Deep down inside, Jack is a big marshmallow," says Allan Fotheringham.

He first constructed his grouchy façade on the streets of his native Glasgow, where Webster was a reporter during the heart of the Depression, and as a British army colonel in the Sudan Desert during the Second World War. After the war, he worked as a journalist amid the flash and trash of Fleet Street tabloid newspapers before emigrating to Vancouver in 1947. As a reporter and later a city editor at the *Vancouver Sun*, Webster was a flamboyant co-conspirator in Vancouver's boisterous journalism during the late 1940s and the 1950s. Webster was a character straight out of the 1928 play *The Front Page* by Ben Hecht and Charles MacArthur. The raucous, vaudevillian exuberance of Vancouver's media in those years suited Webster perfectly.

"Jack Webster arrived at the *Sun* the day I left," says Berton, "and he said to Hal Straight, the managing editor, 'I want to be the next Pierre Berton.' But I don't think Webster could be the next anything. Webster's unique. You wouldn't want two of them. One is plenty."

Webster's uniqueness is shown, among many other things, in his disdain for bosses such as Straight. "Straight fired me because I quit," Webster says. "I said to him with my normal panache and sophistication, 'The day you drop dead, I'll be one of the ten thousand people who dance on your coffin for joy.' But later we became friends, and I gave the eulogy at his wake. I guess I had a natural inclination to fight authority. I got thrown out of more offices than I care to talk about."

After working at the *Sun* and a brief fling back in Scotland, where he became the first Scottish private TV newscaster, Webster became Your Roving Reporter for CBC Radio in Vancouver, did interviews for Ross McLean's "Close-Up" on CBC-TV, and in the mid-1960s achieved fame as the most provocative radio hot-line host in the country. Webster also became the West Coast correspondent for "This Hour Has Seven Days," furthering his reputation as an aggressive, in-your-face interviewer. His style and what he calls "my raspy, brattish voice with all its inflections and sneers" and its thick Scottish burr enhanced his tough-guy image. But, he says, "I usually asked a nasty question with a bit of a sparkle in my eye." Asking nasty questions catapulted Webster into stardom.

As much as financial insecurity and guilt over a lost child and his wife's lobotomy drove him, as he says, to journalistic success, he also got there through his love of and flair for theatrics. "Webster's a born ham and a very good ham," says Fotheringham. "And I suspect he was hired by 'Front Page Challenge' to fill the blustering bombast role that Sinclair had." Years ago, Fotheringham christened Webster as Haggis McBagpipe, the mouth that roars. "I was always a bit of a ham, and later that made me a natural on television," Webster says.

"When Webster discovered that he could hold his own with showbiz types, he also discovered he was a performer, and he really started to work at it," says Cameron Bell, who ran the news programming at BCTV – the private Vancouver television station – at the time it wooed Webster away from radio. Although Bell was instrumental in designing the TV phone-in show that brought even more fame to Webster, it was at BCTV that Webster's smouldering hostility towards Bell was born. "Once at BCTV," Webster recalls, "I was sitting around the desk one morning, and we were having quite a jolly little time since we'd had a good program. Cameron swaggers over and says, 'What the hell have you got to giggle about?' I said, 'Listen, you son of a bitch, get out of my way.' I went up to management and screamed my head off about him."

"Yes, we had differences," Bell says. "There was one problem about a cameraman assignment. He didn't take kindly to my questioning something, and he issued some kind of arbitrary order. So we had a rather large and colourful discussion. Other than that, he and I got along, I thought, very well." "Cam was nominally Webster's boss, but Webster was a star and wasn't going to have any kid push him around," says Fotheringham.

Although he had denounced television twenty-five years earlier in a *Vancouver Sun* front-page series, Webster was a smash hit with his own TV show. "He loved the camera," says Juliette, a longtime friend of

Webster. "It was kind to him, and he was very comfortable and loose on camera. He wasn't trying to be a peacock. He was just himself."

After the death of his wife, fifty years as a journalist, and nine years on his own TV show, at age seventy-one, Webster decided to slow down. The CBC had approached him once before about going on "Front Page Challenge" and now producer Ray McConnell tried again. This time Webster leapt at it, even though he'd been nervous the first time he'd been a guest panellist. "In fact, I was paralysed with nerves," he says. "It wasn't easy for a wee boy from the West Coast to come out and sit beside the great Berton." But taking the job on a regular basis was, he says, a joy, even though he was still nervous. "I'm always nervous," he says. "I am not secure. I think that if you're a fully secure person, you're not much of a reporter."

Webster's insecurity was intensified when his old nemesis, Cameron Bell, became his boss on the show. "Although Jack had been a great guest questioner, as a full-time member of the panel, latterly, he wasn't comfortable doing the show," said Davis. "He was inhibited by the producer, Cameron Bell. They were kind of tough on him. Jack's value on the show was a sort of curmudgeon, a gruff Scot who came up with some very funny stuff. In a sense, a replacement for Sinclair. Whereas with Cameron there were times when Jack was cut out of the show entirely. Foth was once, too. It really upset the panel. We had a knock-down, drag-out fight about that with Cameron. Jack was always being put down and criticized, which was a shame. They were missing what he could bring to the show."

"He would rarely go to his strength," says Bell. "His journalistic ability is to extract information from people in a friendly way. The width of his brogue is inversely proportional to the depth of the story. When there is nothing happening, he'll put in the burr, but when there is something he wants to bring out, he's excellent. Sometimes you could see flashes of it, but he was, I think, very much intimidated by the others." "Once in a while," says Fotheringham, "Cam would take him off and talk with him like the kid trying to tell the teacher."

In his retirement, at least, Webster has a storehouse of memories of confrontations with the rich and famous. He recalls that even Pierre

Trudeau was puzzled by him. "After one of my first interviews, Trudeau walked out of the studio saying, 'Why does Webster shout at me all the time?' His aide said, 'Oh, don't worry about that, sir. He shouts at everybody.'"

At first Webster regarded Trudeau as "the most arrogant, supercilious SOB I have ever met as a politician. Trudeau had that cold, biting Jesuitical form of questioning." Once, Trudeau was late for a live radio interview with Webster, who ad libbed for several minutes until the prime minister arrived. "He finally comes in. I said, 'Good morning, Prime Minister. How are you doing?' He said, 'Fine until I saw you!' Well, you know that shakes you coming from the prime minister, and it took me fifteen minutes to get back on my feet." Even so, he came to admire Trudeau because he was honest. "Interestingly, I called him prime minister, but I called Joe Clark just Joe."

Mila Mulroney once was offended by Webster when, on the air, he asked her, "How heavy are you?" "One hundred and thirty-nine pounds," she said, prompting Webster to tell her she was five pounds too heavy. "She was aghast and saw it as rudeness on my part. I was just trying to be funny. The next time I saw her a couple of months later, I said I was sorry. She forgave me and pecked me on the cheek."

His encounter with Shirley MacLaine was a different story. "She told me that as a Roman emperor I had my way with her some two thousand years ago, and it was all very exciting," Webster says. "She told me that I was the most intriguing combination of her father and Archie Bunker. She made advances on me that caused me to sweat profusely." He jokingly told her to act her age, which at the time was fifty-two. "You're very sexy," she told Webster. He recalls, "I looked and sounded like a small boy in love."

If he was in love with Shirley MacLaine, he was in awe of Queen Elizabeth when he met her at a dinner party in Vancouver. He recalls, "As they began to leave the table, the Queen turned to Prince Philip and asked, 'Where's my handbag?' 'There on the floor,' he said. 'Well, pick it up!' she snapped. And he did, just like any of us would."

Webster admits his fiery style is cooling as he ages. "I don't think I have any great anger left in me now. I don't go about screaming and shouting. Too bad. I miss it."

A Parade of Characters

Fred Davis's smooth hosting of "Front Page Challenge" hid from the public the many raging egomaniacs, drunken loudmouths, and tedious bores who came calling. For eighteen years Lorraine Thomson was the program co-ordinator and den mother to the guests, persuading them to come on the program, taking them to dinner, catering to their every whim, holding hands with the nervous, and calming down the arrogant.

Sarah Churchill, Sir Winston Churchill's daughter, was one of Thomson's biggest challenges. Before each program the guests rehearsed briefly, but Churchill, says Thomson, "was so drunk it was not possible to rehearse with her. I told her, 'We're going back to the hotel because you're not feeling well.' She said, 'No! No! I've got to rehearse.' But we managed to get her into my car. We turned onto Yonge Street in the midst of traffic, and it was pouring rain. Suddenly she opened the car door. Cars are whizzing by and the rain is bucketing down, but she gets out of my car and starts to run down the middle of Yonge Street. So I leap out of the car, leave it in the middle of the street, and run after her. Finally, I get hold of her and drag her back to the car, and she's hitting me with her purse all the time and screaming. I get her in the car and take her to her hotel. Up in her room, I get her calmed down, undressed, and put to bed. I ordered her some food, and she fell asleep after she had a bit to eat. I then leave, figuring she's going to sleep through the show. Lo and behold an hour and a half later who turns up at the studio but Sarah Churchill, slightly more sober but not totally, and announcing, 'It's time for me to go on.' "

While Thomson was trying to sober her up, producer Ray McConnell was worrying about putting Churchill on the air. He told the panel, "We have a problem with one of our guests. Actually, I have to tell you the guest is drunk. It's entirely possible I may have to cancel the guest." At one point, Betty Kennedy remembers, McConnell told the panel, "I've got to tell you that the guest is now standing out in the pouring rain directing traffic on Yonge Street." Finally, McConnell told them, "We are going to go with the guest." "We were all just holding our breath," says Kennedy.

"We say, 'Okay, let's see what happens.' So we bring her out, put her on the air, and believe it or not she gets through the interview," Thomson says. "Later on we got a lot of letters saying, 'Why did you put poor Miss

Churchill on when she obviously was ill.' Of course, we couldn't have told the audience that she was drunk as a skunk."

When Sarah Churchill's brother, Randolph, made his "Front Page Challenge" appearance, he fully lived up to his reputation as a riotous drunkard. The first problem was that he went to the wrong studio. A guard phoned Jim Guthro to say, "Mr. Guthro, there's a man standing here who says he is Randolph Churchill, and he's angry because he can't find the studio." He was also very drunk. Guthro arranged to get him to the studio, and his first words on arrival were "I want some whisky!" "What kind of whisky?" asked Guthro. "You damn fool," Churchill replied, "there's only one kind of whisky – Scotch!"

"After he had his Scotch, he started to get a cigarette but didn't have a match," Guthro remembers. "The writer John Aylesworth pulled out his lighter, but it was a trick lighter, and as he opened it, it played a woman singing, 'Do you wonder where the yellow went when you brush your teeth with Pepsodent?' He glowered as if to say, 'These bloody colonial fools!' I said to Fred, 'Let's cross our fingers on this show.' "

"He'd certainly gotten at the grape that day," Davis recalled. "He was in a foul mood, swearing and cursing the CBC and all of us." He was monumentally offended when the story chosen for him to represent was the Yalta Conference where he'd been an aide to his father. Davis said, "He stormed into the studio and said, 'What the hell are we talking about this for? I've made headlines myself.' "

Guthro told Davis, "If he's like that on the air, we're going to throw him off!" To which Davis replied, "Great, what are you going to do while the commissionaires and stagehands throw him off?" "Well, we'll cut to you and you can fill for ten minutes," replied Guthro. "It would have been like cutting away from a fight in a hockey game," said Davis. "Who the hell could fill when the son of Sir Winston Churchill is being hustled out of the studio? But he came on, and as soon as the red light went on, he became Mr. Charm and coherent even though he was half cut."

Another misbehaving guest was the swashbuckling Hollywood star Errol Flynn, who demanded airline tickets and expenses for his mistress, Beverley Aadland, as well as for himself. Because of his reputation regarding alcohol and women, he was handled gingerly by make-up artist Margaret Epp. "He needed a lot of make-up packing because he was pretty dissipated," says Guthro. "Margaret was dabbing it on and suddenly he grabs her by the buttocks and pulls her towards him. 'Sit down on my knee and face me and then put the make-up on,' he says. 'We've got to have some fun.' 'Oh no, Mr. Flynn,' Epp said, 'I couldn't do that. At the CBC we're not allowed to touch the performers anywhere but their face.' And then she extricated herself from his clutches."

Another story of a Hollywood star involves actor Joan Fontaine when she was chatting in the green room before her appearance. Producer Don Brown recalls, "She said her first major film was with Bing Crosby. It was being shot in Alberta, and she was taken onto the set to meet Mr. Crosby, whom she was in awe of. She was introduced, and he didn't say, 'How do you do?' or anything. Just, she said, three words: 'Do you fuck?' It completely disillusioned her."

Actor Tallulah Bankhead was renowned for the variety and number of her romantic escapades. Brown remembers her sitting in the green room before a show, whipping her hair with a handbrush and then deciding she wanted a different brush. "George, hand me the other brush," she said to the "assistant" she had brought from New York. "I'm not George, I'm Harry," he replied. She looked closely at him and said, "Oh yes, George was last week."

The most aloof Hollywood star Brown encountered was Bette Davis, who said she didn't want to be bored waiting to go on the show and left the studio to drive around in her limousine until it was time to go on. "She assumed we were riffraff and didn't want to mix with us," says Brown.

Probably the most exuberant drinker "Front Page Challenge" ever entertained was the Irish playwright Brendan Behan. He made it through the program without a problem, but then Guthro took him to a bar where trumpet player Roy Eldridge was performing. Guthro left them to carouse together. When Behan returned to the Royal York Hotel, he got involved in a fracas in the lobby. "I was phoned by the manager, who said the police were going to take him to jail for causing a disturbance," says Guthro. "I said, 'Don't do that – let him sleep it off.' They finally agreed, although I think they did take him to jail and then brought him back to the hotel. He was at one point loudly denouncing the critics with his line that they were like eunuchs in a harem who see the act done every day but can't do it themselves." A less serious drinker was conservative editor William Buckley, whose only request was "Please, a six pack of Molson's."

Don Brown, who succeeded Guthro as the show's producer, remembers booze being a problem for the singer Ginny Sims of the Kay Kyser Band. Just before the show, the make-up artist told Brown, "Don, we've got a problem. Ginny Sims is stewed to the gills." As Brown remembers it, "I think she had taken a bath in gin. I went into the make-up room to see her in her chair, weaving while sitting. And she was a nasty drunk." "You don't like me, do you?" she said, to which Brown replied, "Whether or not I like you is irrelevant. All I'm interested in is whether you give us a show tonight." After that she began to sober up and went on the air.

It wasn't booze but drugs that worried producer Ray McConnell when actor Janet Leigh was a guest. "She was sniffing coke backstage," he says, "and I was very concerned about that. No matter what she was asked, she would go into one of her scenes from a movie." There was another drug problem with a guest when he was on camera for a program called "VIP," which was an offshoot of "Front Page Challenge" and featured a long interview with one of the guests. In this case it was not a human guest but an RCMP dog called Cloud Two, whose acute sense of smell had helped in the capture of several criminals. "While I was interviewing his RCMP handler," says Lorraine Thomson, "Cloud Two kept shifting his eyes left and right, looking at the various technical people standing around, and his head kept darting around. I had no idea what was happening with the dog."

Eventually the taping had to be stopped because of the dog's mounting excitement. Steve Hyde says, "The officer told me, 'Somebody in here has got some marijuana. Tell them, for God's sake, to get out of the studio so the dog can settle down.' So I said, 'Whoever's got the grass, piss off because the dog's gone bananas. You're not going to be arrested.' A couple of guys walked away, and the dog lay down on the floor and was fine after that."

The guest with the bluest language was unquestionably the famous fan dancer Sally Rand. She arrived for an edition of "Front Page Challenge" being done in Halifax, in the midst of one of the city's worst snowstorms. There was a problem at the airport because the driver sent

Kate Reid, one of the great actors, performing as Nellie McClung in a CBC-TV drama. *(National Archives of Canada, MISA 14571)*

The late Bruno Gerussi, who starred on the stage and television, achieved his greatest fame in the long-running TV series "The Beachcombers." He was bitter when the series was cancelled. *(Courtesy of the CBC)*

"The Country Gentleman," Tommy Hunter, sang his way into the hearts of viewers for twenty-six years. His backup group, The Rhythm Pals, was part of his success: left to right, Marc Wald, Mike Ferby, and Jack Jensen. *(Robert C. Ragsdale, courtesy of the CBC)*

Wayne and Shuster produced the greatest comedy act in Canadian TV history. Here they are seen with dancer Lorraine Thomson. Frank and Johnny's fierce battles were legendary but never personal. *(Courtesy of the CBC)*

"Our Pet" Juliette, the blonde queen of Canadian television, waged war against her directors, but her voice and style won the hearts of viewers. With her Saturday night post-hockey show, she was the most popular singer on Canadian TV in the 1960s. *(National Archives of Canada, MISA 16143)*

"I ain't hurtin' to be a star," said Anne Murray when she began her career, but she knew she was good. In the late 1960s, Murray started as a barefoot country music singer on "Singalong Jubilee" out of Halifax, but she quickly zoomed to international stardom. *(National Archives of Canada, MISA 16154)*

Gordon Pinsent starred in many a CBC drama and shot to fame as a Mountie in the early 1960s series "Forest Rangers" and later in the lead role on "Quentin Durgens, MP." After a flirtation with Hollywood, he came back to CBC-TV in, among other projects, "A Gift to Last." *(National Archives of Canada, MISA 16147)*

Although he's been a TV star for more than two decades, Al Waxman is best remembered as The King of "The King of Kensington," in which he co-starred with Fiona Reid for five years. He later starred in the American series "Cagney and Lacey." *(National Archives of Canada, MISA 16145)*

Ernie Coombs, a.k.a. Mr. Dressup, and some of his puppet pals who entertained Canadian children for twenty-nine years on CBC-TV. *(Fred Phipps, courtesy of the CBC)*

Bob Homme as The Friendly Giant began his show on CBC-TV in the 1960s. After a long, twenty-five-year run, the program's cancellation was stayed for one year when a CBC reporter got wind of the story. *(National Archives of Canada, CBC 10020)*

CBC announcer, newscaster, and anchorman Alex Trebek learned the ropes of game-show hosting on the quiz program "Reach for the Top." Trebek's near-photographic memory and smooth demeanour led him to become the internationally known quiz master of the popular American show "Jeopardy!" *(National Archives of Canada, MISA 16150)*

Leslie Nielsen was a noted actor in early CBC-TV dramas before Hollywood called him to comic stardom. He turned to comedy after he decided his bowlegs made him an odd-looking Hamlet. *(National Archives of Canada, MISA 16155)*

"Front Page Challenge" was the granddaddy of all TV network programs, lasting from 1957 to 1995. Left to right: Pierre Berton, who joined the cast the first year, Allan Fotheringham, Jack Webster, Betty Kennedy, and Fred Davis, the host from 1957 onwards. (*Courtesy of the CBC*)

The most unforgettable character on Canadian TV and an irascible panel-list on "Front Page Challenge," Gordon Sinclair met his match in "Ma" Murray, the feisty B.C. publisher Margaret Teresa Murray. (*National Archives of Canada, MISA 16148*)

Patrick Watson, host of the controversial, groundbreaking public affairs series "This Hour Has Seven Days," was a quintessential interviewer. He went on to become chairman of the CBC. *(Fred Phipps, courtesy of the CBC)*

William Shatner began his career in space on the CBC's "Space Command" in the 1950s and wound up in Hollywood as Captain Kirk of "Star Trek." *(National Archives of Canada, MISA 16159)*

to pick her up was looking for a luscious blonde beauty in high heels. "He couldn't find her, but since he was carrying a sign, a thin, saggy, lined woman of seventy or so went up to him and introduced herself," Lorraine Thomson recalls. "She was just about the tiniest person I've ever seen, about four foot ten, and you'd never recognize this former fan dancer without her make-up and wig."

When Rand arrived at the studio, the snow had piled up to about three feet, and as she plunged through it, she cried out, "Christ, the snow is so deep it's right up to my hot box!" Her tough-talking broad reputation was evident, too, when she told a reporter that she only sunbathes in the nude "otherwise my tits look like headlights." As she struggled through the Halifax snow and into the studio, "Front Page Challenge" writer and *Toronto Star* columnist Gary Lautens asked her if she had brought her ostrich plume fan because it would be, he told her, "a wonderful touch of nostalgia." "Fuck nostalgia," Rand replied. "Where's the dressing room?"

Producer Don Brown was terrified she'd use that kind of language on the air, but she didn't, although Gordon Sinclair had a lively time after the show in the green room discussing what, if anything, she wore behind her fans. Sinclair always enjoyed asking daring questions of the more exotic female guests who came on the show. Another striptease artist who appeared on the program was Gypsy Rose Lee. "We told her to be careful of Gordon Sinclair, the bald guy," said Fred Davis. "And she told Gordon, 'After my striptease vaudeville days, I'm used to old bald-headed men like you sitting in the front row with their hotel-room number etched in lipstick on their forehead.' Gordon just laughed." To disguise her voice, Gypsy had put marbles into her mouth, writer Alex Barris recalls. "And later she told us, 'That's how you become an actress. When you lose all your marbles, you're an actress.' "

Sinclair was enchanted, too, when another guest, Beverley Harrell, the madam of the Cotton Tail Ranch in Nevada, a well-known brothel, gave him a free pass. She'd been on the program discussing prostitution as a business, waving a gold and silver cane and the longest fingernails Sinclair had ever seen. "She charmed Gordon, and he was just thrilled to get a free pass to the Cotton Tail Ranch," Thomson recalls. "I don't think he ever used it though." The madam also charmed the technical crew, and Steve Hyde remembers her telling him, "Let the crew know, if they come, I'll give them a deal."

Hollywood star Cloris Leachman didn't use her charm on the panellists, but did seem to fall in love at the first sight of Gary Lautens. "She took a real shine to Gary," Thomson recalls. "She was all over him, stroking his hair, whispering into his ears. She wanted to go home with him. Gary, of course, was a very shy person. He looked over at me as if to say, 'Get this woman away from me!' " Someone eventually did.

The most frightened guest was Martha Mitchell, the wife of Richard Nixon's attorney general. She knew most of Nixon's Watergate secrets and spilled many of them on the program, all the while terrified that the U.S. Secret Service and FBI were following her. "She was one scared lady," says Thomson. "I had dinner with her, and afterwards she asked me to come up to her hotel room so I could help her search under the bed, in the closets, and outside the window. She wouldn't stay in a room by a fire escape for fear somebody would get at her. She told me the FBI had injected her with something and had her confined to a hospital for being a drunk, for fear of her giving away secrets about Watergate. Eventually, the things she told us turned out to be true."

Broadway musical star Ethel Merman was one of the program's most costly guests. She flew up for a show, pocketed both her fee and her cheque for expenses, and then left the CBC to pay her hotel bill. Occasionally a guest panellist was caught off guard, as when columnist Peter Worthington found himself questioning his father, General F. F. Worthington, a onetime soldier of fortune, war hero, and founder of the Canadian Armoured Corps. "I don't know whether to call you General or Daddy," said Worthington.

Some government leaders were not particularly good on the program, Pierre Berton recalls. "Clement Attlee, the former British prime minister, wouldn't answer any question except with yes or no. And French Prime Minister Pierre Mendès-France for some reason wouldn't talk about anything but milk."

Occasionally a president or prime minister had to be gently ordered about. When Indira Gandhi arrived as a guest, she was surrounded by an entourage of sycophantic officials. She was slow in getting seated, and floor director Steve Hyde had to intervene. To the incredulity of her officials, he said, "Put your little ass over here right now, dearie," which she promptly did. Hyde, a onetime British navy tar, had a penchant for being irreverent with the high and mighty. When Pierre Trudeau made his appearance on the program, Hyde kept calling him Peter, and when the pudgy world-famous violinist Isaac Stern was the guest, Hyde told him, "You sit over here, Tubs."

Of all the Canadian prime ministers who appeared on "Front Page Challenge," the most memorable was Pierre Trudeau, not for what he said on the air but for what happened backstage. He, Margaret, and their baby, Sasha, arrived in a stretch limousine, pulling up in a driveway just inside the back door of the studio. "I was there to greet him," says Ray McConnell. "He bounds out of the car and we shake hands. Then Margaret comes around holding Sasha in her right arm. Trudeau said, 'Margaret, I'd like you to meet the producer of the show, Ray McConnell,' and she stuck out her right hand. Both the RCMP guard and I blanch, but she manages to grab the baby just before it fell."

While Trudeau was doing the program, Margaret and Sasha stayed in the car. At one point a passing technician looked in through the open car window in goggle-eyed astonishment, then ran over to Fred Davis to say, "Jeez, have you seen that? The prime minister's wife is breastfeeding her kid just off the green room." When the program ended, Trudeau came offstage with Lorraine Thomson. "I was saying what a wonderful job he'd done," Thomson says, "when Margaret came up to him, handed him the baby, and said, 'Here, the baby needs changing.' I said, 'Over to you, Daddy,' and Trudeau took the baby into a private dressing room to change the diapers. I got the sense he was a frequent diaper changer."

Later Margaret Trudeau came on the program several times herself and told Thomson that her secret wish was to be a TV interviewer. "She was a sixties flower child, but I never found her a flake," says Thomson. "In fact, there was something of the waif in her." Betty Kennedy agrees. "Margaret always struck me as being terribly vulnerable. Like somebody who really needed someone to protect her, from herself mostly."

Producer Cameron Bell recalls Margaret on her last "Front Page Challenge" appearance, chatting about the break-up of her marriage to

Trudeau. "She basically said, 'I blew it. If I had to do it again, I wouldn't do it that way.'"

The guest who awed everyone was Eleanor Roosevelt. Fred Davis said she was "the most important guest we ever had. It was very early on in the show and the Americans wouldn't even listen to us before. They thought of Canada as a land of Eskimos, igloos, and Mounties, and thought it was a four-day trek by dogsled. But Eleanor Roosevelt opened the door for a lot of VIPs to start coming to Canada. She was a charming, charming woman who even urged Harry Truman to come on, but he couldn't. She told us, 'Whatever the fee is, I want you to donate it to the March of Dimes.'"

Roosevelt not only opened the door to political and diplomatic VIPs – such as Averell Harriman, her sons James and Franklin, Jr., Harold Wilson, Hugh Gaitskill, and Sir Alex Douglas-Home – but also to sports heroes like Mickey Mantle and Gordie Howe and to a parade of Hollywood stars. Even though he was a world-famous comedian, Groucho Marx was nervous about being on the program and asked everyone to call him Groucho, not Mr. Marx. "Groucho was a revelation to me," said Davis. "When we got off the air, he grabbed my arm and said, 'Was I okay? Did it work? What do you think? Did it seem okay?' Here's this giant of comedy wondering if he'd been all right."

In the green room after the show, Groucho took off his jacket and asked Davis and his colleagues what they thought of his suspenders. Davis said, "They were navy blue with yellow birds flying in them and quite wide. We're all saying, 'Oh, they're very nice, Groucho.' He replies, 'Yeah, well, my wife got them for me in Paris. She thinks I'm a faggot.'"

One guest who didn't impress Thomson much was popular singer Tony Bennett. "Great singer but dumb," she says. He didn't impress Davis either. "It was painful," Davis said. Bennett was to talk about civil rights, which he strongly supported, but, apparently, mostly with his presence. He was quite inarticulate under the panel's questioning. "Tony Bennett was one of the worst guests we ever had," adds Ray McConnell. "He really didn't know why he was on the show."

"Jayne Mansfield," Davis said, "was portrayed in all her movies as a sexy, dumb blonde, but she was one bright lady and had a great sense of humour. Zsa Zsa Gabor, dismissed by some as being an airhead, was a very thoughtful person offstage. She took the trouble to remember our names." "She darling-ed me to death," says Don Brown. When B.C. newspaper publisher Margaret "Ma" Murray, on the same program, kept referring to her in the green room as Za Zu, Gabor repeatedly said, "No, no, darling. It's Zsa Zsa," but to little effect. Before coming to the studio, Gabor lost her diamonds down the washbasin at her Royal York Hotel suite. She explained, "I was cleaning them with a toothbrush. Everyone cleans their diamonds with a toothbrush."

One not especially affable guest was Veronica Lake, a onetime Hollywood siren whose trademark was her blonde hair falling over her eye. "Her every other word was 'fuck,'" says Brown. "I asked her if she would be okay on the air without saying that word. 'Oh, I won't say it,' she assured me and she didn't. But she started in again as soon as she went off the air. She couldn't form a sentence without using the word."

Perhaps the most dramatic "Front Page Challenge" guest was Soviet defector Igor Gouzenko. Fred Davis and producer Jim Guthro had lunch with him in 1958, several weeks before the program, at a back table in a downtown Toronto restaurant. Guthro remembers Gouzenko demanding, and getting, $1,000 for his appearance, more than double the usual fee. Gouzenko also insisted on being called Mr. Brown. "He was really paranoid about the whole thing," said Davis. "He was sure 'they' were going to get him. He sat in the green room before the show with his bodyguard and scowled around at everybody. Then his guard searched the studio for bombs."

Gouzenko insisted on wearing a black hood so he couldn't be identified. And then, even though his face was covered by the hood, he asked to have make-up on his face. Just before going on the air, he said, "Wait a minute, you've got to disguise my voice. I'm not going on because where I live people will recognize my voice even under the hood."

Technicians quickly found a special mike that distorted his voice. "On the air," said Davis, "he was nervous, so his accent got thicker. The panel and I didn't know what the hell he was saying, with his accent thickening, the hood muffling his voice, and the neck mike distorting it. The panel just asked questions and hoped something was emerging. We went on for about twelve minutes with him. I thought, 'I hope the people at home are understanding this because I don't know what this guy is saying.'" Alex Barris says that after the show, Larry Mann and Gouzenko walked down Yonge Street for half a block before Gouzenko realized he was still wearing his hood.

One of the prickliest guests was one of the CBC's own producers, the iconoclastic current affairs producer Ross McLean, who took the opportunity to dump on CBC stars. He said the personalities of popular TV singers Wally Koster and Joyce Sullivan were "a well-kept secret," and he said prominent musician Jack Kane could not "speak three consecutive sentences without stumbling." When he finished, Davis thanked him, saying, "Ross McLean, it's been mildly pleasant."

The Fun Is Over

For Davis, Berton, Kennedy, Fotheringham, and Webster, the joy of "Front Page Challenge" stopped when CBC vice-president Ivan Fecan ordered producer Cameron Bell to put more "edge" into the show by going after headlines and dealing with significant contemporary issues.

"You know, the show isn't fun anymore," Berton said at one point to Bell's deputy, Helen Slinger. Berton remembers Slinger responding, "You're not supposed to have any fun. . . . You're supposed to be putting on a program," "But," he says, "the secret of putting on a good show is having fun."

Fun was not what Fecan had in mind when he first called Bell, a successful, hard-headed combat veteran of Vancouver's news wars. "How would you like to get on an airplane and see me in Toronto?" Fecan said. "Well, I have a meeting tomorrow," Bell replied. "Could I come Thursday?" "Tomorrow!" Fecan demanded, and so the next day Bell flew to Toronto. At their meeting, Fecan told him, "I want to move 'Front Page Challenge' to Vancouver, and I want to put some edge into it, and I want you to produce it." Bell says, "I took that to mean he wanted stories that were more sharply focused, more likely to make news, and more likely to be thought relevant." Bell went for a walk around the block, came back, and told Fecan, "Okay. You've got four of the better journalists in the country. It shouldn't be hard to put an edge on it."

Bell hired Slinger as his deputy. She had been a CBC News executive producer in Vancouver, had worked in the CBC Toronto newsroom, and had previously been hired by Bell when he was at BCTV. Together they fashioned the new edge for "Front Page Challenge" and ran smack into the stone wall of Berton, Kennedy, Fotheringham, and Webster.

"My task was to revive a television show that was failing," Bell says. "I had to bring more than simply the personae to the public. We could not run the show on celebrity alone – that's where the friction was. Their favourite guest would be wearing an Order of Canada pin. They wanted the official Canadians."

Not only did Bell and Slinger want different kinds of guests on "Front Page Challenge," they wanted more emphasis on the issue highlighted by the guest and more control over the panel's questioning.

"Cam and Helen were trying to run the show totally," says Berton. "They were trying to tell us what questions to ask."

"Pierre used to say, 'The talent is the reason why the show is there, why it's lasted thirty-eight years,'" says Fotheringham. "I used to say to Cam, 'You're going to tell Pierre Berton how to interview? Come on now!' If they could have scripted the whole show, they would have."

"We don't need questions at our age and experience, for Christ's sake," says Webster. "And also you can't do suicides and child assaults and buggery in Newfoundland for more than a short time, otherwise it becomes depressing."

"They had their own agenda in each show," Kennedy says. "The shows were enormously well researched, although a lot of them were terribly, terribly gloomy. But they said, 'This is the story!' and that's what they wanted.

"When Roberta Bondar was on they wanted her to say there was great sex discrimination in the Armed Forces, but she was not about to say that on the air. So we futzed around on that far too long. There were other aspects to her story we should have been into. But they had their idea of the story they wanted. At the end they would say, 'You didn't get what we wanted out of that.' They would have been perfectly happy to have scripted every word we said. We were all angry."

"Helen was a card-carrying feminist," says Fotheringham. "She wanted to have issues, wife-beating or alcoholism or discrimination against Indians. They tried to shift the emphasis from headline people to people who presented issues, but were nobodies. We kept saying, 'Sure, bring on the issue if you want, but have it with someone who's been in the headlines.' I said to Pierre, 'If I have never heard of her and you've never heard of her, she doesn't exist, and she shouldn't be on the show.' "

To get more control and provide more polish to "Front Page Challenge," Bell decided to edit the program instead of doing it live, or live to tape. "It increased their effectiveness," Bell says. But the only thing it increased insofar as the panel was concerned was their distress. "When you edit, you lose spontaneity," says Kennedy. "I objected to the editing," Berton adds. "We all did. They cut out Foth once. They cut out Webster, too, and I raised hell. I wrote a letter to George Anthony [the executive in charge of the show], and he wrote back saying, 'No, the producer is in charge.' To them, the panel was not the most important element, the news stories were. The panel was secondary."

"I was the first one to be cut out altogether, and I couldn't bloody well understand it," says Webster. "I bitched about it, but nothing happened. When they did it with Fotheringham, the shit hit the fan. You can't have a guy up in the introduction and then not be seen again. The editing took every piece of zip out of the program. Cam acted like a dictator. He wanted to teach us the lesson that he was the boss."

The cuts were made, says Bell, because "it wasn't a competent piece of work, or the questions were not appropriate. Being a producer ain't always easy." Bell was furious that the panel, led by Berton, went behind his back to protest some of his decisions to his bosses in Toronto. "I told them," Bell says, " 'You do that again, and I'm out of here. If that's what you want, do it. I'm not going to put up with that kind of nonsense.' " At one point Fotheringham ran into Ivan Fecan and complained about problems on the show. Fecan mentioned it to Bell, who asked if he wanted to talk about it. "Not really," said Fecan, and they didn't. "If you want change," says Bell, "change means complaints."

Another bone of contention was the mini-documentaries aired for each guest – up to two minutes long – that served to emphasize the issue involved. "Cam was thinking in terms of a news program," says Berton. "He was not entertainment-minded." A further source of tension was the possibility that one or more of the panel might be fired. When he took over, Bell proposed there be rotating questioners. "We made a list of possibilities," Bell says. "There were about sixty of them. Toronto did talk to us briefly about it, but concluded that there wouldn't be a program without this cast. The other thing I was told was that none of the panel wanted to be the first off, but if the boat was going down, they didn't care. Before I became involved, there were meetings on this, and what I was told was that Allan and Pierre were of the opinion that with two other panellists they would have a stronger program."

Berton has a different perspective. "I was approached about Betty and Webster and I said, 'Look, these people are my friends. I'm having no part in this at all.' They wanted a younger woman, they wanted youth." At one point Berton had suggested Vickie Gabereau be added to the panel, and another possibility discussed was TV personality Carole Taylor. When pressed, Bell says, "If it had been up to me, I would have kept Betty and Pierre. Betty had by far the most respect of the underlings, and she was the only one who showed any consistent empathy for the guests. Pierre is one of the hardest-working guys I've ever known. He'd throw in colour and he'd sense when things weren't lively and he could make a contribution."

Almost yearly since the 1970s, CBC management had considered cancelling "Front Page Challenge," but never did because of the program's star power, its inexpensiveness, and its popularity. But after years of being shifted around in the TV schedule, being shunted off to a time when the private affiliated stations didn't have to carry it, inevitably the program had lost much of its audience, and finally, in the spring of 1995, the CBC pulled the plug on its longest-running TV show.

"Somebody outside the arts and entertainment programming said the way to do it is on the eve of a long weekend, and suddenly the wheels went into motion," says Bell. "They told me the night before and asked me not to tell anyone. They said they were going to phone Helen, but they didn't reach her."

After they rejected the CBC suggestion to have a bang-up farewell lunch, Fotheringham, Berton, Davis, and Webster gathered at Kennedy's home outside Toronto for a private dinner and wake, exchanging stories over smoked salmon and beef tenderloin.

Alone of the other panel members, Kennedy got a phone call from Helen Slinger, who said she'd enjoyed working with her. None of the panel heard from Bell. In response to a card she had sent Perrin Beatty, congratulating him on his appointment as CBC president, Kennedy received a phone call from him, thanking her for the card and assuring her that he had no role in the cancellation of "Front Page Challenge." "I'm terribly sorry about 'Front Page,'" he said, "and I would like you to know that I didn't do it. That wouldn't be within my purview."

In its thirty-eight years, "Front Page Challenge" outlasted ten CBC presidents, a technological revolution, and a sea change in television viewing. "The program format was genius," says Bell, the last of seven program producers. "It gave you three runs at a story. You had the headline and its set-up, then the game, and then the interview. But more than that, you got to meet the newsmaker in a non-official capacity. You got to see his human side. The format was just brilliant."

Sadly, that brilliance disappeared from the screen unhonoured and unmourned by the CBC.

7

Legends, Devils, and Other Journalists

The greatest number of legends in Canadian broadcasting spring from the off-air hijinks of journalists. Rivals clearly exist among actors, musicians, singers, and sportscasters, but nowhere are there quite so many vivid characters as among the news people. And, perhaps not surprisingly, with journalists, talent and devilry often go together.

Their reputation may have begun with the fun-loving, mercurial founder of the CBC News Service, Dan McArthur. Stubborn, defiant, and profane, he waged war with CBC bureaucracy throughout the 1940s and early 1950s and won the hearts of his news employees with his ferocious defence of CBC News integrity and his exuberant late-night singing, drinking, and concertina-playing with the boys. He also loved writing and reciting raffish limericks and was once fired from the CRBC for "vulgarity" in reading one of them on the air.

The flamboyant McArthur was the CBC chief news editor for thirteen years starting in 1941. He wins the prize for the most vivid memos ever written by a CBC executive, an example of which is in the appendix. He demanded "rigid factuality," objectivity, and accuracy from his editors and denounced the interference and ignorance of "fat ass . . . poor old dyspeptic bastard" bureaucrats. He insisted CBC News must never be "a government mouthpiece," believed the news was "a public trust," and hated any sign of "showmanship" in the news department.

Despite his apprehension about showmanship, his newscasts during the war years featured the two men with the highest profile in news broadcasting at the time: anchorman Lorne Greene, the Voice of Doom, and Matthew Halton, Canada's best-known war correspondent. The sonorous tones that won him fame on the CBC later took Greene to an acting career in Hollywood. His colleague, Halton, also had a dramatic flair and brought emotion and even poetry to his reportage. "He dramatized everything," said his friend and fellow war correspondent Charles Lynch, "and he kept accelerating the danger he was in, in recounting some of his exploits. I told him that, by God, one day he was going to get himself killed in his stories." Halton thrived on danger and wanted to capture the sounds of battle in his reports. Lynch recalled that on D-Day, as he and Halton splashed ashore in Normandy one hour after the initial assault, Halton threw back his head and exulted, "This is not a day to work. It's a day to live!" Shortly after that, in a pause in the fighting, they took refuge in a brothel in a small coastal town, where they sampled the wine while Lynch pounded the piano and Halton and several other correspondents sang along. Halton got to Paris before most of the troops. He was greeted with a kiss by a beautiful, well-armed resistance leader named Christianne, and sent back the first network broadcast out of the newly liberated French capital.

The bureaucrats whom McArthur so hated once admonished Halton's recording engineer Art Holmes for losing a CBC camera. It went missing in the Mediterranean when his ship was torpedoed. Nevertheless, his request for an allowance to buy a replacement camera was rejected with the stern warning that he should "remember there's a war on."

The triumph of Halton and his fellow war correspondents overshadowed a couple of unfortunate wartime broadcasts. Canada's formal declaration of war was reported in a CBC news bulletin read by announcer Austin Willis, interrupting a music show. Willis remembers he broke into "Smoke Gets in Your Eyes," read the bulletin officially putting Canada at war, and then returned the network to the strains of "Inka Dinka Doo." Five years later, reacting to a mistaken news agency report, the CBC announced the end of the war with Japan two days early and, to Prime Minister Mackenzie King's eternal embarrassment, put on a victory speech he had previously recorded.

An embarrassing but less serious incident occurred shortly before the outbreak of war when the King and Queen were in Canada for a royal visit. As they sailed home out of Halifax, the CBC announcer waxed poetic while their ship moved away from the dock. He reported that the Queen was smiling and waving goodbye and, without indicating he was now speaking of the ship, said, "and now she is turning towards us her broad, beautiful white stern."

That gaffe rivalled one some years later by CBS reporter Larry LeSueur while reporting the news on the night of President Dwight Eisenhower's inauguration in Washington, D.C., which featured two Presidential Balls. LeSueur blithely announced, "And now we take you to Washington where both Presidential Balls are in full swing."

Its wartime coverage put CBC News on the map, and, as CBC postwar radio program director Harry Boyle says, "You had the feeling that come ten o'clock every evening, every radio in the country was tuned in to the CBC to find out what was going on." Even so, CBC News at the time was essentially a rewrite news service with, as the postwar years rolled on, the addition of a few freelance contract foreign correspondents contributing voice reports. There were no national reporters on staff.

It was television that changed everything for CBC News. McArthur, as a stubborn news traditionalist, quit as chief news editor because he felt TV was too frivolous and personality-driven to be taken seriously as a news medium. Indeed, in the early months of television, there was no newscast. "Television news is for the birds," McArthur told one of his successors, Donald Macdonald. But McArthur, who was so right for the times when the CBC News Service was being established, was wrong for the television era. "Television put us into the news-gathering business," says Macdonald. Reporters, foreign correspondents, and cameramen were hired as, for the first time, CBC began collecting the news as well as disseminating it. And there was no reporter among the news gatherers more vivid than Norman DePoe.

Norman DePoe

He drank, he sang, he smoked. He was cantankerous, autocratic, defiant, impetuous, and contemptuous of CBC bureaucrats. For all that, Norman DePoe was the best political broadcast reporter Canada has ever produced, and for a decade or so, his face was better known than the prime minister's.

Nobody in journalism and few in public life had his encyclopedic knowledge and understanding of Canadian politics. With his raspy growl, his Edward R. Murrow good looks and insight, and his ability to boil down a complex story into a lucid, two-minute report, DePoe was made for TV. He could and would quote from Plato to Pierre Trudeau and Thomas Hardy to John Diefenbaker while ruthlessly digging for a story. "Norman had the smell of news, the look of news, with that staccato delivery and that intensity in his eyes," says his CBC Ottawa colleague John Drewery. "There was an urgency in his voice. He combined the abilities of a philosopher, a hard-boiled reporter, and an old-time vaudeville performer."

That combination of talents made DePoe unbeatable as a TV journalist. In his Press Gallery heyday, politicians respected and feared the influence he had in his reports on the nation's political health, particularly since, until the mid-1960s, his was the only TV network voice regularly coming out of Ottawa. DePoe was also a fervent Canadian patriot, even though he was born in Portland, Oregon. His nationalistic pride was vividly on display at a 1966 New Year's Eve party when, as midnight arrived, he insisted the merrymakers sing not "Auld Lang Syne" but "O Canada" to begin Canada's hundredth year. With tears of pride and emotion in his eyes, he led the singing. Everyone joined in, except for a newly arrived British journalist, Alan Edmonds, who scoffed at the spectacle. DePoe broke off the singing and with eyes aflame and fists cocked, he shouted, "Shame!" at the astounded Edmonds. But before he could switch from verbal to physical abuse, DePoe was wrestled away, and he sourly returned to his rendition of "O Canada."

DePoe's emotions were always close to the surface, and tears would trickle down his craggy face at Christmases, birthdays, and special celebrations. "He cared so deeply about so many things," says his second wife, Mary DePoe. "He was a very honourable man. I cannot remember him telling a lie, not even a white one, and if he were disappointed in people, or if they weren't honest, he would be deeply hurt."

DePoe was a workaholic who also drank and sang and argued long into the night at the Press Club. His aggressiveness would intensify as the evening wore on, and then woe betide anyone he felt was being intellectually dishonest or misquoting the classics. He rarely mentioned his wife of the time, and six boys and one girl. "They just did not seem to be part of his agenda," says Drewery. "I only ever heard him discuss his family once, while we drove to Montreal. He was talking about his son. 'John,' he said, 'I hope you spend a lot of time with your boy as he grows up because I didn't and I'm paying for it now.' "

The first time CTV reporter Craig Oliver met DePoe was at the Press Club late at night. "He had a bunch of presents at his feet and he was drinking," says Oliver. "I asked who the presents were for, and somebody said, 'Oh, it's his kid's birthday.' I guess he never got there."

Over the years DePoe drifted away from his marriage and fell deeply in love with the daughter of a socially prominent and politically influential editor. Official Ottawa was scandalized at the romance between what was felt to be, with some justification, a married roué and a naive young girl. Her mother personally called Prime Minister Pearson to ask him to break up the relationship, a colleague of Pearson's says, but, although the prime minister sympathized, he did nothing.

When DePoe was assigned to cover the medicare strike in Saskatchewan in 1962, he was lectured three times by his bosses not to stop off in Winnipeg to see his girlfriend. Before getting on the plane in Toronto, he borrowed someone's guitar, put on a western hat, and sang to the waiting passengers everything from "Onward Christian Soldiers" to "Home on the Range." "He was just looped," says colleague Bill Cunningham, who flew with him.

On the plane his producer gave him another lecture and a warning. "Norman, I understand love as well as the next man," said Don Cameron. "But if you get off in Winnipeg, I've got to suspend you." They discussed the nature of love for a couple of hours, and DePoe's determination to see his paramour increased with every drink he downed. When the plane landed in Winnipeg, he got off, never did get to Regina for the medicare strike story, and was suspended.

DePoe was not alone in his hijinks; those reporters who went on to Regina to cover the medicare story set a standard for devilment rarely equalled in the annals of journalistic mischief. The owner of the motel where they were staying was initially enthusiastic to be the host of what he felt were big TV stars. But after one party that featured loud singing, raucous laughter, and martinis poured inaccurately from a second-floor balcony into glasses on the ground floor, the owner declared, "I don't care who you guys are. This is the medicare crisis, not Custer's last stand. Another night like last night and out you go!" While all this was going on, coverage of the doctors' strike was superb, and included a face-to-face, live-on-air confrontation between the two sides, neither of which knew it was about to happen. The encounter helped break the strike deadlock.

While DePoe missed the Regina revelry, he had more than enough of his own, including an adventure in Paris, where he'd been sent to cover Prime Minister Pearson's visit to the French capital. A highlight of the visit was a reception at the Élysée Palace. DePoe had been enjoying vodka and brandy all day, and when colleagues came to take him to the reception they found him snoring contentedly, stark-naked in his bathtub, clutching a brandy snifter. He was hastily awakened, poured into his formal clothes, decorated with his medals from his days as a Canadian Army captain in Italy, and carted off to the palace. He had trouble standing, let alone walking and talking, and Pearson, who knew DePoe only too well, was horrified as he saw President Charles de Gaulle moving in DePoe's direction. A diplomatic disaster loomed. But when de Gaulle pointed to one of his Italian campaign medals, DePoe snapped to attention, crisply said, "*Oui, mon général,*" and for two or three minutes they conversed in French before the petrified eyes of Canadian diplomats and journalists. De Gaulle moved on, the spectators heaved a silent, collective sigh of relief, and, with a deep gulp of wine, DePoe slumped back into his torpor.

At the conclusion of the trip, Pearson had a less successful encounter with DePoe. As the other reporters were settling into the plane taking the prime minister and his entourage back to Ottawa, DePoe arrived, suffering from the mother of all hangovers. With a throbbing head and heaving stomach, he shuffled by Pearson and threw up either on or just missing the prime minister, at which Pearson exclaimed, "Oh, Norman, for heaven's sake!" "Norman was sick as a dog on the plane," Donald Macdonald says. "I don't know how we avoided not having to get rid of him right then and there. Certainly there was a lot of pressure from CBC Ottawa."

"But Norman was brilliant," Macdonald adds. "There was nobody quite like him, and we needed him. We had to hang on to him at any price as we developed the news service. Nobody else could have gotten away with the things he did, but he had such shining talents. Most of us felt that Norman had to be protected from himself."

At a time when drinking among Ottawa correspondents was prodigious, DePoe's consumption impressed even his colleagues. "A normal day," says John Drewery, "would see him have a couple of vodkas in the morning and maybe a couple of beers, then a couple of glasses of wine at lunch, followed by three or four vodkas in the afternoon, and then over at the Press Club at night he'd start drinking seriously." No wonder that, in his memory, Ottawa's National Press Club named one of its bars the DePoe Bar.

During his palmy days in Ottawa, DePoe drunk was better than most of his colleagues sober. In Quebec for election day in 1966, he guzzled vodka all evening in the press room, until his voice became slurred, his face was flushed, and his clothes were rumpled. A half-hour before airtime, he staggered off to a typewriter, pecked out his story on Daniel Johnson's victory, and at airtime delivered a lucid, insightful account, by far the best report broadcast by anybody that night. When he returned to the press room, his fellow reporters, who had feared a disaster, broke into applause as DePoe went back to the bar for another vodka.

Time and time again that scenario was repeated. Before his filmed reports, he would often be slouched and mumbling, but when the camera was on, he was suddenly alert, vital, and compelling. On live election programs or political conventions, his depth of knowledge and insight gave a lustre to political reporting that has never been matched. "He reached people with a kind of journalistic magic," said Charles Lynch.

At night he would often be called away from the Press Club to do a late-breaking story for "The National" from a studio in the nearby Chateau Laurier Hotel. The studio was remote-controlled from the CBC station miles away, so no one at the station was ever aware of how much DePoe had had to drink, although it didn't seem to matter because regardless of his condition he would come through with his usual brilliance. But as he grew older and drank more, cracks began to appear in his professionalism. On one occasion a glassy-eyed DePoe was introduced on "The National," but as he began to speak he started to hesitate, repeating himself and searching for words. His head sank lower and lower, and the instant he had signed off, his head thudded to the table. There he remained, snoring for more than an hour before the CBC arranged for someone to take him home.

DePoe's friends and colleagues who were concerned about his alcoholism occasionally tried to steer him away from his self-destructive drinking, although they more often joined him. "He'd sleep with a bottle of gin or vodka under his bed, gulping when he'd wake up in the middle of the night," says Donald Macdonald. When he was on live or recording a program, he would sip a glass of what appeared to be water, but which in fact was vodka or gin.

Macdonald once arranged to get DePoe into a Toronto clinic, but before going to the clinic, DePoe went on an all-day drinking spree with some colleagues. He also was easing the pain of a romance gone wrong. A fellow journalist, Peter Reilly, decided to be a good Samaritan and escort him to the clinic. Reilly loved liquor as much as DePoe, and both were quite looped when they arrived late at night at the locked front door of the clinic. After pounding on the door, they were finally let in, but confusion arose over who was to be admitted. The admissions nurse was new in Canada and didn't recognize DePoe, but she did have DePoe's name on her list of people to be admitted. When Reilly went down the hall to look for the night doctor, DePoe declared that he, in fact, was Reilly. John Drewery, who had been drinking with the two much of the day, was sitting in a bar across from the CBC when DePoe returned with his tale of switched identities. "He told us," Drewery says, "that Reilly, protesting wildly, had been detained at the clinic overnight, and he regaled us with a graphic description of Reilly being placed into a straitjacket and borne away, struggling and protesting."

The confusion was cleared up the next day, and DePoe was installed in the clinic for several weeks. It brought, however, only a temporary respite from his alcoholism. "Norman knows intellectually that he has to stop drinking if he is to live much longer, but he doesn't know in his gut," the clinic doctor told Macdonald. "He'll be back."

Macdonald feels DePoe needed or wanted the alcoholic stimulation to buttress his self-assurance in the face of ferocious competition, relentless and ever-present deadlines, the stress of performing live on television, and the challenge of being famous.

"He wanted life to be larger than life, and he was always augmenting it," says Nada Harcourt, who became a senior CBC program executive and once dated DePoe when she was a news script assistant. "He enjoyed the glamour and a sense of style, but he also had a quality of being a vulnerable boy. He loved the sense of power he got from his television prominence, but he had an inner feeling of 'Do I deserve this? Can I satisfy this? No, no, I can't.' That's one reason why he drank."

"Norman drank a lot because he got bored very easily," says Mary DePoe. "He thought he was a very charming fellow and the life of the party when he was drinking. But I don't really know what devils were chasing him, even though he went through a lot of doctors, a lot of dry-out centres, and a lot of soul-searching. Near the end, when he was in such pain from pancreatic cancer, the doctors would give him Valium, but he'd wash it down with vodka. He figured he wasn't going to get better, so why not do what he wanted to."

He often had long conversations with writer Morley Callaghan about Paris and Spain in the 1920s, and once fulfilled a fantasy by fighting in a Spanish bullring with yearling rejects from a professional ring. "He just had to live this Hemingway fantasy and get into the bull ring with a cape," says Mary. "The bull charged, and his horn caught Norman's thigh. I was in the stands screaming and thinking, 'How am I going to get Norman's body out of Spain? If I can get it to London, then I'll be able to get it home.' But it was just a bruise. He loved it."

DePoe's drinking accelerated in proportion with his increasing frustration with new bosses who had little tolerance for his carousing and less respect for his talents. They wanted more obedience, but DePoe offered them only contempt. He left television after a confrontation with TV news head Mike Daigneault, who had just joined the CBC from a Montreal newspaper. "Daigneault and Norman were just war in the night," says Mary. "At one point Norman threatened to punch him out, and he was taking off his coat when somebody grabbed him. He also wanted to kick the shit out of Daigneault's boss, Denis Harvey. Norman was just on a collision course with authority."

DePoe's defiance of authority is ironic in light of his sentimental attachment to the military, gained during his Italian campaign service in the war. He adopted a parade-ground demeanour at times, and on occasion he'd bring home from the Press Club West Coast broadcaster Jack Webster, who had been a colonel in the British army. They would parade about DePoe's home, shouting orders to each other. "The two of them would be marching up and down with broomsticks, being soldiers on parade into the dawn," says Mary.

DePoe's hero in journalism was *Maclean's* magazine Ottawa writer Blair Fraser, who was like DePoe in his emotionality and philosophy, if not in his appetite for alcohol. When Fraser died in a canoeing accident, DePoe was devastated. "A part of Norman died with Blair," says Mary. He was infuriated that "The National" gave only a fifteen-second mention of Fraser's death. In a memo to his editors in Toronto, he sarcastically wrote, "I would like to put on the record my appreciation of the fact that you found time even to mention the death of Blair Fraser. . . . You found those 15 seconds without even a picture of a Canadian who was greater than any of you shits will ever be."

DePoe was as reckless with money as he was with booze, spending it faster than he earned it and piling up bills. "When we really were broke," says Mary, "we'd go to a fancy restaurant like Winston's and order the best and have a good time." DePoe also miscalculated his CBC pension, getting less in retirement than he thought he would receive. Despite his profile, DePoe's paycheque at its height was only about $30,000 a year. "I never wanted to be a millionaire," he said near his death in 1980. "All I ever tried to do is report as honestly as I could. . . . All I want on my tombstone now are the words, 'He was a good reporter.'"

Characteristically, DePoe's will provided funds for a Toronto Press Club drink-as-much-as-you-like party after his funeral. Those there that night swear they could hear his raspy voice belting out an Irish lullaby above the bacchanal.

DePoe's escapades made him memorable, but his reporting made him legendary. In bringing the news to Canadians, he played, in his sunshine days, a fundamental role in helping us become more aware of ourselves. No broadcast journalist did it better.

The Correspondents

Although he yearned for the job, Norman DePoe was never a foreign correspondent, as management feared him being out of sight. He was, however, right at home with the lifestyles of most of the CBC foreign correspondents. "Correspondents were the Spitfire pilots of CBC journalism," says Donald Macdonald, who nursed them in his role as chief news editor during their most boisterous years in the 1960s.

How such a mild-mannered soul as Macdonald could coax journalistic brilliance out of such a ferociously competitive, workaholic, hard-drinking, wild-living, temperamental bunch of characters is a mystery. A small-town New Brunswicker, Macdonald joined CBC News in 1941. He was always a writer, an editor, or a manager and never a reporter, and yet he understood both the professional and personal emotional needs of his rambunctious charges. He put old-fashioned news values into a contemporary TV context while simultaneously counselling some of his charges about their liquor intake and helping to straighten out the complicated love affairs of others. For some correspondents he had to do both.

"They were all charming, engaging, hard-driving," says Bill Cunningham, who, at different times, was a correspondent himself and their boss. "They never talked about mortgages, wives, families, money, or anything practical. Nothing counted except their addicting job."

It is the correspondents' job to be in the thick of world events, facing the threat of snipers, booby traps, tear gas, and capture during wars, revolutions, and uprisings; interviewing presidents, prime ministers, and revolutionaries; investigating plots; and sitting around in bars endlessly waiting for something to happen. Unlike most contemporary journalists, correspondents in the 1950s and 1960s also spent considerable off-the-record time with leaders and would-be leaders who spoke openly in private in a way that's rarely seen today.

Knowlton Nash found covering American politics had its lighter moments, such as when he interviewed a topless shoeshine girl in San Francisco about the economic proposals of then would-be California governor Ronald Reagan. "If Reagan, gets in," she said, "there goes topless right out the window, and there goes a lot of jobs." Reagan himself defended both his conservatism and his acting at a small barbecue for like-minded friends, including actors Andy Devine, Robert Taylor, Walter Brennan, and Buddy Ebsen. "Damn it," Reagan told Nash, "I was not such a bad actor. Really not bad at all."

As a correspondent in Washington, Nash privately heard a constant stream of obscenities pour out of the presidential mouth of Lyndon Johnson, a characteristic no one reported at the time. LBJ particularly liked the word "shit." He talked of "horseshit," "bullshit," "ratshit," "catshit," and, at the time of a coup in Vietnam, referred to it as "that coup shit." "I may not know much, but I know the difference between chicken shit and chicken salad," he shouted at Nash during one Oval Office briefing. At the same briefing, he startled reporters around his desk when he said of a political rival, Henry Cabot Lodge, that "the goddamn son of a bitch can't find his ass with both hands." He said another politician "doesn't know enough to pour piss out of his boots." Of the prime minister of a small country, he said, "I've got his pecker in my pocket." Out of the public eye, he picked and scratched everything, from his nose to his ears, his rear end and his crotch, and he referred to his private parts as "Jumbo." He liked to tell stories of getting reports from State Department officials – "cookie pushers" he called them – while he was sitting on the toilet. He apparently felt that position gave him leverage over his briefers.

Personal chats with Jack and Bob Kennedy were far less sulphurous, although at times Jack Kennedy had a sharp tongue. He once called prime minister John Diefenbaker "a prick" and "a son of a bitch." Bob Kennedy once told Nash, "My brother thought Diefenbaker a contemptible old fool. In fact, my brother really hated only two men, one was Sukarno [the dictator of Indonesia] and the other was Diefenbaker." When Nash chatted with Diefenbaker privately about Kennedy, the prime minister said Kennedy was "a hot head . . . a fool . . . and a boastful young son of a bitch."

Such comments are not likely to be voiced in conversations with correspondents these days because ever since Watergate political leaders have been leery of revealing to journalists, even confidentially, their true thoughts.

But private conversations abounded in the 1950s and 1960s. Michael Maclear chatted with Fidel Castro and Jawaharlal Nehru, Norman DePoe with a series of Canadian prime ministers, and Stanley Burke with most European leaders. Sometimes conversations took place informally in hotel rooms while the leaders were travelling or in some exotic locations, as when Nash met Cuban revolutionary leader Che Guevara. Nash met Guevara in a Cuban sugar-cane field where Guevara, with about fifty armed guards, was cutting cane. He told Nash he liked John Diefenbaker because Diefenbaker hated Kennedy. Guevara agreed to do an interview in which he was to drive a tractor up to a point beside the camera, get out, and begin the interview. Unfortunately, as it was being filmed, Guevara turned his tractor the wrong way, and the producer, Don Cameron, chased after him swearing and yelling, "No! No! This way. Oh God, you idiot!" Ominous clicks were heard as the startled guards raised their guns, but Guevara smiled at the wildly gesticulating Cameron, nodded, turned his tractor around, and did it again. "Good boy!" shouted Cameron.

Don Cameron

Don Cameron's creative instinct sometimes put his correspondents on the spot when he tried to enliven dull programs with opening antics. Nash, who hadn't been on horseback since he was a child riding a pony, hung on for dear life atop a giant horse as he, at Cameron's insistence, galloped into a thundering herd of about three hundred cattle to deliver his opening commentary for a Latin American summit conference being held in Uruguay. On another occasion Cameron had Nash scamper over a rooftop in Atlantic City and interview a flagpole sitter as the opening for a program on a Democratic presidential nominating convention.

Cameron worked exuberantly at the edge of disaster, almost always pulling it off, but sometimes he ran into trouble, as he did in covering Martin Luther King's "I Have A Dream" speech in Washington. The problem was that he had only one microphone at the Lincoln Memorial, where King was to speak from the top of the steps, and before King began, Cameron was orchestrating a number of interviews. He had each correspondent toss the microphone to the next when they'd finished using it, but one toss was mis-aimed and the microphone hit interviewee Marlon Brando on the side of his head, stunning him momentarily. More trouble came when the program was aired that night. It had been a remarkably peaceful demonstration, and Cameron wanted to highlight that aspect. As usual, however, he and the correspondents were doing everything at the last minute. The station from which the CBC was broadcasting back to Canada happened to be airing to its local audience a historical program on an earlier march that had turned violent. As Nash read his narration about the peacefulness of King's march, errant technology was sending the local signal to Canada. Viewers heard Nash's description, but saw riots, soldiers, machine guns, and a lot of blood.

As executive producer of "Newsmagazine," Cameron was the correspondents' ringmaster, directing their efforts and, as often as he could, accompanying them on jaunts around the world. At the drop of a news bulletin, Cameron would fly off to Hong Kong, Saigon, Beirut, Tel Aviv, Buenos Aries, Moscow, London, Paris, Washington, or anywhere something was happening. "Don's idea of a good time was to be on the great silver bird, lighting up that first cigarette, having a martini, flirting with the stewardess, and going anywhere," says Bill Cunningham.

He revelled in the adrenalin surge that comes from being in the middle of a war, a riot, a crisis, a disaster. News was his life, and when he wasn't covering it he was in a bar talking about it. His narrow escapes and daredevil escapades were fuelled by rum and martinis, and driven by his sense of mischief.

Cameron had a remarkable instinct for television journalism. He knew what would elevate a humdrum report into a fascinating story, and he knew how to design a program to assist public understanding of a complicated issue. He was a seat-of-the-pants production genius.

More than most, he relished female companionship, and many women found irresistible his little-boy-lost demeanour and scampish grin. Wherever he was – in a London hotel, a Fifth Avenue apartment, the Montmartre, or on the streets of Saigon – he'd cry, "I need someone!" His reputation spread among hotel bell captains in Asia and Europe, and once when a CBC crew checked in the Hilton Hotel in Hong

Kong, the bell captain, seeing CBC stickers on their luggage, asked, "Where's Mr. Cameron? How's my crazy friend? He some fella. My! My! Oh, he like ladies."

In Saigon he once was befriended by a policeman who perched him on the back of a Vespa motorcycle, and together they spent the entire night going from party to party and girl to girl. They returned in time for Cameron to begin his morning assignment with his colleagues.

Even a heart attack did not slow his hyperactive libido. Hospitalized in Toronto, Cameron was brought back to health by a stunning nurse, who at one point provided too much care for the hospital's liking. Inopportunely, the head nurse came upon Cameron and his angel of mercy one night as they cuddled under his oxygen tent. The nurse was fired, and Cameron was judged well enough to go home to recover. No wonder his nickname was Craze.

In time he became head of CTV News, moderating his style only slightly as he rose in the executive ranks. He died in 1991 at age sixty-six.

Journalistic Rock 'n' Rollers

Cameron was not the only peripatetic journalist to enjoy amorous adventures in his hours away from the job. One correspondent pushed his romantic luck when he took his Russian bride on a honeymoon to Paris, but left her with another correspondent for a week while he gambolled along the Rhine with an old German flame. When his frolic was over, he returned to Paris, picked up his bride, and continued the honeymoon. Another hot-blooded correspondent had, by awkward coincidence, three girlfriends all living in the same Toronto apartment building and had to carefully time his visits to avoid confrontation. His timing failed on one notable occasion when, after an afternoon dalliance with one, he ran into his second friend in the apartment lobby. He quickly said he was about to visit her, and they trotted up to her apartment. A couple of hours later, as he was again walking through the lobby, he was stunned to run into his third playmate. Again, he said he was just coming to visit her and wearily trudged up to her apartment. At midnight, thoroughly exhausted, he repaired to a nearby bar where he met several correspondent colleagues and, with a wan smile, reported on his encounters.

One London correspondent came home early from an assignment

in Vietnam to find his girlfriend entertaining two of his colleagues in bed. Another correspondent fell head over heels in love with a Toronto reporter much younger than him. One day at his foreign base, he told his wife he was going to the store to buy a newspaper and then took a cab to the airport, flew to Toronto, and joined his young lover, never to return home again. Still another, on assignment in Rio de Janeiro, had a madcap affair with a Copacabana beach girl named Lulu. For a couple of years, he jetted between his home base and Rio until he shifted his romantic inclinations to another hemisphere. A broadcaster whom the correspondents respected for his amorous adventures was producer, writer, and actor Lister Sinclair. "He wasn't really a handsome man," says make-up artist Elaine Saunders. "But he was like Trudeau. His brain was sexy. Go figure! He just dazzled them with his brains."

The correspondents more than lived up to the old sailor's dictum of a girl in every port. Away from home half to two thirds of the time, these fast-moving, fast-living correspondents seldom had the home life most people know. Their predilection for female company may have stemmed, in part, from the real danger they faced in wars and revolutions and in part because of the need for release from the constant tensions of fierce competition, ever-present deadlines, and the fear of losing self-confidence. Those who were married either had wives of extraordinary understanding and patience, or they married and divorced several times. One veteran correspondent says, looking back on his salad days, "My mistresses would always complain that they wanted to get married and be treated as a wife, and my wife always complained that she wanted to be treated like a mistress."

Drinking was another refuge from the correspondents' chaotic pace, and sometimes it had its advantages, as Matthew Halton once discovered. He and correspondent James M. "Don" Minifie were partying in a London hotel during a Second World War blitz attack. Minifie later said he was "on the wagon" at the time, but that Halton was collapsed on the floor from his liquid intake when bombs started falling nearby. Minifie went over to a window to look out. Suddenly a bomb exploded, smashing the hotel windows and driving glass splinters into Minifie's eye while Halton snoozed blissfully on the floor. He lost an eye and swore never again to go on the wagon.

"Why did we drink so much?" asks Bill Cunningham. "Well, because it was fun. It was a great party. If we weren't out chasing a story, we'd have four rum and cokes for lunch and for dinner another four rum and cokes and some wine, and then we'd sip brandy or rum or whatever through the night. Only the serious drinkers like DePoe or Reilly would drink much for breakfast. It was a lifestyle, a camaraderie. I thought the party was going to go on forever. It didn't."

The camaraderie was rooted in sharing the same dangers, the same deadlines, the same personal and professional pressures. The correspondents were a band of brothers (there were no female CBC correspondents in this era), and like brothers, they had their rivalries and ferociously protected their beats. Once, in Paris, reporter Bill Boyd was knocked flat by Paris correspondent Doug Lachance, who thought Boyd was London correspondent Don Gordon poaching on his turf.

A similar territorial possessiveness set Far East correspondent Tom Gould's teeth on edge when CBC reporter Peter Reilly joined him in Saigon for a program on Vietnam. "They just seemed to hate each other's guts," says producer Bill Harcourt, who was assigned to put the program together. "They were either yelling at each other or they were each sending cables of resignation to Toronto."

At one point in the assignment, Don Cameron, who was in Saigon as executive producer of the program, got into a battle with Reilly over the affections of a young lady from Tu Do Street. When Harcourt came upon them, Cameron was choking Reilly. "The son of a bitch tried to kill me!" Reilly complained.

Reilly's sensitivity and sentimentality made him that rare kind of journalist who instinctively understands both the basics of good journalism and the importance of translating a story into vivid TV pictures. More than any correspondent of the period, except for Michael Maclear and Morley Safer, Reilly knew the critical importance of TV production values. Later Reilly was briefly head of CTV News but quit in a public spat with CTV director John Bassett, became a Conservative member of Parliament in a short, pyrotechnical political career, and then later was a correspondent for CBC's "the 5th estate." His runaway emotions never ebbed, and he died at age forty-four in 1976, a victim of his lifestyle.

Norman DePoe was a better reporter than Reilly, but he had less interest in production values than his colleague. Their rivalry sometimes had an edge, but they were more friendly than Morley Safer and anchor Larry Henderson, who were constantly at war. Rivals Stanley Burke and Michael Maclear once tangled at a now legendary dinner for CBC foreign correspondents in Toronto.

It was an annual dinner at which an award called the Bull's Pizzle, an elaborate corkscrew, was given to the correspondent who had committed the most outrageous act of defiance against the CBC bureaucracy during the preceding year. Burke won one year for the most creative expense claim. He had moved from New York to Paris and tried to claim his children's nanny and a small yacht in his moving expenses. Minifie won another year for an emotional condemnation of management's refusal to let News use colour film. "Blood is red, damn it!" he had thundered at management officials. But his passion got him nowhere at the time.

The dinner highlight one year, however, was not the awarding of the Bull's Pizzle but a clash among Burke, Maclear, and Gould over a young woman. It developed into a general mêlée when a bowl of won ton soup was poured over one correspondent's head, another correspondent was grabbed by the throat, several slid to the floor, more due to alcohol consumption than fisticuffs or wrestling, and chairs were overturned and dishes were smashed or hurled at the wall. Chinese waiters looked in, appalled and petrified at the spectacle, shrieking in Cantonese above the din. When the police arrived, the private dining room was a wreck, but after paying for the meal, the broken crockery, and the chairs, and being warned never to return, the scratched and bruised correspondents went to a nearby bar together to finish off the evening – all except Maclear, who went to the hospital where his neck was put into a brace.

It was a sorry-looking group, including Maclear in his neck brace, that met with management the next morning to discuss, among other things, expense accounts.

While Burke's expense account won the Bull's Pizzle, the expense account of a London-based cameraman won almost as much admiration from the correspondents. He would overestimate his excess baggage voucher for camera equipment and use the difference to pay for a long-legged blonde companion who travelled much of the world with him and became known as Miss Excess Baggage. Bill Cunningham was particularly inventive with his account, with claims such as $50 for "piranha repellant"; flights on "Gaucho Airlines," which didn't issue receipts; "wharfage fees"; and "research assistance." A correspondent in Africa put down $100 for a "snack for Baluba Tribesmen," and correspondents visiting Seoul would routinely bring back hotel bills from the General Walker Hotel with daily charges for "Korea Plan." That lasted until an eagle-eyed news manager named Ron Johnson discovered that "Korea Plan" meant room, meals, and young lady. He ordered that, in the future, only American Plan and European Plan at hotels were acceptable.

Sometimes, though, oddly labelled expense claims would get past the bookkeepers. PACR was one such claim. It was a favourite until it was discovered to be an acronym for Pissed Away, Can't Remember. One correspondent claimed a fee for Increasing Joy Forever as an expense item. It turned out to be the name of a geisha girl who had done some research for a news report. Producer Don Cameron listed a fee of $150 for the rental of three hundred head of cattle used in the opening of a program in Uruguay. Perhaps the expense account admired most by the correspondents was that of NBC correspondent Jack Perkins, who was being reassigned from Hong Kong and whose account listed "Moving expenses and personal junk." It was approved. It was only later that NBC management discovered "personal junk" meant precisely that – the boat he'd bought for himself in Hong Kong.

Expense account ingenuity was rarely done for personal gain, it more often was necessary to cover expenses such as bribery and other costs that were beyond allowed limits, but had to be paid to get a story. Inevitably the correspondents all wound up spending some of their own money on their stories, and that, plus the reality that being a character is expensive, is why most correspondents were usually broke.

Today's correspondents are a different breed. Bill Cunningham says, "The ones today are much better educated, much more disciplined, more conscious of their responsibilities, and much more anal retentive. You just don't have the characters anymore. The managers have squeezed them out and taken over."

Mike Duffy

One of the few remaining characters in Canadian TV news is Mike Duffy, although even he has, in his later years, become less outrageous and more conformist. In his CBC Ottawa days, his cherubic shape and distinctive style, his insider knowledge, and his hard digging made him a memorable on-air personality. Duffy didn't quite live up to Norman DePoe's standard of liquid intake, but he came close, and, like DePoe, he enjoyed partying to the wee hours. He also enjoyed food, which partly accounts for his expanding presence on the TV screen. He's been known to devour two complete dinners at a sitting, from soup to pie and ice cream.

His on-air style was intimate and gave the impression of letting the audience in on political secrets only he knew. No one had more sources on Parliament Hill than Duffy. "He had an incredible number of contacts," says Peter Mansbridge, who was Duffy's Ottawa colleague in the mid-1970s. "He knew everybody, every politician, their wives, their kids, and where to find them at eight in the morning or eight at night. He knew everything that was happening. And he was certainly a character." His mischievous demeanour made him friends but occasionally got him into trouble, such as the time he was doing a live report from Edmonton. In a brief warm-up to check out the satellite feed, Duffy was chatting with the anchor in Toronto and, feeling frisky, portrayed himself as a pornographic fiction writer. In a flight of torrid fancy, he vividly depicted himself as a lusty Lothario arising from his mistress on a well-used bed, graphically offering details of their lovemaking. As a private conversation it was hilarious, but Duffy and his colleagues forgot that thousands of Canadians with satellite dishes could pick up on this kind of pre-program warm-up, and one of them who did on this occasion was Prime Minister Brian Mulroney and his wife, Mila. Mulroney apparently thought it was funny, but Mila was appalled. It was a graphic lesson that even off the air you can be, in fact, on the air to some.

Some of that Duffy ebullience has subsided with age and with becoming a program anchor for CJOH in Ottawa, CFTO in Toronto, and other stations operated by Doug Bassett. The changes in Duffy, in a way, reflect the changes over the last twenty or thirty years in the style of correspondents and in news anchors.

The Anchors

The faces and voices that millions of Canadians identified most closely with the news are those of the anchors. Unlike almost any other country, in Canada the news anchors are the real stars of television, much more so than singers, actors, or musicians. Canadian gossip magazines, such as *Frank*, more often feature journalists and anchors than entertainers. "With our entertainment stars, while they are extremely talented, there is the sense that unless they've made it in the States, they're not big enough. That doesn't happen with journalists," says Peter Mansbridge. "Our journalists have a sort of aura about them which has come down from generations."

That's not always true, however, as Mansbridge found out when he was speeding from Toronto to Ottawa one night and was stopped by a policeman. When the officer looked at his driver's licence, he said, "Peter Mansbridge!" Thinking his celebrity status might save him from getting a ticket, Mansbridge smiled brightly, "Yes, that's me." "Well," said the policeman, "you and I were in Scouts together in Ottawa in 1959. Those were great days. It's amazing, I never thought I would bump into you again." He paused and then said, "So tell me, Peter, what do you do now?" Mansbridge said he worked for the CBC. The policeman said, "Oh," and handed him a speeding ticket.

While Lorne Greene was the first TV news anchor as host of "Newsmagazine," where he reviewed the week's news, Gil Christie was the first anchor of a daily news report. It was inserted at the top of a weekday interview and talk show called "Tabloid." January 25, 1954, saw the first separate daily news program, anchored by the temperamental, much-travelled Larry Henderson. Within a couple of years, the program was seen coast to coast, and, to his delight, Henderson became a national celebrity. He resigned when his demand for a salary of $25,000 was rejected, and Earl Cameron, described as being "as Canadian as wheat," took over as anchor. Seven years later Cameron was dumped by Bill Cunningham, who had become executive producer of CBC-TV News. He brought Stanley Burke in from out of the cold as a correspondent to be the anchor.

Burke loved the attention he got, but hated the confinement of the studio. "It's a very humbling experience to realize that just because you sit there and say some words every night that somehow people think you are endowed with an aura," Burke says. The "words" to which Burke referred are seen by the anchor on a teleprompter that rolls the script in front of the camera so that the anchor appears to be looking directly at the audience. Before such devices were available, producers tried different ways to have the anchor look into the camera instead of having their head down reading the script. CBS producer Don Hewitt, who now produces "60 Minutes," once tried to have anchor Douglas Edwards read Braille script. The idea was to have him look straight into the camera while his fingers flicked over the Braille bumps. It didn't work because Edwards couldn't learn Braille.

As news anchor, Burke was frustrated by union rules that, at the time, forbade him from writing scripts for "The National." He turned his energies to speaking on behalf of a few causes, particularly the cause of the Biafrans in their struggle for independence from Nigeria. He became so involved that he quit the CBC to spend his time lobbying the Canadian government to be more supportive of Biafra. He went on to become a writer and a newspaper publisher in British Columbia.

The fiery-tempered, highly skilled journalist and announcer Warren Davis stepped briefly into "The National's" hot seat, but a few months later his frustrations over the same restrictive union rules erupted, and to avoid murder or suicide, he quit. During his short tenure, he had had many temper tantrums involving high-decibel cursing, smashing furniture, falling off his anchor chair in anger on one occasion, and throwing a typewriter out a window on another. "He used to kick the walls in, literally," says longtime colleague Lloyd Robertson. "I remember one time he got so angry he drove his fist through a wall and actually broke his hand. The union drove him just crazy. They would goad him because he dared to have an office in the news room, and they would throw notes under his door saying, 'You're an asshole' and 'You can't read the news.' One night just as 'The National' went on the air, he snarled at one union man, 'You son of a bitch!' and a bit of it got on the air. He threatened people and he could not control himself."

Lloyd Robertson

When Davis left, Lloyd Robertson moved into "The National" anchor seat and stayed until he was wooed away by CTV in 1976. Robertson hasn't always been the calm, smooth anchor that he appears to be. Nerves got to him once when he was anchoring a motorcycle race on ice and was opening the program on the track as the race got underway. The plan for him to finish his opening just as the motorcycles came into view behind him should have given him ample time to move off the track before they raced by. The timing, however, was off slightly, and halfway through his live opening, the sound of oncoming motorcycles told him something was wrong. He took a quick glance behind him and saw that they were heading straight for him. He says, "I thought, 'I'm getting out of here,' and I simply took off. Live on camera, I threw the mike over the boards, scrambled over myself, and wound up on my rear."

Robertson's introduction to hosting network programs was similarly abrupt. As a beginner he was co-hosting the Queen Mother's presentation of colours to the Black Watch with veteran announcer Byng Whittaker, who was known to imbibe generously. After an evening of drinking, Robertson went to a breakfast meeting with Whittaker to plan the program. A huge breakfast and a bottle of Scotch were on the table, and Whittaker jovially ordered his tyro co-anchor to drink up. "I can't drink at eight o'clock in the morning," Robertson said to himself. So he sipped his Scotch from time to time, watering it down when Whittaker wasn't looking. Then he went to the bathroom and threw it down the sink. "Byng promptly poured me another one. I went through three or four Scotches, and he finished most of the bottle while eating his eggs," Robertson remembers. On the live program, Whittaker got angry at the director who was giving him instructions over his earphones, yanked off his headset, and threw it against a wall, shattering it to pieces. "It's your show, kid," he said to Robertson. "Take over!" And with that he headed out of the studio in high dudgeon, leaving Robertson to carry on alone. "That's when I really became a broadcaster of live events," says Robertson. "That was my baptism by fire."

Another moment of terror for Robertson came when he was opening "The National" at the Montreal Olympics in 1976 and got trapped on the roof of the CBC building. With a beautiful view of Montreal behind him, Robertson had taped the opening a few minutes before airtime, giving himself plenty of time to get from the roof down to the studio to do the rest of the program. Unfortunately, he discovered that the elevator doors were locked, so he and his crew began walking down, trying to find an unlocked door on a lower floor. They went down three or four flights and found all the doors locked. "So we went back up to the roof and began yelling down the seven or eight storeys to attract attention," says Robertson. Eventually a security guard came to the roof, but by this time "The National" was due on the air. Thirty seconds before air, someone grabbed reporter David Halton as he was walking down a hallway, thrust a script into his hands, and told him he was anchoring "The National." Three minutes after Halton began, a puffing Robertson arrived and took over.

When Robertson was anchoring the news on a prime-time program called "Week End," the producers tried to enliven the opening by having Robertson walk over to the desk, which looked like an ironing board, at the same time as it was pushed out towards him by a technician hiding behind a wall. The manoeuvre didn't always work, however. The desk got stuck a couple of times, and a few times it came out too quickly. "Sometimes it zoomed out at me, and once I almost became a soprano," Robertson says. "But most of the time I managed to duck out of the way. Eventually we gave up on the idea of shoving it out."

Robertson's most agonizing moment in broadcasting, however, was making the decision to leave the CBC to anchor the CTV News. "What you have to understand is that I was a baby of the CBC, and the CBC was my home," he says. "Departing my beloved CBC was the most traumatic event of my life. I felt as though I'd kicked my mother in the stomach."

He decided to go when CTV said it would let him report and write as well as anchor, which union rules at the CBC prevented him from doing, although that restriction was soon lifted. Robertson joined the venerable Harvey Kirck as co-anchor of CTV News, soon dubbed by one columnist "The Happy and Grumpy Hour." While Kirck thought a co-host was not a bad idea, he was "a little twitchy" about maintaining his status. Because he'd been working at CTV for thirteen years, he successfully demanded that he be paid 13 per cent more than Robertson. "I don't think Lloyd knows that, but he raised my salary a whole lot," says Kirck. Raising the salary was one thing, but raising a seat was another. At a rehearsal Robertson's chair was raised so he would appear the same height as the six-foot-four Kirck. "He got a little testy about that," says Robertson. At the next rehearsal, Kirck's chair was lowered so he would match Robertson's height. "But he raised his chair up again so he was higher than I was," Robertson says. "Then the producer wanted to raise my chair." Finally, Kirck glowered at Robertson and the producers, saying, "Goddamn it, the chairs are going to stay they way they are and that's that!"

After so many years at the CBC, Robertson lived in dread that his past would come back to haunt him, and a year or so after his switch, it happened. "I'm Lloyd Robertson. For CBC News, goodnight," he said at the end of the CTV News, leaving Kirck open-mouthed, saying, "What?"

Robertson had trouble of a different kind a short time later when he was the innocent victim of a water-pistol fight in the CTV newsroom that broke out just before the news went to air. One editor decided to escalate the fight by hurling a pail of water at his adversary as the victim came through a door to the newsroom. "When he thought the editor was coming through, he threw the pail of water," says Robertson. "Unfortunately I happened to be just coming back from the make-up room at that very moment. I came through the door instead and got soaked." Robertson was due on the air shortly and ordered the culprit to rush out and buy him a new shirt and tie in time for the program.

Kirck also had the occasional problem. Once while on the air, he was reading his teleprompter faster than the technician was rolling it, and he glared into the camera and said to a mystified audience, "Keep up with me!" He'd thought he was in rehearsal and talking to the technician. Occasionally Kirck got snarled in election coverage gone wrong, as in the 1974 federal election when there was a disastrous computer breakdown at CTV. Kirck and his colleagues simply stole the results from CBC and added a bit here and there. "It was agony, faking it like that," he says. On another occasion, as the news went to air, the transmission lines from Ottawa went down, but the producers didn't know it. When Kirck introduced an Ottawa item, nothing came up. Kirck hastily introduced another Ottawa story, which also didn't appear. That happened several more times, and to fill the eight minutes of missing stories from Ottawa, Kirck ad libbed and read obscure news agency stories. It was a nightmare, and as the newscast ended, Kirck signed off by saying, "I'm Harvey Kirck, I think." In one way, this was an appropriate comment, since Kirck is not his original name. His real name is Harvey Krick, but one of his early radio producers kept calling him Kirk. "It sort of stuck and so I just changed the letters around," Kirck says.

Like so many of his colleagues, Kirck's taste for wine and women has got him into trouble. "I've never met a woman I didn't like nor had a drink I didn't enjoy," he says. Eventually he went on the wagon for good, in 1984, and, after twenty-one years on daily news, he quit to do on-the-road feature pieces for "Canada A.M." and curmudgeonly pieces for "W5." He lost his job in 1987 in a CTV budget-cut blood bath that saw several CTV News veterans pushed out. "I'm still bitter and angry about that," Kirck says. "I probably always will be."

When Robertson left CBC, he was replaced on "The National" by Peter Kent and then Knowlton Nash. In a decade of anchoring, Nash, like Kirck and Robertson, has had occasional problems, including wishing everyone Happy New Year on Halloween. Another time, confused about the metric system, he reported on a storm in Britain which, he said, had dumped twenty-three kilometres of snow. In advance of an interview with U.S. Senator Wayne Morse, he told the senator that he would tap his knee under the table when it was time to wind up the live interview. When that time came, Nash tapped the senator's knee. Morse stopped dead in mid-sentence and glared at Nash. "Why are you grabbing my thigh?" he demanded. "To tell you, Senator, that your time is up," said a red-faced Nash.

Embarrassing moments abound in TV news broadcasts because of their last-minute nature. Once, on "The National," a picture of Adolf Hitler appeared instead of a picture of Richard Nixon. The mistake was caused by a mix-up between back-to-back stories on Nixon and the anniversary of Hitler's death. Another accidental switch occurred on stories of Dr. Henry Morgentaler and a hog industry report. A photo of a pig popped up instead of Dr. Morgentaler and then his picture appeared in the hog story. A technician pushing a wrong button caused utter confusion in a story about Soviet President Yuri Andropov threatening retaliation against some White House action. At the precise moment Andropov was speaking, the TV screen switched to a movie running on another channel. Viewers saw a cowboy slugging someone and saying, "Take that!" However, the technical miscue that produced the biggest storm of protest occurred not on the news but in the midst of the children's program "Sesame Street." Technicians with some idle time on their hands had downloaded a hard-core porno film from a satellite channel. Then someone pushed the wrong button. In the middle of a scene between Big Bird and Bert and Ernie, suddenly there was action of a decidedly different character. "For a minute and a half, we had a slice of hard porn. There was hell to pay over that," says CBC English network public relations head Tom Curzon.

Children's programming figured in another incident, this one the news department's fight over studio space. "The National" and "The Friendly Giant" shared the same studio, which meant desks, chairs, and lights had to be moved every day. When the news shifted to 10:00 P.M. in 1982, producers demanded some permanent space in the studio, but Friendly and his colleagues Rusty the Rooster and Jerome the Giraffe refused. A boardroom showdown was held between the director of "The National," Fred Parker, and Friendly, who had been Parker's childhood TV hero. For half an hour, Parker argued with Friendly, a.k.a. Bob Homme, a five-foot-eleven, soft-voiced, and gentle sixty-three-year-old who was very protective of his space. The Friendly–National crisis was ended, however, by a compromise that gave "The National" permanent use of about one third of the studio.

Anchors occasionally have problems with introductions, and when he was a correspondent in Washington, Knowlton Nash was once introduced as Knowlton Wash from Nashington. Another time he was introduced as George McLean. A more alarming beginning to the news occurred when a floor director was so emphatic in throwing Nash a cue to begin "The National" that his finger struck the edge of the camera and blood spurted over the script. Nash wiped it away and continued with the program. When he was anchoring the news on CJOH in Ottawa, Peter Stursberg had a habit of rushing into the studio at the last minute with little or no time to read over his script before going on the air. On one occasion his writers gave him a different opening.

Without a pause or a smile, he read, "Good evening. I'm Peter Rabbit and here is the news."

The Brain Drain

Canadian broadcast journalists are highly prized by American networks, and over the years many of them, especially from the CBC, have been lured south. Canadian reporters are generally better trained in both TV journalism and production and have experience in covering stories more complex than the fires, robberies, and murders that so dominate local American TV news shows. "You look around the networks in the U.S.," says Morley Safer, "and you keep tripping over Canadians. They're not being hired because of their accents. They're hired because they're very good, very well-trained reporters."

Safer, who now stars on the CBS program "60 Minutes," was an early recruit for the Americans, as was Peter Jennings, who now hosts the leading ABC television news and is the best of all American network news program anchors. Since then, American networks have scooped up dozens of other reporters and anchors, offering them considerably more money and a much bigger playing field. Most of them go eagerly, although some, such as Morley Safer, have gone by accident.

When he was a CBC correspondent, Stanley Burke hankered for an American network job, and he sent to New York a tape of an annual year-end CBC correspondents round-table program in which he had taken part. CBS officials looked at it and were impressed, not with Burke, but with Safer, and offered Safer a correspondent's job, which he accepted. "Stan was not amused," says Safer. "But I have Stanley Burke to thank for my CBS job." Safer's boss at the time was startled that CBS hired Safer. He'd called Safer "Mumbles," and said he'd never make it as a correspondent.

Safer's wry sense of humour appealed to the CBS recruiters. In the tape they reviewed, Burke, as a Paris correspondent, had commented that it's a myth that the French are great lovers and bad businessmen. "Does that mean, Stanley," asked Safer, "that the French are bad lovers and good businessmen?"

Peter Mansbridge

One anchor who resisted a million-dollar siren song from the Americans was Peter Mansbridge. CBS News president Howard Stringer wanted Mansbridge to host the network's morning show and tempted him both with dollars and talk of a future as Dan Rather's successor. Mansbridge, however, said that, on balance, he'd rather stay in Canada. He'd been urged to stay by colleagues, including Nash, who proposed to Mansbridge that, since he wanted to leave the anchor desk of "The National" in a year or so anyway, he would accelerate his departure to enable Mansbridge to take over in a few months' time. Over a post-midnight cup of cocoa, they agreed, and the next day when Stringer and his colleagues flew to Toronto for what they thought would be a final and successful wooing of Mansbridge, he told them no. They thought Mansbridge was just negotiating, and kept improving the salary and fringe benefits they were offering. They were stunned when Mansbridge gave a final and emphatic no.

For Mansbridge, it was a long way from the days in 1968 when he first discovered he had a good broadcast voice. He was filling in as a flight announcer at the airport in Churchill, Manitoba, when a passenger asked him, "Have you ever thought of being in radio?" The passenger was the manager of the local CBC Radio station and suggested to Mansbridge that he give up his job as a ticket agent and freight manager. He did. During his first night as a CBC trainee, the local night man left Mansbridge alone while a network program, "Between Ourselves," was running. Suddenly the network line went dead, and a terrified Mansbridge opened the microphone to utter his first words on radio: "One moment please." The program came back on in a few seconds. Later, Mansbridge was given the job of preparing a three-minute local newscast, and eventually he was posted to the CBC Winnipeg newsroom. His first live TV assignment was as co-host of the airport arrival ceremonies for Princess Margaret, who was flying into Winnipeg. He had been told the first person off the plane would be the princess, so as the door opened, he announced, "And there she is, Princess Margaret." The only problem was that it was an Air Canada flight attendant.

If that was a professional embarrassment for him, an even bigger one was going bald. "I started to lose my hair when I was twenty-five, and I kept thinking, 'This is going to stop any chance I have for moving ahead in television.'" When he was covering a trip to China by Saskatchewan Premier Allan Blakeney, he was excited to discover a Chinese miracle cure for baldness. He'd been directed to a small shop on the Shanghai waterfront that offered him bottles of one hundred pills each, and he was told, "Take fifteen a day for seven days, stop for a month, and then do it again the next month." Mansbridge thought this would not only cure his baldness, but he could make a fortune as well. "How many bottles have you got?" he asked the clerk, adding, "I'll take them all." He carried one hundred bottles of the baldness pills back to Regina, where he was based, and took them to the Regina medical health officer, who happened to be Chinese. He examined the pills and then announced, "Mr. Mansbridge, these pills will do nothing for your hair. They're aphrodisiacs. But, Mr. Mansbridge, would you give me one of the bottles?"

His worries about going bald led Mansbridge to comb what hair he had with considerable creativity. After he became a network anchor, he had the make-up artist rub a colouring into his scalp "to make it look like I had hair," he says. "It worked for a while, but the more hair I lost, the more area that had to be covered." "Now you have to powder his scalp so it doesn't shine," says Elaine Saunders. "He was very, very sensitive about being bald."

The CBS job offer finally eased his balding worries, especially when the anchor CBS hired instead of him had even less hair. "For me, that was a turning point," Mansbridge says. Anne Murray is a fan of Mansbridge, partly because he's bald. "There's a guy with balls!" she says. "There's a guy with a bald head who reads the news. Atta boy! I like a guy like that."

Because of the new, politically correct ethic in journalism that frowns upon private contact between journalists and politicians, Mansbridge was roundly criticized once when he and about fifty other guests went to dinner with Prime Minister Brian Mulroney at 24 Sussex Drive. He was labelled "a Tory hack" by some and admonished by many columnists and commentators. When a similar dinner invitation came from Prime Minister Jean Chrétien, Mansbridge's bosses told him he could not go. Now, whenever the prime minister or an Opposition party leader asks him to a social occasion, he has to refer it to senior CBC executives for a decision.

The high profile of news anchors also has drawbacks in their personal lives. Few people get more space in the gossip magazine *Frank* than Mansbridge, especially during the break-up of his marriage to Wendy Mesley. Since both of them were prominent TV personalities, their marriage and subsequent split wagged many tongues. While co-workers tiptoed around the separated couple, Mesley and Mansbridge managed to remain respectful of each other as colleagues. "God, those two handled it with such class," says Saunders, who has powdered and painted both of them. "Privately, he never said anything negative about her and she didn't about him. Now when they're together in the make-up room or on the set, they seem like good friends."

The publicity both over their parting and his subsequent relationship with TV star Cynthia Dale was painful for Mansbridge. "The gossip magazines here are not about show business, not about actors, but mostly are about the news business and journalists," says Dale. "In a way, we're more British in that, more like *Private Eye* and less like Americans, who focus on show people. As a news person, it's harder on Peter, whereas for me, I'm a performer, an actor, and we don't care if people are talking about us because that's what they should be doing." Mansbridge is lucky, though, says Saunders, "because Cynthia is a real homemaker, and he needs a woman who can be supportive in that way."

Another trial for Mansbridge was the ill-advised experiment of "CBC Prime Time News" at 9:00 P.M. and the subsequent return of "The National" at 10:00 P.M., along with the controversial departure of Pamela Wallin as Mansbridge's co-host. In retrospect, bringing Wallin into "Prime Time News" was almost inevitably going to set CBC News ablaze. It didn't seem that way at the time, however, for, like Mansbridge, Wallin was a highly regarded journalist with a track record and on-camera talent and appeal.

Pamela Wallin

Saskatchewan-born and -bred, Wallin began her professional life as a social worker at the penitentiary in Prince Albert. Her journalistic career started when she was asked to fill in for a sick friend who hosted a local CBC noon-hour radio program. She became a radio producer, moved to the CBC in Ottawa, then to Toronto as a researcher for "As It Happens."

After a two-year stint at the *Toronto Star*, she went back to Ottawa to work for CTV, where she became a nationally known reporter and host. As have all hosts, she has had her embarrassing on-air moments, including one where she referred to German Chancellor Helmut Schmidt as "Helmut Shit." She had trouble of a different sort with Liberal Leader John Turner at a garden party for reporters. It had been raining, and Wallin made a remark to Turner about her high-heel shoes sinking into the grass. Grinning at the male reporters around him, he responded, "Well, jeez, Pam, those high heels. I bet they've been under a lot of beds, eh?" "I laughed, but I was shocked," says Wallin, "and my initial assessment was that he'd had too much to drink. John is a good ole boy, a slap-you-on-the-back type, and he has a problem showing friendship for women."

Some time later during a TV interview, Wallin, who had heard stories of Turner's drinking, asked whether he had a booze problem. He said he sometimes overindulged, but it never affected his work. Off camera, he told Wallin, "Jeez, Pam, that was pretty rough." Wallin says "Most people believe I did it in retaliation for the shoes, but I didn't."

Drinking has been a major hazard for many Ottawa reporters as well as politicians. "All those guys," says Wallin, "were drinkers, womanizers, and hell-raisers, but that behaviour is no longer acceptable because we are scrutinizing politicians in a personal sense to a degree we never have before. You can't run around out there whooping it up and ask a cabinet minister about having a drinking problem. The standards apply to both sides."

Wallin found Pierre Trudeau a tough interview. On one occasion he took exception to a question from her about whether he would resign, and he lectured Wallin on the electoral system. "He just wiped the floor with me for all the viewers to see," she says. "I was mortified." Even so, Wallin was shaken to see how Trudeau's break-up with his wife, Margaret, affected him. "He seemed so tough, that nothing fazed him, and yet, in the House of Commons, he looked like a man beaten. It killed him, and to see him so vulnerable made us all sit back and say he's really hurting."

When Wallin left Ottawa she became co-host with J. D. Roberts of CTV's "Canada A.M.," but she found her co-host an uninspiring partner. "He's a very nice guy, but he really didn't understand some of the things he was doing," she says. She recalls once going to Los Angeles to interview actor Warren Beatty. She and Roberts were talking on the air about the interview when he said, "Well, have a good time. I hope you don't end up like Annette Bening, knocked up." Beatty and Bening had had a romance and she was pregnant. "When J. D. said that on the air," says Wallin, "I was just stunned. When we got off the set, I said, 'J. D., do you not understand that you cannot say knocked up on television? The implication is that I'm going to sleep with Warren Beatty. You can't do that!' He looked at me as if I were speaking Greek. He just didn't understand."

Worse for Wallin than her co-host's unfortunate comments was what she felt was his knowledge of news events such as the constitutional debates or political and economic issues. "He was," Wallin says, "a video jockey." Eventually, Roberts went to CBS in New York, where he now anchors major specials and occasionally fills in for Dan Rather.

The 3:15 A.M. wake-up calls for "Canada A.M." finally got to Wallin, and she was excited when rumours began circulating that she might be asked to join Mansbridge in co-hosting the CBC prime-time news and current affairs hour, replacing Barbara Frum, who had died in the winter of 1992. Mansbridge was part of the CBC's mating dance to hire Wallin. "I had coffee with Peter one morning at a restaurant because somebody told me he had concerns, and Peter had to be onside," Wallin says. "It was over something personal he thought I'd said. I told him I hadn't said it, and wouldn't. We were both in the middle of pretty difficult times. His marriage was coming apart and mine had just come undone, so it was not the pot's job to be calling the kettle black."

Mansbridge was satisfied and encouraged his bosses to hire Wallin, whom he had first met when he was reporting from Saskatchewan a dozen years earlier. At one point, Wallin says, "We had talked about him coming to 'Canada A.M.' when he was concerned about his future." Now, however, she was joining him at the CBC, and the deal was made in a flurry of long-distance phone calls among CBC officials in Toronto, her agent who happened to be travelling in Europe at the time, and Wallin, who was in her home town of Wadena, Saskatchewan for the grand opening of a beauty parlour she and her sister had started. "It's the most exciting job in Canadian journalism," the workaholic Wallin enthused when the hiring was announced.

"Pam, it's good to have you here," Mansbridge said as "CBC Prime Time News" began its 9:00 P.M. misadventure. Trouble loomed immediately. The program had a fuzzy focus, and as time would prove, the new hour was a disaster. After a while Mansbridge became decidedly unhappy. "The place was such a mess," he says. "The different time, the change in format, it was just a nightmare."

It was especially a nightmare for Wallin. "A lot of people were resentful of me," she says. "I had no allies, no team. There was resentment that I wasn't Barbara. I'm sure it offended a lot of people that I sat in her office, that I sat in her dressing room. The people who had worked with her on 'The Journal' did not identify with me in any way. And there was no connection with the news side. That was Peter's group. They were his writers, working in his style. But I had a different style. It's a pain in the ass when you try to write news scripts for different people. If I said I wanted a verb in a sentence, they got mad. I think they saw it as an affront."

"The CBC culture is a funny thing," says Larry Zolf, a colleague of both Wallin and Mansbridge. "It helps to have a long history and knowledge of where the bodies are buried." Wallin had neither, and she also felt her previous CTV and CBC experience didn't count for much among the writers, editors, and producers of the 9:00 P.M. program. She says, "People would say to me, 'That's not the way Barbara would have done it.' The 'Journal' people were used to Barbara and the news people were used to Peter. I guess I never had a chance. I can't change my personality. I can't say, 'Oh, I'll read anything you write and do any interview you want me to.' I have my own opinions."

Because of those opinions from the strong-willed Wallin, her colleagues nicknamed her "Pamzilla," "Pambo," and "Pamattola." "Pam Wallin, she's a tough nut, and she's demanding," says Elaine Saunders.

"It's awful to have people stop talking when you walk into a room," says Wallin. She hated the long meetings "Prime Time News" involved and had strong feelings not only about scripts and interviews but also about lighting, camera angles, and make-up. "Pam is very talented, but she never built her own constituency, and you have to do that at the CBC," says Lloyd Robertson. News executives became restless with Wallin, and so did Mansbridge, who preferred a solo role in the newscast. Before long, the hour was divided into Peter and Pam sections, removing her from the newscast. "My presence on the screen was deliberately cut back and minimized," she says. "It was an untenable situation, and I was desperately unhappy."

The acidic chemistry between Mansbridge and Wallin may have had its roots in their previous on-air work, Wallin thinks. "I had always worked as a co-host," she says. "My whole experience was working as part of a team. Peter had worked as a reporter and 'The National' had been a solo act. Despite his best intentions at the beginning, if they were in fact there, that's not what he wanted. In the end, he wanted his own thing. And who would want to share if they didn't have to?"

As the 1995-96 season approached, her contract was not renewed, and after rejecting a proposal to work on the CBC morning show from Halifax, she negotiated a deal with the CBC for a prime-time interview and phone-in program on its Newsworld channel. The program, called "Pamela Wallin Live," is produced by her own company.

When the program returned to its 10:00 P.M. time slot as "The National," "the 5th estate" veteran Hana Gartner stepped into Wallin's shoes as co-host of the rejuvenated hour. Gartner can be just as dogged as Wallin but is more knowledgeable about the sometimes Byzantine workings of the CBC. "Hana's very tough. She's a passive resister," says Saunders. She's also a witty workaholic with a less aggressive style than Wallin.

With a new co-host, a new (old) time of 10:00 P.M., and a return to the old title of "The National," the news hour started in the fall of 1995 what executive producer Tony Burman calls its "long march back." In the spring of 1996, with audiences well above a million and with eleven Genie nominations for the program, Burman announced, "We're back!"

Trouble at CTV

At the same time that Wallin's unceremonious departure from "Prime Time News" was a front-page story, CTV suddenly announced the firing of Lloyd Robertson's heir apparent, Keith Morrison. Morrison was a CBC and CTV veteran and until recently had been CTV's golden boy. He had been brought back to Canada from Los Angeles, where he was a highly paid anchor of local news and also reported for NBC, as CTV president John Cassaday's personal choice to succeed Robertson. The plan was, in time, to ease Robertson away from the CTV newscast and into documentaries and anoint Morrison as the new network news anchor. At the time of Morrison's hiring, Robertson was sixty. He asked Morrison, "I have to know, Keith, what Cassaday has told you about my job." "He's promised it to me," Robertson remembers Morrison replying. Robertson felt the graceful thing to do would be to step aside in a couple of years when his contract was up, and after a friendly discussion with Morrison, he told Cassaday he would do exactly that. In the meantime, Morrison would co-host "Canada A.M." and occasionally fill in for Robertson on the news. At the end of the first year, Robertson says, Morrison asked if he could fill in more often. Robertson estimated that with holidays and assignments, Morrison would be doing the news anchoring about a third of the time. As 1995 began, Robertson felt he was being squeezed to leave earlier than his contract expiry in September 1996, when word came back to him that Morrison had been saying to colleagues that Robertson might not live up to his commitment to leave. That outraged the normally placid Robertson. He told Cassaday, "You've got to stop this man. You've got to shut him up."

"I said till I was blue in the face that I would live up to my commitment to go in '96," he says. What also angered Robertson were reports that Morrison was telling friends that when he substituted for Robertson in January 1995, the audience ratings went up. "I was really angry with Keith," Robertson says. "I felt a bit betrayed. I had given up my job for this guy, and here he was seemingly trying to crowd me out early."

Meanwhile, Cassaday was hearing rumblings over Robertson's departure from several CTV board members, and there was also discomfort among CTV News bosses that Morrison was doing some work for NBC. Although Cassaday had high regard for Morrison's skills as a documentary-maker and believed that his distinctive style would enhance CTV News, he finally succumbed to these pressures and announced Morrison's dismissal. The would-be news anchor was stunned by his firing, feeling he had been unfairly and arbitrarily treated. It was a sentiment shared by a good many in broadcasting who themselves had been roughed up by the fast-changing and sometimes brutal world of broadcast journalism.

8

Flops, Hits, and Controversies

The tensions, rivalries, and jealousies that characterized the broadcast news hounds over the years were almost matched by the aggressive talents of current affairs producers, editors, and hosts. The 1960s saw the introduction of daring and defiant current affairs programming that flouted conventionality – and CBC management. "This Hour Has Seven Days," produced by a current affairs team led by Douglas Leiterman and Patrick Watson, reached new heights of popularity with an innovative style of in-your-face TV journalism, and then tried to overthrow a CBC president.

In the early years of radio, CBC current affairs programming had been earnest, insightful, somewhat academic, and occasionally provocative. The arrival of television changed everything in current affairs programming just as it had for news, and the personification of that change was an iconoclastic loner, Ross McLean.

Ross McLean

Ross McLean produced information programs that masqueraded as entertainment. His irreverent mix of the serious and the ridiculous was seen on the first daily current affairs program on television, "Tabloid," which began with an interview with the controversial anthropologist

Dr. Margaret Mead and ended with an interview with an Egyptian belly dancer, Samia Gamal. Another program featured an item on carrier pigeons, one of which got loose and remained in the studio for several weeks, feeding on technicians' leftover sandwiches. It was nicknamed the Mad Bomber because whenever the studio lights went on, it would swoop down and occasionally drop deposits, once splattering "Tabloid" host Dick MacDougal on the forehead during an interview.

McLean's pioneering efforts to popularize current affairs programs peaked with "Close-Up" in the late 1950s and early 1960s, a weekly network program that, in Pierre Berton's words, "was the daddy of all the information shows like '60 Minutes,' 'The Journal,' or 'the 5th estate.' They all owe their life to Ross McLean's 'Close-Up.'" Everybody who was anybody in TV journalism clustered around McLean, including Berton, June Callwood, Charles Templeton, J. Frank Willis, Jack Webster, Allan King, Daryl Duke, Patrick Watson, and Douglas Leiterman. McLean's list of interviewees, which included the gangster chief Lucky Luciano, Anne Landers, and President Tito, illustrated his style. He counterposed the famous with the infamous, controversy with serious issues, on the theory that you had to shock, surprise, and entertain before you can effectively enlighten. He was aiming at the average citizen rather than the knowledgeable élite and was, indeed, the father of contemporary TV current affairs programming.

At the same time, McLean was a wicked-tongued *enfant terrible* who was openly contemptuous of his bosses and cruelly articulate with his staff. He called one of his bosses "sloppy . . . a regular drunk," another "Queegian," and a third, "an idiot." He tried to be a Svengali but was often a Simon Legree.

Patrick Watson says McLean was "a superb teacher, but he also was complicated, tyrannical, and incredibly insensitive to other people's feelings, particularly women's feelings. He was a very insecure man. He had a real problem with intimacy because of his own feelings of vulnerability. It surprised me when he got married because it seemed to me that the vulnerability of marriage would be intolerable for him. His wife, Jean, used to say of Ross that he was the only man in the world who never looked down when he took a pee."

Before and after his marriage, McLean regularly squired beautiful women on his arm. Clyde Gilmour, whose radio program in Vancouver was produced by McLean, says, "I heard from several women that Ross was quite a panty-grabber."

"He could not abide fools, and he had his hates," says June Callwood, who went to high school in Brantford, Ontario, with McLean. "He was bitterly cruel to some people, and he was a cold taskmaster. But for all that, he was a creative genius. As a student he was shy, stand-offish, smart, lofty, and not popular."

Later Callwood and McLean worked together at a Brantford radio station and at the local newspaper. Callwood went on to work primarily in print journalism, but their paths often crossed on the TV shows he produced. As his reputation spread, he got "a huge offer to go to the States," she says, "but he turned it down. I thought that he was a little scared of the big pond."

McLean prided himself on his ability to verbally lacerate his adversaries. "He didn't open his mouth unless he had a phrase ready," says Watson. McLean once confessed to Callwood, however, that it wasn't all as spontaneous as it seemed. "I'm always afraid I won't know what to say," he told Callwood. "When I go out for an evening, I rehearse how I will phrase things and how I'll tell a story." When Peter Gzowski interviewed him for *Maclean's* magazine, he told McLean that he hoped to capture some of his wit in the article. "Ross immediately pulled from his pocket a list of his more memorable ad libs and gave them to me," Gzowski says. "That act has stuck in my mind for thirty-five years. Giving me his *bon mots* was so descriptive of who Ross was."

Another of McLean's traits was his unceasing attempts to reshape his female hosts. He constantly told them what to say and how to say it so he could combine their beauty and his mind. "Ross, if nothing else, wanted to spend his life playing Pygmalion," says producer Ray McConnell. "He wanted to take perfection and make it really good." "He was a star maker," says Murray Frum, whose wife, Barbara, went through the McLean "treatment." "He was totally impossible – mercurial, irrational. He'd love you one minute and hate you the next. He always wanted to change you. He loved you for what you were, and then once you were under his sway, he had to change you, to influence you."

McLean had trouble dominating Barbara Frum, however. "Ross

always was a little hesitant about Barbara," says Frum. "She wasn't the usual bimbo. I don't think he ever had a screaming match with her. He never drove her to tears. Nobody ever drove Barbara to tears."

He came close, though, according to Barbara's good friend June Callwood. "He all but wrecked her confidence for television," Callwood says. "When she did programs for him in the late 1960s, he just rode her. He had mean things to say, and I remember how shattered she was by the raking over the coals that Ross used to give her. Ross did admire her brains, but he decided to mould her into something else, and they became frightfully antagonistic. She felt he was a destructive force. She might have learned from him, but it was hatefully done."

McLean kept his hypersensitive interior protected under a tough manner and masked his compassion and friendliness with sarcasm and a brittle wit. When Callwood's son was killed in a motorcycle accident, Callwood and her husband, Trent Frayne, put his ashes into a stone urn that McLean had given them some time before as an anniversary gift. When she told him, McLean was deeply moved but said, "So that's all you think of my gift."

With a trail of bridges burning behind him, McLean found it difficult to get a CBC job when "Close-Up" ended, in spite of his recognized genius for television. When he was hired by "This Hour Has Seven Days" in the mid-1960s, he was paid in his wife's name because he was on a management blacklist. It wasn't until late in the decade that he again produced programs under his own name. But he never achieved the creative heights of his early years, and became a symbol of the past in the present.

"Ross was a shit disturber who didn't know how to give or bend," says Sydney Newman. "His last years were very tragic. He spoiled his life somehow. People finally get fed up with a guy who is shit-disturbing all the time." When he died, he was writing for "Front Page Challenge" and had taught broadcast journalism at Ryerson Polytechnical Institute in Toronto. In his own way, he had been the driving force in making current affairs television popular, taking it out of the realm of academia and getting it into the streets.

Patrick Watson and Douglas Leiterman took McLean's popularizing approach one step further with "This Hour Has Seven Days," the most popular, most controversial current affairs program ever produced in Canada. Although it lasted only two seasons, it left an indelible standard for both success and excess and was almost as dramatic behind the screen as on it.

Larry Zolf

One unusual aspect of the program, noted by "Seven Days" reporter Larry Zolf, was the prevalence of leg problems. "For some reason we had a lot of wooden legs at 'Seven Days,'" he says. "There was Watson and Warner Troyer, and Leiterman had a bad leg from infantile paralysis. And there were other producers, like Bob Hoyt, who had a bad foot, and at one point Sam Levine broke his leg and was hobbling about on a crutch. Sometimes you couldn't tell whether it was a 'Seven Days' editorial meeting or a meeting of the Crippled Civilians Society."

Zolf remembers when he and a young researcher took award-winning journalist Warner Troyer to his hotel room after a party in Ottawa. Done in by alcohol, Troyer immediately fell asleep on the bed. The researcher thought she should at least take off his shoes so he would be more comfortable. "She got the first shoe off all right, and I said nothing to her about Warner's artificial leg. She didn't know about it," says Zolf. "Then she tugged at the other shoe and tugged and tugged. Then with a big yank, off came the shoe and his leg. She passed out, and I thought, 'Well, I guess I'm going down to the bar.'"

Zolf had another leg problem with Pierre Sevigny, a hero from the Second World War, a onetime associate defence minister in John Diefenbaker's government, and a key player in the Gerda Munsinger sex and spies scandal in Ottawa in the 1960s. Assigned to interview Sevigny, who had lost a leg in the war, Zolf was met at Sevigny's front door by the former cabinet minister, who hit the reporter on the shoulder. "Then I just lost my temper," says Zolf. "I kicked him, hit his leg, and his wooden leg came unstuck and went sailing onto the lawn. But he kept swinging at me and hopping around on one foot and yelling. I figured I could outrun him and ran to the car and took off."

Pugnacious interviews were a "Seven Days" feature, and one interviewer hired was Pierre Trudeau, who had earlier rejected an offer to be the program's host. In one hot-seat session, however, the producers judged Trudeau to be insufficiently aggressive and told co-interviewer Zolf to take over the questioning. The person being interviewed was Trudeau's future political adversary, René Lévesque. "Originally I was to be the nice guy and Trudeau the black hat," says Zolf, "but he didn't fill that role at all, and they told me, 'Drop him. Take control of the interview,' and I pushed him right out."

Zolf now feels "Seven Days" was too aggressive in these interviews. "Sometimes we brutalized people," he says. "Made them less human beings. That's where the war between journalists and politicians started."

Not only was Trudeau too restrained in his interview style, but, Zolf says, he was unable to tell jokes. Years after their "Seven Days" work together, Zolf was asked to prepare some humorous material for a speech by Prime Minister Trudeau. Zolf felt Trudeau delivered his lines limply. "You couldn't deliver a joke in a Brink's armoured car," he told Trudeau. "You've got no sense of timing."

Zolf started out as a teaching assistant at the University of Toronto and then found his way to the CBC and "Seven Days." There, his opinions frequently got him into hot water, as when he offended Vancouverites by saying that "Vancouver is just like Winnipeg with mountains." He's been sued several times, including once for describing a book as being so wooden "it reeked of Dutch elm disease." He got into a public feud with columnist Allan Fotheringham after Dr. Foth ridiculed Zolf's humour. Zolf himself says he has "an Iago streak" and used to enjoy poisoning the well by telling bar acquaintances that a friend had said the acquaintance was "terrible in bed."

Zolf used to drink like a maniac but has now given up. He had a cancer scare a few years ago and says he doesn't want a sudden death. "I'd prefer a lingering death to a quick one so I can watch TV and phone people," he maintains.

"Seven Day's" focus on confrontation, controversy, and sex sent CBC senior management into a frenzy, including executive vice-president Capt. Ted Briggs, who was particularly offended by stories on homosexuality. He claimed they were irrelevant in Canada and advised colleagues that, for example, there were no homosexuals at all in Saskatchewan.

The show's mocking impudence and illuminating dramatics were finally too much for the CBC's managers, and they ham-handedly killed the program. The resulting public outcry and parliamentary hearings rocked the government, spurred the resignation of CBC president Alphonse Ouimet, and generated more headlines and hostility than the crisis a quarter-century later over the documentary depicting an aspect of Canada's role in the Second World War, *The Valour and the Horror*.

"Seven Days" not only warred with CBC management but also with the news department, which denied Leiterman and Watson access to its files, tapes, and film. At one point "Seven Days" operatives broke into the news library, outraging the news staff. The union issued a formal denunciation of the "Seven Days" team, calling them "masters of harassment, of stealth and of cloak and dagger . . . unscrupulous and diabolical . . . charlatans with little or no experience."

There also was conflict within the "Seven Days" unit even while the program was fighting the news department and CBC management. Zolf criticizes Watson's co-host Laurier LaPierre, whose passionate commitments brought a new style to current affairs programming, saying, "Laurier was mostly bombast and bullshit." LaPierre was himself assailed by personal problems at the time. "He was torn by his role in the program and brutally pummelled by his wife, who thought his television work was embarrassing, stupid, and absolutely inimical to his academic career," says Watson. "When the divorce came along, his wife had a detective on his tail. He'd been reckless. He lost everything."

Although he was portrayed as co-leader of the "Seven Days" revolt, Watson says he didn't enjoy the fight. He was particularly dismayed with the program's senior producer and field commander of the rebellion, Bob Hoyt. "Hoyt was an American and didn't know Canadian sensitivities," Watson says. "I had to persuade Doug to put the brakes on him from time to time. Hoyt's objective was glory. He was, in my judgement, a conscienceless man. He simply saw it as an adventure. I don't think there was any sense of purpose in Hoyt at all. No sense of the public good . . . I felt a bit contaminated by the whole thing."

Because of his role on "Seven Days" and his subsequent TV programs, Watson, who had begun his broadcasting career at age fourteen as an actor in the CBC series "The Kootenay Kid," became one of the best-known CBC journalists. "The finest, fairest, most intelligent craftsman ever produced by the public affairs department," Ross McLean once said of Watson. And yet Watson says, "I never considered myself to be a journalist. I always thought of myself as a theatrical producer putting journalism into a theatrical frame."

In his early years as a producer, Watson was angered when he was assigned to public affairs programming instead of the children's department, where he really wanted to go. But with his broadcasting talents and his lifelong passion for magic, he managed to bring to current affairs television an excitement that it had never had before.

Peter Gzowski

The "Seven Days" trauma may have led to a pause in aggressive current affairs programming, but it did not stop it. In 1976 the CBC launched a late-night talk show spearheaded by Peter Herrndorf, then head of current affairs, called "Ninety Minutes Live" and awkwardly hosted by Peter Gzowski. A hugely successful radio host at the time, Gzowski was apprehensive about his TV adventure, saying, "You're up there naked in front of the camera every night." He had good reason to be uneasy. Almost immediately he faced a barrage of blood-seeking critics inside and outside the CBC, including Ross McLean. In a memo, McLean pronounced the show a "blend of gaucherie and gangling hostmanship . . . sub par and warmed over," adding that if the show continued, "it will confirm my bleakest view of this company's infinite capacity for self and public torment." McLean himself had used Gzowski as host on a short-lived late-night show a few years earlier and had tried to make Gzowski adapt the style of American comedian Dick Cavett, who was hosting his own talk show at the time. "Later, when I was on radio," says Gzowski, "somebody called Ross to ask how come Gzowski works on radio but did not on TV. Ross told him it was because on TV I tried too much to be like Dick Cavett."

Gzowski was devastated by all the criticism. He struggled on, sometimes with guests who brought him more trouble, such as poet Irving Layton, who read to Gzowski and the audience a poem entitled "The Farting Jesus." Layton said since Jesus was human, he therefore "went to the bathroom, excreted, and farted." A storm of protest erupted, and

Layton defended himself by claiming bad taste has a place on television. Besides, he added, "I just said Jesus must have broken wind."

Artist Don Arioli also caused a stir with his on-air discussion with Gzowski about sex education for children. A salacious conversation full of *double entendres* accompanied a display of Arioli's cartoon characters, Jimmy Penis and Victoria Vagina. Gzowski said it was educational, but in truth, it was quite scatological.

"Once we had a disco queen whose eyes were streaming and her nose running as she sang," Gzowski remembers. "'What's the matter?' I asked, and she said, 'I'm allergic to the white paint on the microphone.' The band just cracked up, but here I am, a guy from Toronto who had never seen anybody stoned on coke."

Gzowski also had trouble handling the self-described "world's greatest groupie," a young lady named Cherry Vanilla who kept pulling down her blouse to reveal more of her ample bosom, distracting Gzowski. When he innocently asked her what a groupie does, she replied, "Basically, you go to bed with rock stars."

"They were trying to make Peter into Johnny Carson, and it just didn't work for Peter," says Mary Lou Finlay, who filled in for him occasionally. "I think he marks that time as the worst year of his life."

One of Gzowski's problems was that he didn't like the way he looked on TV. "I was all tense and artificial," he says. "He had acne as a teenager, practically terminal acne," says Elaine Saunders. "You could see the pockmarks, and his acne robbed him of his confidence, as it did Tommy Hunter. It was almost as if he was doomed before he started."

Another problem for Gzowski, according to Saunders, is that he was too intelligent for the program. "To be good on TV like Letterman and Leno, you can't be too smart," she says. "And that was Peter's problem, because he thought about things."

Gzowski also was irritated by having to worry about whether his collar was sticking out or his glasses were reflecting the light. He was irked when, after a show, people would comment on how he and his guests had looked rather than on what they had to say. "On radio, people argue substance with you, but on television, it's style," he says. "And also I had no idea how bad I would be. I can't blame anyone for this because I was seduced more than I was raped by television. This was not going to be sophisticated like Johnny Carson, and yet everything was based on that. I went along with it, although I didn't understand it. But it didn't work. Ed Sullivan didn't try to be sophisticated. It was very simple. That's why Rita MacNeil works. I'm jealous of Rita MacNeil. I wish I'd been like her. . . . It was so hurtful. I had never before experienced being criticized personally. I didn't realize this would happen. I'm not over it yet."

Another TV program that caused problems in this era was a cheeky current affairs show called "Up Canada," designed to poke fun at the antics of Ottawa politicians. One sketch involved a fictional womanizing member of Parliament from British Columbia who left his wife at home and frolicked in and out of bed in an Ottawa apartment with his secretary. Unhappily, the character bore a disturbingly close resemblance to a real and prominent MP, all except for the mistress. The fictional MP was called George Fraser. The real MP was John Fraser, who later became Speaker of the House. The real Fraser lived at 1200 Rideau Terrace, while the fictional Fraser lived at 22 Rideau Terrace. The real Fraser represented a West coast riding, while the fictional Fraser represented the West Coast riding of Nookie in the Islands. The real Mrs. Fraser lived in British Columbia, as did the fictional Mrs. Fraser. All details but the affair with the secretary were uncomfortably similar. The real Mrs. Fraser took offence as did the real MP, who was hooted at in Parliament as "lover boy!" The CBC promptly killed future episodes of the romantic adventures of Mr. Fraser.

Barbara Frum and "The Journal"

No current affairs programming came close to matching the impact of "This Hour Has Seven Days" until "The Journal" went on the air in 1982. The inspiration for "The Journal" came from CBC vice-president Peter Herrndorf, who was now head of English TV, and executive producer Mark Starowicz provided the creative perspiration. The personification of "The Journal," however, was Barbara Frum.

Partnered with "The National" in a 10:00 to 11:00 P.M. daring scheduling of journalistic programming, "The Journal" was an instant success.

Industry naysayers, who had warned it would be too serious a program for prime time, were astonished. "On that first night, I remember Herrndorf being in tears because it had happened," says Murray Frum. "He was just overwhelmed."

There were many reasons for the program's triumph: the drive provided by Herrndorf and Starowicz for "The Journal" and by executive producer Tony Burman for "The National"; the talent and exuberance of the producers, researchers, reporters, and editors; and the CBC's handsome financial commitment. But the special ingredient was Barbara Frum.

Through a decade of hosting "As It Happens," Frum had become radio's most prominent current affairs personality. As an interviewer, she was insatiably curious, dogged, and serious. As a private person, she was compassionate, realistic, and small "l" liberal. She was rich, born to wealthy department store owners from Niagara Falls, and married to a highly successful real estate developer. "I never had to work for money," she once said, "so I value the fact that in my life I don't have to do things I don't approve of."

Her first radio work was in the 1960s on a CBC program hosted by Lorraine Thomson called "Audio," in which she talked about taking underprivileged inner-city children to the art gallery, the museum, and other cultural locales. She began doing more freelance work for radio, as well as writing articles for Peter Gzowski, then the *Toronto Star*'s entertainment editor, and for *Maclean's*, *Chatelaine*, and a television column for *Saturday Night*. Ross McLean liked her aggressive interviewing style, brought her into television in the late 1960s, and then tried to mould her to his approach. "There was no outguessing Ross," says Frum's husband, Murray. "When she did serious, he wanted funny. When she did funny, he wanted serious. He drove them all nuts. You just never knew with him."

McLean's successor as producer of the daily Toronto dinner-hour current affairs program that Frum hosted was the veteran newsman Don Cameron, who also sought to change her because he thought she was "too argumentative." At one point in 1970, she came into the studio to do an interview and found someone else sitting in her chair. "You're not doing this interview," the producer told her. "In that case, I won't do any interviews," she said and walked out, thinking she would never work for the CBC again. A few weeks later, however, she got a call from a CBC Radio executive asking her to audition for "As It Happens." She got the job and began her rise to the top of Canadian broadcasting. "She loved radio because it was so personal," says Murray. She also loved the sudden switches that characterized "As It Happens," which meant one minute she was interviewing a farmer who grew the biggest pumpkin in the world and chatting with Indira Gandhi the next.

She liked, too, the locker-room conviviality among the young researchers, editors, and producers. "Barbara in many ways was one of the kids," says Mark Starowicz. "She found us oddly fascinating. She came out of a fairly straight background and we were a wicked 1960s gang. She knew everything about everybody's life. If somebody was pregnant, she would tell Barbara first. People would go to Barbara with the most private details."

As a young researcher, Pamela Wallin was also impressed with Frum. "She was a grown-up and we were all kids," says Wallin. "I learned a lot from her over those 'As It Happens' years." Wallin noticed that Frum was much more at ease doing interviews by telephone than in person. "She never wanted to interview anybody face to face," Wallin says. She liked the freedom, the independence, that a phone call gave her. She could be so tough with people on the phone, but if you put them in the studio, she just got so incredibly nice."

Even on the phone, however, Frum occasionally had to handle some difficult people, such as the cranky Harold Ballard, who owned the Toronto Maple Leaf hockey team. At one point during an interview, Ballard told her to shut up. He went on to say women on radio were a joke and that their best position was horizontal. Afterwards Frum sent a joshing but sarcastic note to him, signing it, "Your favourite BROAD-caster, Barbara."

Wallin and her co-workers were puzzled about the expensive and sometimes bizarre clothes, Frum wore. "She had a monkey-skin coat that used to drive us all crazy," says Wallin. "It would hang on a peg inside the radio studio like a bundle of monkeys hanging there. Barbara was quite wild in her clothes and money was no object." One reason for Frum's odd apparel is that she wanted to support young fashion designers.

Years later, on "The Journal," clothes became even more important to Frum. Her "Journal" colleague Bill Harcourt says, "In the eyes of some, she had an odd sort of clothes sense. Often she would bring to the studio a whole bunch of dresses or blouses, and while we were watching on the screen up in the office, she'd hold up a blouse or dress to the camera and say, 'What do you think of this one?' I thought she was always very well-dressed, but we were very glad she was persuaded not to use some of the stuff she turned up with."

Her "As It Happens" co-workers gossiped about her wealth as well as her clothes. "She was rich, which was a real novelty for us," says Wallin. "Barbara came to work in a Jaguar – I think she and Murray had matching Jaguars. I didn't even know what a Jaguar was at the time."

Frum's deep compassion is illustrated by the help she gave both the former cabinet minister Judy LaMarsh and controversial Ottawa columnist Marjorie Nichols when they fell ill with cancer. "Judy was at home dying and had no money," says June Callwood. "Barbara could have given her own money but that would have embarrassed Judy, so she phoned a lot of prominent Liberals and said, 'You owe Judy. She can't pay her rent, so you're part of that rent as long as she lives. Send a cheque to me.' She wanted a way to help so Judy wouldn't have to be grateful to her."

Wallin, who was close to Marjorie Nichols in her last months, says Frum would call Nichols in Ottawa twice a week to try to cheer her up with gossip and jokes. Frum also acted as a den mother to the "As It Happens" staff. "If somebody's love life was a mess or if there had been a death in the family," says Wallin, "she always said something personally and privately to them."

When Mark Starowicz took over as executive producer of "As It Happens," he and Frum were soon at loggerheads over the show. "We had terrible explosions," says Starowicz. "It was frosty. She was a very strong-willed person and always involved in the program." After a couple of months, Frum called him. "We got together at a greasy spoon and spent two or three hours there arguing," he says. "Out of that came a mutual trust, a handshake agreement that lasted twenty-five years, although we did continue to argue."

"Their backgrounds were different, and they did not think the same way, but they fed off each other and had great respect for each other," says Murray.

When Starowicz went to television to launch "The Journal," he had Frum in mind as a possible host. The combination of Frum and Patrick Watson as co-hosts was discussed, but Starowicz felt that while Watson was a superb long-form interviewer, "we weren't going to do that kind of a program," he says. "We needed a sharp questioner." Turning down Watson was difficult, as there had been considerable speculation that he would be a co-host. "I asked Herrndorf if he'd promised Patrick the show, but Peter said no, only that Patrick would be seriously considered as host," says Starowicz. "Not being asked to be the host of the 'The Journal' probably hurt."

Instead, Starowicz persuaded Watson to be a documentary-essayist, but that agreement collapsed in arguments among Watson and "The Journal" staff. Watson went off to New York to host the short-lived CBS cultural channel. Publicly he criticized "The Journal" as being too "mechanical," "glib," and "controlled."

Starowicz thought of other possible hosts for "The Journal," including ex-CBCers Peter Jennings of ABC and Robin McNeil of PBS. "They were all in love with the notion that they could repatriate a big-name Canadian," says Murray. "When that didn't come about, it became logical to go to Barbara, especially for Mark." Starowicz told her, "This program is going to be television's Normandy invasion!"

Frum was initially reluctant to take the job, however, because she loved the freedom she had in hosting "As It Happens," and thought that TV's technical demands and complexity would limit her. As well, she remembered Ross McLean's bitter comments on her earlier performance as a TV host. When she first saw the set for "The Journal," she said, "All that stuff scares me. There's just so much of it!" She was also advised by friends such as June Callwood not to go to "The Journal." "I didn't want to see somebody doing to her again what Ross had done," says Callwood. "Look," Frum told Callwood, "it's a new show, and if I don't start at the beginning I won't get it." She said later, "I felt I'd be a coward if I didn't do it. I didn't want to be a coward."

"I think she succumbed because of the challenge of it," Murray says.

"She felt that if she didn't do it, she would always wonder if she could have done it. She always loved pushing herself."

"She did it out of a sense of duty," says Starowicz. "She was not a natural for television and she knew it. She was terrified of it. But she was determined."

"They wanted her so badly they negotiated one hell of a contract and Murray helped her with that," says Callwood. "She got the whole summer off and other holidays and that was almost unheard of."

She used the time off to read and travel to trouble spots in the world at her own expense. "I kept telling her, 'Who pays money to go to a war zone?'" says Murray. "But that's what we did on our holidays. She felt she had to do this. Lying on a beach was not her idea of a good time. She wanted to learn something. Wherever she spotted trouble coming, she wanted to go there, Yugoslavia, Yemen, Morocco, Romania."

When the decision about who was to host "The Journal" was finally made, the program, uniquely, had two women sharing the role. "Why the hell not?" said Starowicz as he hired Frum from radio and blonde, blue-eyed Mary Lou Finlay from CTV's "Live It Up," a prime-time consumer show. Finlay, who had guest-hosted on "Ninety Minutes Live" and co-anchored "Take 30," had started her TV career inauspiciously on a local Ottawa show. "I'd never done TV, and nobody told me to look into the lens of the camera," she says. "There was a TV set over at the side of the set and I saw myself on it. We were live and I just looked at myself as I talked." "What the hell's she looking at?" cried the producer, who ordered her to look into the lens. She also had a nervous facial tic for the first few days of TV. "My eye kept blinking and I kept smiling, and it looked like I was winking at the audience all the way through the show," she says.

When Starowicz asked Finlay to co-host "The Journal," she was uncertain. "I hemmed and hawed because, although it was very exciting, I knew it was going to disrupt my life totally," she says. Starowicz reiterated his line that the launch of "The Journal" was like the invasion of Normandy. Finlay finally succumbed when Starowicz and a colleague took a cab at dawn to her home and, carrying a bunch of roses and her morning newspaper, knocked on her front door. "I told her," he says, "This is a battle for the country, for sovereignty. How can you say no?" She couldn't.

"Mark had a knack for infusing in his people the notion that 'The Journal' was the most important, exciting thing that had ever happened in television anywhere. And we believed him, or a least half of you did," Finlay says.

While the program itself was a success, the Frum–Finlay duo was not. Frum did most of the major interviews and Finlay was clearly uncomfortable. She felt increasingly confined in the studio and did not like doing an interview by talking to a blank wall. The hosts could hear but could not see the person they were interviewing; the picture was inserted later to get a higher-quality production. It was thus essentially a radio interview, as Frum had done for a decade on "As It Happens." But Finlay felt embarrassed. "We were cheating. You're doing it blind, but the audience is going to see the guy you're interviewing joking or shaking his head. I thought television was getting to be more and more fakery and smoke and mirrors."

She also found the job tedious – "just unspeakably boring," she says, with many "long, lonely" waits in the studio between interviews. "I just didn't have enough to keep me occupied," she says.

"I made a mistake," says Starowicz. "We were going to be a quick-paced magazine, and I figured we would need two interviewers to keep up the pace. But the program did not need two interviewers. It needed the centrality of one. The problem was we had two talented people, both eager to work very hard." "It wasn't comfortable for Mary Lou," says Callwood, "and Barbara didn't like the idea of there being two hosts, she just didn't think it worked."

Nor did Finlay, who says, "Because I spent so much time on the show doing so little, that's why I went away first to Harvard for a year and then out in the field to do documentaries for 'The Journal.'" Later she became host of radio's "Sunday Morning" and then went on to host "Now, the Details," a radio program on the media.

"The Journal" and its partner "The National" quickly became an informational must for the nation, and as its influence grew, so did

Barbara Frum's. "One of her strengths as a journalist was that she asked the questions her neighbour wanted answered," says Peter Herrndorf.

Despite the grinding hours and tensions, she loved the job. She was, however, tough on herself. "Tougher than anyone else would have been," her husband says. As her TV reputation grew, he started joshing her by calling her Queen after someone wrote a song called "Barbara Frum, Queen of Canada." She enjoyed the nickname, as she did the wickedly satirical take-off done about her on "CODCO" by impressionist Greg Malone.

To provide her with some comfort during the long studio hours, her daughter, Linda, gave her a French poodle named Diva. The dog, says Murray, "was her pal, something she had all day as family. Diva was very important to her." Frum would walk Diva several times a day in the streets and parking lot outside the CBC, and it would curl up beside her in the make-up room or her own small dressing room.

Others were not as enthusiastic about Diva. Complaints filled a file an inch thick, which was known as the Diva File. One problem was Diva's eating habits. Pizza or chicken was delivered nightly to "The Journal" studio and, says Starowicz, "We'd be meeting and eating while Diva was going from wastebasket to wastebasket wolfing down the remains of pizza or chicken. This snarfing dog. Barbara would get up and say, 'Diva! Naughty girl! No. No. I don't want you to do that.' The meeting would stop, and we'd all sit around while she spanked Diva and sent her out of the room. And you could tell by her expression that Barbara felt this was just normal."

Occasionally Diva would misbehave in other ways, leaving deposits in the hallways, most of which Frum cleaned up, but sometimes the chore fell to others. "The technical guys sometimes were unhappy, and often I'd get some Kleenex and clean the mess up," says Elaine Saunders. Murray Frum says a union official once complained to Frum about Diva's deposits, saying, "You can't bring the dog here." "Well," Frum replied, "if I can't bring the dog, then I can't bring me." The dog stayed.

The eulogies for Frum following her death painted her almost as a saint, overlooking her human foibles, such as fussing about her hair, her clothes, the health of her colleagues, and enjoying gossip about journalists and politicians. "Barbara was a great gossip, she loved it," says Saunders. "All the researchers would bring her little tidbits. But in a way, you know, all news is just organized gossip. That's all it is." "Gossip was fun for her," says Starowicz. "It was often romanic gossip. She was gleeful with it."

Frum was just as much a den mother to "The Journal" team as she had been to the staff of "As It Happens." Colleagues with the flu would inevitably hear her telephoned advice to drink lots of hot chicken soup. "When I hurt my back, she sent a cake saying, 'Get well soon, Steve,' " says studio director Steve Hyde. "If somebody wasn't there, she wanted to know what was wrong. She would pen notes and call colleagues to congratulate them on something they'd done." Saunders says, "If she looked particularly good on a show, she would phone you at home to thank you."

Royal Canadian Air Farce comedian Roger Abbott says that when he and his colleagues were just beginning their TV work, "I was sitting home on a Saturday afternoon and the phone rang and it was Barbara. She said, 'I've just been screening one of your programs, and the stuff you guys do is terrific, and I just had to call you.' How often does that happen in our business? Since we were just starting out, she made me feel like a million bucks."

"In her book of life, she must have had a million acts of small kindnesses," says Trina McQueen, who ran CBC news and current affairs at the time.

It's possible that Frum's kindness sprang at least in part from her own vulnerabilities, which she sought to hide from the public and from most friends. One handicap she tried to conceal was a withered arm that she had from birth. "They cut a muscle and she never recovered," says her husband. The arm withered, and she never had the use of it except to carefully turn pages to read a book. "But she was very, very good at masking it," says Murray. "She would always keep her arm close to her side and a lot of people were never even aware of it."

Frum's biggest and ultimately fatal vulnerability, however, was cancer. In 1974 when she was an energetic, thirty-six-year-old, seemingly healthy as a horse, she went for her regular check-up, and the doctor found a lump under her arm. As Murray says, "All of a sudden the doctor tells her she's got leukemia." She was given less than two years to live.

Defiant, impetuous, and brilliant, Norman DePoe was the best political broadcast reporter Canada has ever produced. He had "the smell of news," his colleagues said, and his face was better known than the prime minister's. *(National Archives of Canada, MISA 16158)*

Smiling on the outside but in turmoil within, Peter Mansbridge and Pamela Wallin co-hosted the star-crossed "Prime Time News." After three years, the program reverted to the name "The National." Wallin left for her own Newsworld show, Mansbridge continued as anchor, Hana Gartner joined as host of the magazine section, and the program began its long climb back to popularity. *(Courtesy of the CBC)*

When Peter Gzowski's alarm rings at 3:13 A.M., he starts his long workday as host of "Morningside" on CBC Radio. Affable, sometimes even lovable on air, he admits the pressures of being a broadcast icon occasionally can make him grumpy off the air. *(Courtesy of the CBC)*

Gentle, knowledgeable, and impeccable on his radio program "Gilmour's Albums," Clyde Gilmour can be a mischievous imp in private. He's been on CBC Radio every weekend for half a century. *(Courtesy of the CBC)*

Lloyd Robertson has the best-known face on television, having spent the first half of his career at CBC hosting news programs and doing the same thing at CTV for the second half. He's the only person who has anchored both the CBC's "The National" and CTV's "National News." *(National Archives of Canada, MISA 16137)*

Vickie Gabereau, host of the afternoon CBC Radio network show. Gabereau once ran for mayor of Toronto, campaigning in a brightly painted face as Rosie the Clown. She got 3,200 votes. Gabereau figures she's done 15,000 interviews in her career. *(Courtesy of the CBC)*

The TV News Specials team covering the 1984 Liberal Leadership Convention: Barbara Frum, Peter Mansbridge, and David Halton, then the CBC's Ottawa correspondent. *(Fred Phipps, courtesy of the CBC)*

The Royal Canadian Air Farce got their big break in the early 1970s when they were fired from one CBC Radio show and then hired to do another. Today they star on both radio and television. Left to right: Roger Abbott, John Morgan, guest star Dave Broadfoot, Don Ferguson, and Luba Goy. *(Courtesy of the CBC)*

Jackie Burroughs, left, as Aunt Hetty in "The Road to Avonlea," and Lally Cadeau, her on-screen sister-in-law, starred in one of Canada's most popular prime-time shows ever. The program's sweet gentility was accompanied by occasional tensions backstage. *(Courtesy of Sullivan Entertainment)*

Creative powerhouse Mark Starowicz on location in China. Starowicz was executive producer of "As It Happens," the program that helped revive CBC Radio in the 1970s. Later he was executive producer of "The Journal," which brought new vitality to CBC-TV journalism in the 1980s. He now heads CBC-TV documentary programs. *(Courtesy of the CBC)*

Barbara Frum and "The Journal" became must viewing for millions of Canadians. Along with its partner, "The National," the program set a new standard for TV journalism. When Frum died in 1992, an era ended. *(Fred Phipps, courtesy of the CBC)*

Eric Peterson, Cynthia Dale, and C. David Johnson were the stars of "Street Legal," the longest-running, most glamorous TV drama series the CBC has ever produced. Its last year, however, was fraught with behind-the-scenes disputes. *(Courtesy of the CBC)*

Rita MacNeil is everything a TV star is not supposed to be, but in her "Rita & Friends" Friday night show, she captivates Canadians with her sensitivity and crystal-clear voice. *(Mark Mainguy, courtesy of the CBC)*

Peter Herrndorf, left, and Larry Zolf, veterans of CBC political and creative wars. Herrndorf, the driving force behind numerous CBC program successes, wound up heading TVO, Ontario's educational channel. Zolf, a mischievous *enfant terrible* of TV current affairs, moved from being an on-air iconoclast to a behind-the-scenes research expert. *(Courtesy of the CBC)*

Three leading lights of the CBC correspondents corps in the turbulent 1960s. Maclear and Gould later became independent producers, and today Safer is a correspondent for CBS's "60 Minutes." *(National Archives of Canada, MISA 15653)*

Newsman Mike Duffy, an irrepressible gourmand who had more insider contacts than almost anybody else on Parliament Hill. In the 1980s he moved from political reporting for CBC-TV to his own show with Baton Broadcasting. *(National Archives of Canada, MISA 16162)*

Brian Williams, left, and Don Cherry, right, have totally different approaches to sports broadcasting. Williams follows Foster Hewitt's tradition of "tell-it-like-it-is," while Cherry is the Gordon Sinclair of the ice. *(Courtesy of the CBC)*

"She went through a terrible time in accepting it in the beginning," says June Callwood, one of her closest friends. "It was just awful. Just awful. She was rocked, and there was three or four months of this constant, intense emotion."

"We decided we wouldn't tell the kids because how do you deal with a mother who's dying," says Murray. "They were very young. Then she said she wanted to continue working, but she didn't want to work with people who would feel sympathy for her. She wanted to keep it a secret. I wondered, 'How do you keep these things secret?'"

Globe and Mail TV columnist Blaik Kirby heard she was dying of cancer and called Murray to say he was going to write a story on it. "Blaik," Murray told him, "if you go with that story, the reader will read it in about ten seconds and never think about it the rest of the day. Meanwhile, you'll destroy my kids' lives, you'll destroy a career, and who the hell knows who's dying anyway." Kirby did not write the story and, ironically, he himself was dead a year later.

Her first doctor "was mean and stupid" says her husband, and Frum went to another who gave her no specific time limit, but there were indications she might live another ten or fifteen years. "You don't know when," Murray told her. "All they've told you is what. Most of us don't know what's going to take us out. Nobody knows when. The trick to living is to look at the abyss and keep going. After all, it's terminal from the day you're born. You create enjoyment and you create satisfaction, but the end result is that you're going to die." Frum said she was inspired by endurance and "by people who know that they were born to die and all that matters is how they do in the meantime."

"She had bad moments right after the diagnosis, but she worked that out," Murray says. "She would talk to close friends. She used June a lot. She was very realistic. She never fooled herself. She didn't want to go chasing around to try to find a magic cure. She was a tough lady, and she was grateful for every day she got."

She talked extensively to her doctor as well as her friends, and then, says Callwood, "one day she got herself back together." "It's too bad," she told Callwood, "I would have been a great old lady. But, now, I've done everything I can on this damn thing, and I'll continue to do everything I can, but now I'm getting on with my life."

When Callwood asked her how she could cope with a demanding career and a killer disease, she told her, "I put my other life in a paper bag and close the top and put it outside the door. Then I shut the door, and it's there and I'm here."

"She stared at death for eighteen years," says Murray. "She was reminded of it every day when she had to take a pill and when she went for blood tests four times a year. Near the end she also got radiation treatments and some blood transfusions."

Early on in the disease, she had told Starowicz, "Mark, there are going to be days when I'll have to come in a little late. And also some days when I'm depressed, and here's why . . ."

"I could tell her blood count from the way she'd come into the office," Starowicz says. "If she bounced in, I knew it was okay. She was definitely tough, but she'd cry sometimes. She came to my office after she'd been going from doctor to doctor and maybe she'd had a bad blood test. She had on dark glasses, and she was just streaming with tears. She told me, 'Mark, I was looking around at the world, and this is just so unfair. So unfair.' I think that day she thought it might be one of her last."

Frum knew her time was short. "She always acted like there's no tomorrow because so far as she knew, there was no tomorrow," says Murray. "She was always aware of time as being finite, and that's why she didn't waste a minute of the day. She was always occupied." Callwood says, "She tried to pack everything in. She tried to do everything, to not miss a thing."

She also never wanted to admit when she had a cold or felt tired, although she often did in her last years. "Her skin would be grey and white, terribly white," says producer Bill Harcourt. "And then she'd go into the make-up room and come out looking very different, almost robust and healthy."

A few months before her death at age fifty-four, flu hit her and to her regret forced her to miss much of the coverage of the Persian Gulf War. Even though her energy had flagged and her voice was weak, she would often come down to the CBC. She would stand impatiently on the sidelines saying, "I'm fine, I'm fine," and aching to work. In the late winter of 1992, just after the tenth anniversary of "The Journal," she returned, still feeling under par, but determined to get back into action. In March, running a fever, she interviewed Mordecai Richler, who was alarmed at her condition. "This is as very sick woman," Richler told a producer. "We had been insisting that she go home, but she wouldn't," says Starowicz. "She looked awful. Her face was so strained."

She had a temperature of 104°F, and when she finished the Richler interview, she called Starowicz to say, uncharacteristically, "Mark, I'm scared. I'm really, really feeling run down. I've got this fever. I've called Murray and he's going to take me to the hospital to have me checked over."

"Take care of yourself, and, for God's sake, get some rest," Starowicz told her. "She stayed until the taping was done so they wouldn't lose the show," says Murray, and she went directly from the studio to the hospital. He thought she'd be back at work in a few days. "I didn't think she was going to die," he says. "I thought she was getting better." He was staggered when she started talking to him about her funeral arrangements. "No, no, don't be silly," he told her. "I was totally shocked," he says. "I never wanted to talk to her about death or dying. In a way, I guess I might have done her a disservice. But I'm an optimist and she was a pragmatist."

Two weeks after going into the hospital, Frum died. Murray was staggered by the national outpouring of sympathy after her death. "People across Canada felt as if a piece of their own lives had ended with hers," stated the Montreal *Gazette*. "It won't be the same any more," declared the *Ottawa Sun*. "She never would have believed it," Murray says. "She would have been astonished. As far as she was concerned, she was just doing her job."

When Pamela Wallin was named to co-host "Prime Time News" a few months later, she was taken to Frum's dressing room by Anne Emin, a close associate of Frum. Emin opened the door and said, "We want you to have this room." Nobody had been in it since Frum had died and, says Wallin, "We were standing there crying, and we put our arms around each other. But then we were laughing because Diva's hair was all over the place."

Barbara would have liked that.

9

Radio Reborn

Long before her triumph on "The Journal," Barbara Frum was among the pioneers of a new beginning for the entire CBC Radio Service as host of "As It Happens."

After television entered Canadian living rooms in 1952, radio plunged in popularity. For the next two decades, it limped along, presenting programs that were increasingly out of sync with what Canadians wanted to hear. At the start of the 1970s, Canadians followed hockey on TV, not on radio, got their news mostly from TV, not radio, and enjoyed comedy and music on TV, not on radio. CBC Radio schedules were a hodgepodge of mostly fifteen- and thirty-minute programs with indistinct profiles and few identifiable stars. "We have to redefine the medium," said CBC executive vice-president Laurent Picard, launching the campaign to resuscitate radio. Picard set in motion what became known as the Radio Revolution. It transformed CBC Radio and recaptured much of its audience by offering more meaningful programs than the commercials, pop music, snippets of news, and opinionated phone-in shows that dominated private radio.

In the new CBC Radio, local information programming was sharply increased and longer, star-driven network shows were launched. "As It Happens" had begun as an experiment in November 1968; in 1971, after

Frum became host, the program soared in popularity, partly because of her aggressive yet empathetic interview style and partly because of the metamorphosis wrought by "wunderkind" producer Mark Starowicz. He catapulted a relatively sleepy show into a fast-paced, hard-nosed journalistic centrepiece. Starowicz, son of a Polish resistance fighter, was born in England, raised in Argentina, educated in Montreal, and had been a firebrand at McGill University where he ran the campus newspaper. He went on to write the occasional script for CBC, worked at the Montreal *Gazette* and then for the *Toronto Star*. At age twenty-four, he was hired by CBC Radio in 1970 to work for, among others, Peter Gzowski, who hosted the short-lived "Radio Free Friday." In 1971 he became executive producer of "As It Happens," beginning his meteoric rise in CBC broadcast journalism.

Initially, Starowicz had a hard time enticing senior Canadian politicians to go on the program. "We actually had a beer and wine party when we got our first low-grade cabinet minister," he says. But soon politicians realized that being interviewed by Frum on "As It Happens" added to their profile, and Starowicz's reputation as a program innovator (he calls himself "an editorial civil engineer") resulted, four years later, in his being asked to design "Sunday Morning," an in-depth current affairs program with edge and perspective. It was another success story and led to his appointment as executive producer of "The Journal." This was the biggest challenge of his professional career and the biggest programming risk the CBC had taken since "This Hour Has Seven Days."

By the time Starowicz left radio, it had been reborn, thanks not only to "As It Happens" and "Sunday Morning" but also to the network morning radio shows hosted by Bruno Gerussi, Peter Gzowski, and Don Harron.

"Gerussi: Words and Music," which ran from 1969 to 1971, was the forerunner of Gzowski's "This Country in the Morning." Gzowski's show, with its unscripted informality and focus on the host, typified the radio revolution and helped to change the whole face of CBC Radio. A newspaper and magazine writer and editor, Gzowski had done both TV and radio assignments before "This Country in the Morning." Possibly the biggest challenge he faced on that program and on his later "Morningside" was getting up in the morning. "My alarm is set for

3:13 A.M.," he says, "set that way for symmetry. I read the papers and I get to the office about 5:00 A.M., read more papers, read the mail, read through the research, and then we're on the air at 8:00 A.M. to the Maritimes and Newfoundland." Despite this punishing schedule, Gzowski also reads about a book a day. "He's the greatest," says Vickie Gabereau, his network afternoon talk-show counterpart. "Even though he hums and he haws and takes three hours to ask a question, he gets things out of people, and when he's on a roll, he's unbeatable."

Gzowski, so affable, sometimes even lovable, on the air, can be grumpy and even occasionally anti-social in private. "Grumpy? Well, yeah, sometimes," he says. "I get frustrated by hypocrisy and bureaucracy, and the load of stuff I have to do. I get tired, physically drained. And I have a limited capacity for social affairs. I spend all day talking to people. It's what I do for a living. I don't want to go out after work and talk to people. I don't like all that milling about at parties. I want to go home."

"Peter is a profoundly shy person, and at a party he'll be in a corner," says Gabereau. "He's really quite panic-stricken at times in a crowd." Another problem Gzowski has is his chain-smoking. "I smoke a lot, a lot," he says. "I'm wrestling with trying to stop. It's bothering me, from a health point of view. It's also a pain in the ass. You can't smoke in people's houses, and the CBC's supposed to be smoke-free. They've now set aside a room to smoke in called 'The Gzowski Memorial Smoking Room.' "

Gzowski also is not known for sartorial splendour. "A real unmade bed kind of a guy," says Don Harron, who himself hosted the CBC morning show in the 1970s. The morning program's pace is a killer, says Michael Enright, now host of "As It Happens" and who took over Gzowski's show when he went briefly and miserably into late-night television. "It leaves your brains like guacamole."

When Gzowski leapt into the fire of late-night TV, he was replaced on "This Country in the Morning" by a series of people whose terms were brief, including Enright, Harry Brown, Maxine Crook, and Judy LaMarsh. After them, Don Harron took over for five years. Oddly, the CBC would not allow Harron to do Charlie Farquharson or any of his characters on the program, although once he did do an interview with

Charlie on a book that carried Charlie's name as the author. "I panned it," says Harron.

Having hidden behind his Charlie Farquharson and Valerie Rosedale characters for so long, Harron was uneasy about being simply Don Harron. "In fact, I was never so scared in my life as I was at having to be myself on the radio," he says. "It was one of those moments when you think, 'I'm going to jump out the window.'"

"The CBC wanted him to be a newsman, which he never was," says Vickie Gabereau, who worked as a researcher on Harron's show. "He's an actor, not a newsman. He was afflicted with inflicting puns on the hapless Canadian public. He couldn't stop punning. But it all worked, and he was the first guy to take that show to a million listeners."

His most challenging guest was actress Joan Fontaine, who threatened to kick him in his testicles – "in a vital area you will regret," she snarled – if he talked about a play she had done that failed. "She got really snarky," he says.

Like Gzowski, Harron found the hours and the pressures exhausting, but he had the ability to take quick naps. "He could fall asleep on a rug in thirty seconds," says Gabereau. "If there was a tape on, he'd lie down and, bang, be unconscious. They'd go 'beep beep' into the studio and up he'd jump and be back on the air."

But after five years, Harron quit because he was tired. The timing was ideal for Gzowski, who was at loose ends after the cancellation of "Ninety Minutes Live." "I wanted to come back, but I couldn't because Don had the job," he says. Harron's resignation opened the door, and Gzowski came home to morning CBC Radio after eight years of exile.

As well as doing research for Harron, Vickie Gabereau filled in for him when he was ill and once for the summer. "But I was so nervous about screwing up, I was throwing up," she says. "I thought I'd be found out as an imposter with no education." Gabereau, however, continued to anchor radio shows and work as a TV researcher until she got her own afternoon network program called "Gabereau." Within a few years she, too, was a radio star.

"I like show business and I like to be on the stage," she says, noting that she once ran for mayor of Toronto, campaigning as Rosie the Clown and getting thirty-two hundred votes in the election. Of all the fifteen thousand interviews she's done on the program, she thinks her oddest guest was the world-famous violinist Yehudi Menuhin. "He hung upside down," she says. "He had those boots that you put your feet in, in the ceiling, and he hung upside down to get the blood flowing. He was seventy when I did the interview with him, and he'd hang upside down for two or three minutes at a time."

Gabereau found another interviewee, author John Fowles, "a very scary, brooding, dark, big guy"; actor Robert Culp, "pretty badly behaved"; and actor Robert Stack, "with fascinating little scars behind the ears and looking a little flat-faced." Her first words on meeting writer Margaret Atwood were "Oh my God, you're so short!" The five-foot-two Atwood said, "Nice greeting," and noted that Gabereau is only five foot five. During an interview in England, author Kingsley Amis asked her, "Who's you're next victim?" When she said it was writer Clement Freud, he replied, "Oh God, what a hateful swine, an unbearable schnook! I hope he chokes to death."

While the daily interview programs hosted by Gabereau, Gzowski, and Frum were in the forefront of CBC's radio revolution, new weekly spice was provided by programs such as "Sunday Morning," "Cross-Country Check-Up," "Double Exposure," and "The Royal Canadian Air Farce."

The big break for Roger Abbott and his colleagues on "Air Farce" came when they were fired from the CBC Radio show "The Entertainers." "The department head felt, I guess, a little guilty," says Abbott, "so when we asked him to give us a shot at a show with an audience, he backed us. It worked, and we were on our way." They were on their way to becoming not only a hit on radio but also, some years later, the most popular Canadian series on CBC-TV.

"Oh no, the boy is lost forever!" Abbott's father lamented when his son quit university to work in a Montreal radio station. Abbott's boss at the time was Newfoundland broadcasting pioneer Geoff Stirling, who ran several stations and was a legendary eccentric. "He was an absolute loony," says Abbott. He fired people at whim, talked endlessly about oddball philosophies, would disappear for months at a time, and made a fortune. He also couldn't remember names. He called Abbott "Francine" at times, and at one cocktail party he tried to introduce his wife, but couldn't remember her name and finally introduced her as "Mrs. Stirling." "She seemed used to it," says Abbott.

Partly inspired by Stirling, Abbott took his career into comedy and began working in small theatres with actor John Morgan until they wound up first on "The Entertainers" and then on "The Royal Canadian Air Farce." Because the show's comedy is based on the latest headlines, there has been many an unplanned moment on "Air Farce." One skit about the news had as a character a TV anchor named Romboy Muckfuster. Dave Broadfoot, who was playing the anchor, vividly remembers Morgan announcing, "Now back to our anchor person, Romboy Fuckmuster."

"John turned white," says Broadfoot. "He was in shock that he had said fuck. Don Ferguson went into hysterics, and he fell to the stage on his knees. I said, 'I'm leaving right now.' Everybody was ad libbing trying to get out of the skit."

The fate of news anchors is often the butt of "Air Farce" fun, as when Pamela Wallin was dismissed as Peter Mansbridge's co-anchor on "Prime Times News." "Pam joined us when we were taping in Saskatchewan, and we had her in her home town of Wadena, Saskatchewan, as the local anchor for news, sports, weather, and doing her own commercials for the Wadena House of Hair that she and her sister operated. She was just great." "It was good for me," says Wallin, who was initially leery of being spoofed by the show. "After all the fuss about being bounced, I needed to go back home and say to everybody that I'm alive, I'm standing, I'm okay, and don't you worry about me." At the same time, Keith Morrison had just been fired as co-host of CTV's "Canada A.M.," and "Air Farce" did a show about him in a new job selling zircons as host of the Home Shopping Channel.

Peter Mansbridge and his former wife, Wendy Mesley, were satirized in a skit where Mesley substituted for Wallin as Mansbridge's co-anchor. "We had Peter saying, 'Oh no, not Wendy!'" says Abbott, "and then we had Wendy constantly trying to one up him. We had each one trying to get their chairs higher than the other. Ultimately, Peter's was too high and he fell off. We heard through the grapevine that he was very upset."

Rita MacNeil was also upset at an "Air Farce" TV skit in which a well-padded Luba Goy played her. "When she danced, everything moved," says Abbott. "Rita's weight is part of the picture, and I had told her at the start of the year, 'We're going to get you one way or another this season.'" The Air Farce and MacNeil have their dressing rooms close together, and to avoid MacNeil's wrath at them for making fun of her weight, Abbott, Goy, and their colleagues made sure they taped the program on a week when MacNeil was not in production. "We're chicken to that extent," says Abbott. "We didn't actually have the nerve to do it in front of her," adding, "I'll find some way to make peace with her because she is such a nice person."

Luba Goy, the short and zaftig comedian who portrayed MacNeil, says she prefers radio to television "because on radio I look like I'm five foot nine and have a body that can kill."

Politicians also are uneasy about being featured on "Air Farce." "Be gentle," pleaded Reform Leader Preston Manning before his appearance. "You fellows don't let anybody get away with anything." Brian Mulroney, who was savaged in "Air Farce" skits, told Abbott the show was "very clever." "What he meant is," says Abbott, "'I think you're assholes.' Maureen McTeer wasn't too pleased with the way we treated her husband, Joe Clark, although he thought it was fine."

Pierre Trudeau was the most co-operative of all prime ministers, at one point telling Don Ferguson, who imitated him, "Let me give you a few pointers." "It was fascinating," says Abbott, "to see Trudeau coaching Ferguson on how to do Trudeau."

Lester Pearson was another prime minister who was impersonated by Dave Broadfoot. Once when Pearson rose to speak at a meeting where Broadfoot had offered his impression of the prime minister, Pearson noted, "I don't know whether I'm being Lester Pearson or whether I'm Dave Broadfoot being Lester Pearson."

Robert Scully, the well-tailored, smooth-talking host of the CBC business program "Venture," professed to be upset when "Air Farce" made fun of his $700 suits. "He said his suits were worth much more than that," says Abbott. "And that it was very bad for his reputation to have people saying he was wearing only $700 suits."

Occasionally the comedians tone down their humour if they think they're going too far. In a sketch on the Royal Family, they had the Queen saying, "The way the family is going, I'm getting royally pissed off." They felt that was a little strong, so for the broadcast the line was changed to "getting royally PO'd."

"We're reasonably good at self-censoring, knowing what we can get away with," says Abbott. "When I've gone too far, I have an immediate sense of panic and rush through it as quickly as possible, or make eye contact with the audience and roll my eyes as if to say, 'I have nothing to do with this stuff.' But there is nothing more chilling than the sound of an audience not laughing."

Another problem that periodically afflicts the troupe is giggling. "John Morgan is probably the worst at giggling," says Abbott. "Sometimes it just gets silly and the audience loves it. We try to get back to the script, but often it's pointless."

In the years when Dave Broadfoot was a regular on the show, there was often inadvertent laughter because he consistently dropped his script in mid-broadcast. "The script would just drop out of my hands and be all over the floor," Broadfoot says. "I'd be down on the floor picking up pages while the program continued, and Roger would pick up some, and I wouldn't know where I was in the script. But they all turned it into a big joke. The first time it really was funny, then there was a second time, and a third and a fourth, and it sort of became my specialty. It was really embarrassing. Although, come to think of it, maybe my most embarrassing moment was when I found I was not adopted."

Putting "Air Farce" on television as well as radio was traumatic for the team, given the demands of both media and their kind of humour. But with support from then CBC vice-president Ivan Fecan, they began reaching a far wider audience through TV than they ever had with radio. But for them, appealing to the wider audience can have its drawbacks. "As our audience base widens, sometimes you realize you can't be as tightly focused on satirical stuff," Abbott says. "It's a curse of popularity, but then again may we all be so cursed."

In the spring of 1996, the CBC came perilously close to losing its highest-rated series. The CBC's obsession with budget-cutting led entertainment head Phyllis Platt to tell Abbott and his "Air Farce" associates that they would have to accept cuts of 5 per cent or more for the coming season. This lack of support made the comedians look to their future, and they soon found themselves being ardently wooed by the man who put them on CBC-TV in the first place, Ivan Fecan, now an executive at Baton Broadcasting. After months of haggling over the terms of renewing the show's contract, the CBC suddenly realized that it might lose its premier series. This would have been a programming calamity, and Platt, who had succeeded Fecan at the CBC and who had been preoccupied with saving money, began backtracking on her threat to cut the show's budget. She even enlisted CBC president Perrin Beatty to meet the comedians privately and implore them to stay at the CBC. Eventually, Jim Byrd, CBC vice-president and head of English TV, joined the negotiations. The cuts were rescinded, the proposals sweetened with a long-term commitment, and the "Air Farce" troupe decided to stay.

The bidding war with Baton over "Air Farce" also speeded the lagging negotiations with the hit shows "This Hour Has 22 Minutes" and "Rita & Friends," both of which had also faced budget cuts. "Actually, it all turned out to be a really good thing," says Abbott, "because, thanks to Ivan's interest, the private sector put a high value on a show the public broadcaster was airing." It also demonstrated that the CBC's fixation on budget-cutting was endangering programs that express the basic purpose of the CBC.

Abbott knows the show's popularity won't last forever. "It's going great now, but it could end tomorrow," he says. "We've been incredibly lucky to go the nearly quarter-century that we have, but one of these days it will be over. And I have no idea what I'll do then."

One graduate of "Air Farce" who successfully struck out on his own is Dave Broadfoot. One of the most exciting moments of his career, he says, was being asked to appear on Ed Sullivan's Sunday night TV show. He called his born-again Baptist mother to tell her the news, but her only comment was "Must you work on the Sabbath?" "I said yes, and she was heartbroken." While his mother was devout, his father, he says, was a bigot, "anti-Catholic, anti-French, and anti-this and anti-that." His twin sisters were missionaries in the Far East, but, he says, "Like any good Canadian, eventually they came home to medicare."

On the Sullivan show, Broadfoot was billed as "the Member from Kicking Horse Pass." "Ed wasn't the brightest man," he says. "He thought that's who I really was and introduced me as 'my political friend from Canada.' "

Even surpassing Sullivan, the person Broadfoot remembers most vividly is Queen Elizabeth. He was chatting with her during a royal performance just after singer Anna Russell had finished a comedy song complete with loud barnyard sounds. "I can do those noises too," said Her Majesty, "but not when I'm wearing my tiara." Broadfoot took the opportunity to persuade the Queen that the Garden of Eden was actually located in Canada. "I told her," he says, "that she might not realize it, but history proves that, in the Garden of Eden, Adam was a Canadian, because only a Canadian would stand in a perfectly gorgeous tropical garden beside a perfectly gorgeous naked woman and get excited about an apple."

Broadfoot's scariest moment was at a loggers convention in Kamloops, British Columbia. The loggers had had an exceptionally long cocktail party with little food to soak up the alcohol. Somehow the official who hired him for the event mistook Broadfoot for singer Gordon Lightfoot and announced to the well-oiled loggers, "All right gentlemen, here he is to sing for us, Gordon Lightfoot."

"They could see I didn't have a guitar, but they'd never seen Lightfoot in person so they just thought I was him," Broadfoot says. "I didn't know what the hell to do, so I did an opening joke and a few more. Then one of the loggers jumped up and said, 'Sing!' Another called me 'an asshole' and I said, 'Well, at least we can speak as equals.' Then a big guy came up on the stage, put his arm around me like a vice, and said, 'Now, Gordon, you're going to sing.' I said, 'You don't understand, I'm not Gordon Lightfoot, I'm Dave Broadfoot.' He got mad, so I started singing, 'If you could read my mind love, what a tale my thoughts would tell.' " After the song Broadfoot fled the stage and left Kamloops on the first plane out.

Tall, crinkly-haired, and raspy-voiced, Broadfoot discovered the thrill of making others laugh at age twenty after he left the navy. "I never got over that sound of laughter," he says. "I felt that I belonged on the stage. . . . I'd like to die delivering a punch line."

Over the years comedians such as Broadfoot and programs such as "The Royal Canadian Air Farce" kept alive on radio the tradition of comedy and satire begun by Max Ferguson and Wayne and Shuster. That tradition is carried on, too, on TV by the biting comedy of "This Hour Has 22 Minutes," which features what *Maclean's* has called "the bitch goddess of Canadian political satire," Newfoundlander Mary Walsh. Smashing taboos and jeering at the famous through her madcap characters, Walsh has become a modern-day version of Max Ferguson's Rawhide of forty years ago. The "Air Farce," "22 Minutes," and "Double Exposure" all demonstrate Canadians' healthy ability to laugh at themselves and even more at their politicians. "In the States, if people don't like their leaders, they shoot them," says Roger Abbott. "In Canada, we make fun of them."

One survivor of the radio revolution of the early 1970s is Clyde Gilmour. Every weekend for half a century, listeners have heard the voice of Gilmour. For the first decade he reviewed movies and for the last forty years he has hosted his own show, "Gilmour's Albums." The quiet, gently pedantic on-air side of Gilmour gives no indication of the mischievous imp he can be in private.

In a journalistic career stretching back to the 1930s, Gilmour has interviewed everyone from violin virtuoso Isaac Stern to Hollywood sexpot Kim Novak, and he has sharp comments on all of them. Of comedian Danny Kaye, he says, "He and his wife had a testy relationship. Kaye reminded me of an old song. 'You'll look sweet upon the seat of a bisexual built for two' "; of crooner Rudy Vallee, "He was such a tightwad. All he talked about was money"; of actor Donald Crisp, "Another tightwad"; of the comedians Bob and Ray, "They were funny on the air, but such nice, dull guys to talk to"; of screen siren Kim Novak, "Beautiful, but it was like talking to a robot"; of Peter Sellers, "His own personality was as colourless and polite as the night clerk in a very fine London hotel"; of Cary Grant, "A genuinely charming guy and so considerate."

When Gilmour asked Peter Ustinov whether he thought audiences might soon reject too much sex in movies and on television, Ustinov told him, "No. My feeling is that we're going to discover and exploit some entirely new and unsuspected erogenous zone. The one I'm thinking of is the ear. Think of it. It's ideal. It's circular, there's a cavity in it, and it's surrounded by hair. I can imagine them hiding ears in movies and TV, and people saying, 'For a second there, you could get a flashing look of her left lobe.'"

To Gilmour, Isaac Stern revealed his fascination with baseball. "To me," he said, "a great baseball player is an artist, like a great violinist or pianist. I'm not interested in hitters. All they do is bang, bang, bang. I like to see a pitcher work his way out of a tight spot. But best of all, I like the absolute effortless grace of the way a good shortstop or third baseman can field a tough, hopping ball and a nice easy flip to first base one second before the runner reaches it. To me, that's artistry of the highest kind."

In his days as a movie critic, Gilmour was in Hollywood interviewing stars so often that a senior MGM executive told him, "Your name is a byword with us, Mr. Gilroy." After forty years with "Gilmour's Albums," the program's title has become imbedded in his audience's memory so deeply that he's had people think his real name was Gilmour Zalbums. "People call me Clive, Clift, Clark, and dozens of other variations of Clyde," he says. "The supreme one was from a Chicago movie producer whose version of my name was wildly at variance, calling me Clarp Gebrow."

Gilmour himself has had fun with names, particularly with a certain Mr. Kosmos Kagool. In the 1930s he saw a movie in which a hideous witch by the name of Kagool was burned to death in an African volcano. Gilmour thought it would be amusing if the witch had a son named Kosmos Kagool who lived in Chilliwack, British Columbia, was a member of the junior board of the Board of Chillwack, and was engaged to a nice, dull girl. Gilmour brought Kosmos Kagool to life by slipping his name into the papers as having attended social functions and meetings. He signed Kagool's name to petitions from time to time and put it in the telephone book. By listing Kagool's name at his own address, "I would get through the mail," Gilmour says "two free razor blades, two bars of soap instead of one. This adds up in a year."

He even used Kagool's name once as a byline on a story in the Vancouver *Province*. The story was one Gilmour had written when he was still in the navy and couldn't use his own name. The managing editor of the rival *Vancouver Sun* called the *Province* to ask who the new reporter was. "He's good, and if he's got guts enough to use his byline, then I've got guts enough to use mine," said Hymie Koshevoy, who later became a columnist.

Kosmos Kagool had a particularly heroic war. "When hostilities broke out," says Gilmour, "Kagool became an object lesson to all young men in Canada by joining all three forces simultaneously. Each enlistment was duly reported in various newspapers, and he made appearances on different occasions, with his rank rising and falling unpredictably. In one listing, I had him as Kosmos Kagool, RCNVR, and I once got his name in the Vancouver *Province* as Admiral of the Fleet, Kosmos Kagool, DSO, and two or three other decorations, being in town for confidential discussions. I learned later the top navy brass on the West Coast spent hours trying to track him down so they could honour him in the mess. I managed to get word back to them that he was on a secret mission for Churchill personally and couldn't see anybody." When a new city hall was opened in Johannesburg, South Africa, newspapers in Vancouver and Chilliwack noted that "Kosmos Kagool of Chilliwack, B.C., was one of those present."

For more than sixty years, the name Kosmos Kagool has turned up from time to time, and still does to this day. It even appears in part on Gilmour's car licence plate, which reads KAG 333, for Kagool and thirty-three and a third for the rpm of an LP record.

Clyde Gilmour was born in Medicine Hat, Alberta, but the Depression foreclosed the chance of going to university, and he went to work on newspapers in Medicine Hat, Edmonton, Vancouver, and Toronto, later becoming a fixture on CBC Radio. During the war he was in public relations in the Canadian Navy, where he learned to enjoy drinking and singing, especially the latter. His favourite song then, which even now in his mid-eighties he still sings lustily, has typical mess-room lyrics: "Violate me in violet time, in the vilest way that you know. Ruin me, ravage me, brutally savage me, on me no mercy show. From now on, to sweet words I'll be oblivious. What I need is a gal that is lewd and lascivious. Violate me in violet time in the vilest way." He was once exuberantly singing this in the officers' mess in Ottawa when an admiral walked in. He continued to sing, but notes that "curiously enough, I never made any further advancement in the navy beyond lieutenant."

Years later producer Ross McLean asked him to sing a song dedicated to a printer and his typographical errors. The song was from South Pacific, and Gilmour sang it complete with typos, calling the music, "Sothu Passvekik by Rogers and Hammersnite." To this day, he can still croon, "Smeo enchnated eenvnig."

Gilmour still enjoys singing, but admits he expresses more enthusiasm than excellence. He adds, "To me, the human voice is the king of instruments. The spell a great singer can weave on an audience is really magic of the highest kind." He has, however, kept both his own singing and rock music off "Gilmour's Albums." "I really feel rock is anti-music," he says. "Rock to me sounds like Attila and his barbarians coming in through the living-room window. There are millions of kids now who will have damaged hearing." He does differentiate among rock musicians, however, saying, "The Beatles now sound like the Vatican Choir compared to some of the heavy-metal boys."

Gilmour's fans are fiercely loyal, as one eighty-year-old widow demonstrated when she wrote to Gilmour, telling him of her enjoyment of his voice and his program. She said she always made herself a pot of tea and had a couple of Dad's cookies while listening to him in her bed. When he thanked her, she wrote a second letter a month later saying, "Dear Mr. Gilmour. My oh my, I certainly enjoyed you in bed last night." "I asked my wife, Barbara, to respond," he says.

"I always think of my audience as one person," he says. "I used to hear broadcasters say, 'Some of you,' and I'd think, 'Just talk to me buster! I'm here. Just talk to me!' Radio after all, is just one person talking to another. I don't talk down. I don't talk up to the listener. I just say, 'Hello' and have a conversation."

Gilmour is so precise in his approach that he has a reputation of never making an error. "That's absurd," he says. "I do make mistakes and I make lulus." Sometimes his announcers do as well, and one of them told the audience that the program would feature Ezio Pinza, the Italian operatic bass, pronouncing bass like the fish. "No, Disney has singing fish on his show, but I don't," Gilmour quickly said.

He is particular about pronunciation and music, and he also is a punctuality freak. As a nineteen-year-old, he lost out on a job because his watch wasn't working. "I smashed the watch in the gutter and spent the outlandishly extravagant price of seven bucks for a new watch," he says, "and then I got another and started wearing two watches. I still do and both are never more than a second out." He was astonished when Barbara Frum told him she never wore a watch. "I'm surrounded by watches everywhere I go all day long," she told him. "I always know what time it is, so why should I carry one." "It astounded the hell out of me," says Gilmour.

"Gilmour's Albums" survived the CBC budget cuts because it combined two qualities treasured by broadcasters: it was popular and it was cheap. "All it costs them is my quite modest fee," he says. "Every record is from my own collection." But in his mid-eighties Gilmour's health finally caught up with him and he retired from the airwaves in June 1997.

Clyde Gilmour's gentle enthusiasm enriched the rebirth of radio in the 1970s. "Gilmour's Albums," "Cross-Country Check-Up," and Lister Sinclair's "Ideas" all gave new life to what had been a radio service shrivelling in the face of the mesmerizing, ubiquitous, one-eyed box of wires, tubes, and circuit boards that Canadians were watching for around twenty-three hours a week. Constantly rejuvenating itself with programs such as "Definitely Not the Opera" and iconoclasts like Rex Murphy, CBC Radio has become one of the best network radio services in the world.

10

TV Grows Up

While CBC Radio was transforming itself, television was also changing, becoming less audacious than in its pioneering days, although more polished; less magical, but more pervasive. One change was the switch from live broadcasts to recording almost everything. That not only lessened the tension and excitement but also saw power shift from the studio set to the edit suite. In truth, taping took some of the fun out of television.

CBC series like "Wojeck," "Quentin Durgens, MP," "The King of Kensington," "The Beachcombers," "Hangin' In," "Seeing Things," "North of 60," and a host of others largely replaced individual drama; pop music replaced the classics; and song and dance shows no longer dominated prime time. The CBC also had ceased being the only TV network in the country, and by the 1980s cable had brought in a multitude of American channels.

Although exclusive no more, the CBC still provided by far the most Canadian journalistic and entertainment programming. The new age brought new stars, including John Vernon, Al Waxman, Bruno Gerussi, Gordon Pinsent, Louis del Grande, Lally Cadeau, Jackie Burroughs, Cynthia Dale, David Suzuki, Patrick Watson, Roy Bonisteel, Tina Keeper, and even The Friendly Giant and Mr. Dressup. They and a galaxy of other performers brought stories into our living rooms every night as TV became Canada's principal source of information and entertainment.

Even though most shows were now taped, there were still challenging moments behind the scenes. Drunk performers continued to plague some producers. Studio director Steve Hyde remembers, "Eartha Kitt was absolutely hammered when she came on. She didn't know where she was." The worst for Hyde, however, was a prominent singer, whose name he has mercifully forgotten, who was set to do a love song in a gazebo. She came back from a break filled with alcohol-induced wobbles. "We got her into the gazebo, but she wasn't too steady on her feet, so we put a cord around her and tied her to the back of the gazebo just to hold her up. Even though it was being taped, we couldn't stop production just for her. She sang sort of bending forward, but the cord stopped her from falling down. When it was over, we rushed in and untied her and sat her down."

It wasn't only singers who caused problems. "A big grizzly bear called Gentle Ben had a series that ran for years, and he once did a show for Elwood Glover," says Hyde. Gentle Ben, however, was in a bad mood when Glover brightly introduced him on the air. "First thing the bear does is go for Elwood," says Hyde. "The trainer hauls him off, but then the bear goes after the cameraman. They're down on the floor rolling around, and the trainer is beating the hell out of the bear. Glover is sitting there terrified and crying. Finally, the trainer hauls off Gentle Ben and the program went on."

Glenn Gould, the brilliant classical pianist, appeared on the first prime-time entertainment show when TV began in 1952. "He was not just your average person," says producer Norman Campbell. "In the middle of a hot summer, he came to the studio to do his 'Music of the USSR' wearing an overcoat and gloves. He wanted all the air-conditioning turned off, and the cameramen had sweat pouring off them, but we all knew Glenn, so we went along with him. He was all bundled up until we did a take and then he'd get rid of his coat and gloves. After, he'd put them on again."

Gould would have frozen to death if he'd had to face the kind of conditions international figure-skating champion Kurt Browning endured during the shooting of a couple of TV programs near Rocky Mountain House, Alberta. In forty-below weather, Browning had to skate on a frozen lake in a silk shirt and no gloves. "He had thermal underwear on, and we had a little hut for him to pop into between takes," recalls director Joan Tosoni. "The wind was really blowing, and we had torches out to keep the cables from freezing. He was having a really hard time making one jump, and he got really pissed off because he had to do it maybe fifteen times before he got it. He was mad and frustrated, and he and all of us were freezing our butts off."

In the second show Browning was doing at the same location, a "Singin' in the Rain" number required water to be sprayed on the ice for him to skate through. The shooting lasted no more than a minute at a time because the water flooded the ice. "We had to stop and let it refreeze, and do it again and again. We were cement by the time we finished," says Tosoni. "But Kurt would try anything, and he wanted it perfect."

An actor who also wanted perfection was William Hutt, who played Sir John A. Macdonald in the Pierre Berton series "The National Dream." Hutt was brought up short, however, by a lifelong admirer of Sir John A. – John Diefenbaker. When he visited the set and saw Hutt attired as Macdonald, Diefenbaker said, "Your lapels are too wide! And you're surely not going to wear those shoes, are you?"

Gordon Pinsent

Although he appears to be a suave and confident performer, Gordon Pinsent was anything but when he first starred in television. His CBC-TV début featured him behind bars as a Latin revolutionary who had been badly beaten by the police. "I wasn't satisfied with the amount of make-up I'd been given, so I plastered bloody gauze on my face," he says. His co-star, a young actor also doing her first national TV show, was on the other side of the bars talking to him. "She called my name," Pinsent remembers, "and I crawled over to the bars, which had just been freshly painted before we began the show. I had a long page to deliver, and the words went out of my mind completely. The only thing I could think of doing was to reach through the bars, grab her head, and kiss her. We kissed for a long time while I tried to remember my lines. Her eyes were ablaze with fear, for she didn't have a clue what was going on.

"When the words came back to me, I pulled my face away from her only to see that some of the fresh paint from the bars was now streaking down her cheeks. And worse still, some of the bloody gauze that I had on my face was stuck to her. A little string of gauze had come loose and now formed a bridge between our two faces. The spotlight was on us since we were in a close-up, and I forgot my lines again. So in a terrifying panic, I kissed her again, thereby getting more paint and gauze on her. Eventually I got my lines out, but it was my first introduction to the kind of panic that one can get into in this business. The girl left acting altogether after this."

When he went to Hollywood, Pinsent found others had similar memory problems. "E. G. Marshall in his court scenes used to pin his scripts on the jury, and some of them would have his lines on their foreheads as he faced them," he says.

At one point, taking time out from his TV career, Pinsent was appearing at the Stratford Festival when he was suddenly left at a loss for words. He was holding a pearl in one hand, putting on a glove on the other, and had begun a speech when the pearl squirted out of his hand into the audience. From the tenth row he heard a friend's voice cry out, "Got your pearl, Gordon!"

Pinsent also had trouble in a musical with Kerrie Keane, a Canadian actress working in Hollywood, who had come back to do the show with Pinsent. In one dance number in the middle of a ballroom spin, Keane's boa whirled into Pinsent's face, giving him a mouthful of feathers. The biggest problem with that particular show, however, was not the feathers, nor the bad back that kept Pinsent in excruciating pain, it was Irving Berlin. Berlin's New York agent had assured producers Lorraine Thomson and Alex Barris that Berlin would give the CBC the rights to use half a dozen of his songs. The production was just finished when the ninety-eight-year-old Berlin decided on a whim not to give the CBC the rights to several of the songs. "There was no rhyme or reason to it," says Thomson. "He just decided we could use only half the songs they'd earlier agreed to us using." This meant days of delay and a costly reshooting of the opening and a couple of dance numbers with different music. When it was over, Pinsent came to Thomson's home carrying a bouquet of flowers and a little note that read, "Fuck Irving Berlin!"

"He's a deceptive guy," says Jackie Burroughs, who has worked in several shows with Pinsent. "I always think charming and good-looking people like Gordon are stupid, but he's really smart. He's a writer, actor, singer, painter. Sometimes I think he's too much of a nice guy. Sometimes I wish he were a bit more pushy because he's brighter than most of the people he steps aside for."

As a child, the stage and TV screen did not seem a likely place for Pinsent to call his professional home. "When I was young I had rickets, and I couldn't walk until I was five," he says. "I had a lot of time to sit and get fat. My nickname as a kid was Porky."

In school Pinsent's artistic talents first showed with his drawing ability. "I would draw pictures of my teachers in case I was about to fail," he says. His drawing ability has stayed with him throughout his life, and partly through this interest he has become a friend of the Newfoundland artist Christopher Pratt. He recalls Pratt telling him of the time he wanted to paint nudes but was hesitant to approach the fishermen's daughters who lived in his town, St. Mary's Bay. "He didn't want to go up and down the streets of St. Mary's approaching young ladies and asking, 'Would you mind posing naked?' " says Pinsent. "One day he was driving his car through the rain when he saw walking along the side of the road St. Mary's Bay's only prostitute, who was called Magdalen. Pratt stopped to give her a lift and thought she would be an ideal nude model. He asked if she knew who he was. She said, 'Yes, you paints lighthouses and boats.' 'Well, Magdalen,' Pratt said, 'I don't suppose you would consider sitting for me with no clothes on?' Magdalen took a long drag on her cigarette, squinted at Pratt suspiciously, and said, 'Now, boy, I draws the line at that.' "

Pinsent worked at odd jobs before joining the Canadian Army for three years. He was demobbed in Winnipeg, where, by accident, he found himself in a rehearsal for a play. "The truth is," he says, "I got into this business because I skipped into this darkened theatre in Winnipeg when I was running away from a girlfriend. They were rehearsing, and while I was in there somebody offered me a small part in the play." One play led to another and then led to performances on local CBC Radio and -TV and finally to his network début. Along the way, he met John Hirsch, who had come to Winnipeg from Hungary in 1947. Hirsch became Pinsent's mentor and a dynamic creative force in Canadian drama on stage and television.

Pinsent shot to TV stardom in the 1960s with his performances as a Mountie in the series "Forest Rangers" and as the lead in "Quentin Durgens, MP." He then moved to Hollywood, where he starred in several pictures and came to know many movie stars, including Marlon Brando and Wally Cox. He first met Brando when he was at Cox's home in the hills behind Hollywood. As Cox and Pinsent were sitting in the living room, they heard Brando huffing and puffing his way in through the front door. "Oh God, here's the fat bastard now," Cox said. "I ran all the way from my place," said Brando, stumbling across the room to the kitchen.

"He headed for the refrigerator, grabbed a big handful of chocolate cake, and started mushing it into his mouth," says Pinsent. "He always did just what he wanted. Later I went to a couple of movies with him, and we'd sit there and he'd be shovelling buttered popcorn into his mouth while his wife, Tarita, breastfed their daughter, Cheyenne."

Pinsent adds, "Whenever I was with him, he'd ask me to sing 'Danny Boy,' which was his favourite song. Wherever he went, he had a presence, a peculiar, very strange, and self-absorbed presence."

Pinsent also worked with Robert Young, who played Marcus Welby, M.D., and found that, privately, Young "couldn't be more boring if he tried. Every day before starting to work he would have the cast take a minute of silence." Pinsent enjoyed working with Burt Reynolds, who liked to do his own stunts. "He jumped as though there were springs in his shoes," Pinsent says. "Sometimes I thought his rug was going to fly off." On the other hand, Pinsent found actor George Peppard "a very strange man. He always wanted to look like Anthony Quinn – a glamorous tough guy."

Pinsent had a hard time working with Leslie Caron, as well. "She was going through a bad period and she was just walking through her role," he says. "The trick to being a happy performer," Pinsent says, "is that you have to keep the playfulness with you. It's no good if it's sucked out."

When he realized that Hollywood had sucked much of the playfulness out of his work, Pinsent returned to Canada to make *The*

Rowdyman, which he calls "my own personal Alamo," and went on to do "A Gift to Last" and *John and the Missus*.

One price of being a star, Pinsent has found, is that people point to him on the street and lovestruck fans send him mash notes and, at one point, threw pebbles at his bedroom window in the middle of the night. One woman threatened to kill him after he married his wife, actress Charmion King. Less dangerous, but still bothersome, were a couple of fans who pulled him out of a hotel phone booth in Winnipeg. "The phone just fell and dangled there while this guy pulled me into the middle of the hotel lobby to show me to his wife," says Pinsent. "He didn't say anything to me, but shouted at his wife, 'See, I told you it was him!' The two of them stood side by side looking at me as though I were a piece of art or something. They looked at each other, and she finally said to him, 'Not like he is on TV.' Then he said to me, 'Well, thanks anyway,' and they walked off. I hadn't been able to say a word."

For all his success, Pinsent still frets about his work. "In acting," he says, "you're simply at the mercy of other people's perception of you. It can be a terrifying feeling. The rewards can be great, but there is no steady happiness in this business. There are peaks of joy and valleys of gloom. As you get older, you forget that it was an adventure at one time, that you were able to take the falls. You think, 'I know I'm good. I've had it proven. Then why is it not working now?' You feel you can't take the falls. You say to yourself, 'Gee, I need this. This is all I can do in life.' "

Alex Trebek

In contrast to Gordon Pinsent, CBC announcer and host Alex Trebek went to Hollywood and stayed there, gaining American TV star status as host of the game show "Jeopardy!" Born to a low-income family in Sudbury, Ontario, Trebek entered a military school as a teenager but quit after five days, rebelling at what he calls "the strict and stupid" military rules and regulations. He worked his way through the University of Ottawa as a CBC relief announcer. Peter Jennings and Lloyd Robertson were fellow announcers, although Jennings soon went to the States, and he also worked with Patrick Watson and Norman DePoe. Trebek moved to CBC Toronto a couple of years later and, because he is fluently bilingual, was much in demand for network newscasts, public affairs programs, live-event coverage, concerts, and royal visits.

At the CBC, Trebek quickly rose to the big time and was soon covering not only royal visits but also the World Curling Championships in Scotland, where he learned to eat haggis. "There were decanters of Scotch on each table," he says, "and I realized why they put the Scotch there. You needed it to eat the haggis."

As an announcer – at age twenty-three, the youngest on the network staff – Trebek worked with most of the broadcast legends of the day, including Andrew Allan, Esse Ljungh, J. Frank Willis, Frances Hyland, Kate Reid, Juliette, Bruno Gerussi. "I remember when Barbara Amiel started as an assistant in public affairs," he says. "The criticism of her was that she was probably just an airhead because nobody that gorgeous and with that body could have any brains. I lost track of her, but a few years later when I'd come back to Canada, I'd see her byline and think, 'Hey, she can't be a dummy because she's writing pretty serious stuff.' "

In those early days at the CBC, Trebek was, says producer and writer Alex Barris, "very slick and very good. He could better Fred Davis in terms of being smooth." Trebek is also very disciplined. "He's a typical Jesuit boy," says Elaine Saunders. "He should have been a priest. He has all those Jesuitical rigidities and can be very moody. But he is extremely intelligent and was destined for success."

What Juliette noticed about Trebek when they worked together on a CBC Radio series was that "you never really got to know Alex. He never gave people the feeling that he wanted you to come up and talk to him. On 'Jeopardy!' I'll bet all those contestants are frightened to death of him. He can be very funny, but Alex has never really let loose. I watch him now and say to myself, 'Oh, Alex, let go!' "

As a handsome and very eligible bachelor, Trebek had his full share of girlfriends during his CBC days. "He's a nice guy, but a little temperamental," says onetime script assistant Mary DePoe. "At one point he was engaged to singer Vanda King, but she decided she didn't want to marry him and gave him back his ring. He threw it at her, and when she bent over to pick it up, he booted her right in the backside and knocked her over."

Trebek also dated fellow CBC announcer Jan Tennant, who later anchored Global News. "I used to call her the Head Knit because she was always knitting, even during programs," he says. When she was anchoring newscasts at the CBC, Tennant would read an introduction to a story and when the report came on, she'd pick up her knitting needles and work away until she had to do the next introduction.

Two big Canadian TV shows that spread Trebek's reputation as a smooth, knowledgeable host were "Reach for the Top," a youth quiz program, and "Music Hop," which introduced him to some of the oddities of show business. Trebek has short, curly hair, but that wasn't the look the producer wanted for a music show aimed at young people. "So," he says, "they would bring in a barber every week to straighten out my hair."

But it was "Reach for the Top" that honed his quiz-show skills and set the stage for his career in the States. Alan Thicke, the writer, producer, and performer who had earlier left Canadian TV to work in the United States, recommended Trebek as host of a new NBC quiz program. He got the job not only because of his on-air smoothness but also because of his ability to memorize. The program used a large number of statistics and facts that had to be presented accurately, but because of the style of the program, they could not use cue cards. "That was the hook they used to get me a work permit to get into the States," he says. "They said I had a photographic memory, but I didn't really. I was just able to memorize a lot of stuff."

Prudent as always, when the American agency hired him for the program, Trebek didn't quit the CBC but took his accumulated leave and worked on the show for ten weeks. "I wasn't taking a chance," he says. "I wasn't burning all my bridges." Once the show was picked up for continuation by the network, however, Trebek resigned from the CBC.

Although he's now a Hollywood veteran, having been a game-show star for about a quarter of a century, Trebek still thinks of himself as "just a guy from Sudbury. Basically, I'm a homebody with my family, and I don't care if I never go out in Hollywood," he says.

Al Waxman

In the 1960s, John Vernon as Wojeck and Gordon Pinsent as Quentin Durgens, MP were in the vanguard of new, popular TV drama series, and in the 1970s, Al Waxman's King of Kensington captivated Canadians. "'The King of Kensington' was the first major breakthrough for situation comedy," says Denis Harvey, who was then a senior CBC-TV executive.

Waxman was initially approached to be one of a pool of directors for the show since, at the time, he was both acting and directing. When he was asked to do a screen test, however, he refused, saying, "No, you either want me to do it or not." A pilot was done with a different actor, but producer Perry Rosemond wasn't satisfied. He then saw Waxman in another show and decided he was the perfect King, and TV history was made.

Waxman has been on the stage since he was twelve, playing pirates and ogres in a CBC Winnipeg radio series called "Doorway to Fairyland." He also wrote, directed, and acted in a short play about the cartoon character Dagwood Bumstead, which he put on in a neighbour's recreation room, charging two cents for kids and five cents for adults. "We raised two dollars and fifty cents, which we gave to the Red Cross," he says. Later he acted in radio dramas for Andrew Allan and Esse Ljungh, inspired by the stage electricity of his idol, Al Jolson. "I must have seen *The Jolson Story* twenty-seven times," he says. "I was just smitten by Al Jolson. He had such an unbelievable impact on the audience, and I wanted to do that too."

With co-star Fiona Reid, Waxman soared into stardom on "The King of Kensington," although at the start, he says, the CBC thought the series would last only thirteen weeks. It aired from 1975 to 1980 and led to a call from Hollywood for Waxman to take a starring role in the cops and robbers series "Cagney and Lacey" with Tyne Daly and Sharon Gless.

"I was one of the first people to get over six figures at the CBC, but in five years of 'King of Kensington' I didn't make what I made in one year of 'Cagney and Lacey,'" he says. "But apart from money, making it in Hollywood was very important, and I was a little bit in awe. Then all of a sudden, I realized that I've had more experience than those women. They should be in awe of me."

Like all actors, Waxman fears forgetting his lines. "I've had this same nightmare often over the years, and it is that I go onstage and forget my script," he says. "I'm standing there empty. It's disastrous, and then I wake up. In reality, it's a nightmare that has never happened, but I've had embarrassing moments in auditions where your confidence just drops out of you. As I've gotten older, with more reputation and therefore more at stake, I've gotten worse at auditions."

Occasionally auditions can have surprising results, such as when Waxman was partnered with Robert De Niro in trying out for a movie role in New York as a Jewish gangster. After the audition he was, instead, offered the role of an Irish cop. He also was once offered a role opposite Elizabeth Taylor, whom he had fantasized about since seeing her as a youngster in *National Velvet*. "They told me, 'You're going to have a bedroom scene with her.' She was particularly fat at the time, but she was always beautiful, fat or not. But I said, 'Just my luck. I get to go to bed with Elizabeth Taylor when she looks like me with a wig on.' In the end, I couldn't do the movie because I couldn't get away from 'Cagney and Lacey' for the time needed."

Being fat has preoccupied Waxman all his life, and he's been in and out of spas and been an off-and-on dieter most of his career. He'll lose sixty pounds, but then gain most of it back because he loves to eat. "I'm a pretty strong-minded individual, but one of the weaknesses I've allowed myself is weight. It's an overwhelming weakness, and there have been many roles I have not gotten because of the weight."

Along with his hectic, high-energy pace, weight was a factor in the heart attack he suffered while doing "Cagney and Lacey." The first sign came when he was driving to the set and was hit by heavy chest pains. He thought of going to the hospital but said to himself, "Jesus, no. I'm directing a film, and if they hear I've gone in for this, maybe they'll think I'm an insurance risk. Hell, I haven't got time for this." A couple of years later, he had more pains and wound up having a heart bypass operation. He was helped by a masseuse on the "Cagney and Lacey" set, who, for a dollar a minute, gave massages to the stars. She also played tapes and provided soothing words for Waxman, who worried whether he'd live through his heart problems. "She gave me a mantra," Waxman says, "and told me, 'There's no way you're going to die. You have to think, I Am.' I would lie there on my dressing room floor on the set, and as she was doing the massaging, I would be saying 'I Am' over and over again."

Waxman takes his acting seriously, forever looking for characters to absorb into his TV and film roles. "As an actor you have a sort of filing cabinet in your mind," he says. "If you're sitting in the subway, you're always studying people and you file them back there in your mind. They'll show up some day in one of the characters you portray."

Of all the show-business people he's encountered in Hollywood or in Canada, the most stimulating, understanding, and creative was John Hirsch, the emotional Hungarian from Winnipeg who was a mentor and hero to Waxman, Gordon Pinsent, and many other Canadian actors. "Hirsch cared, he really cared," says another performer, Allan Blye, who knew him in Winnipeg when Hirsch was artistic director of the Manitoba Theatre Centre. He inspired many actors because, says Blye, "he knew what the spirit of the actor was all about. His spirit was totally with the artist."

Waxman found that out in a confrontation he had on "The King of Kensington" set. As he always provided his crew and guest stars with little gifts, flowers, and small parties, Waxman was outraged when he got a memo from the production staff stating he wasn't treating guest stars well enough. "I went berserk with anger, ballistic, because it was the exact opposite of what was the case," he says. He charged up to the control room to confront the show's writers and production staff, demanding, "Who sent this? I will not go back onstage until there is an apology." Nobody apologized, and Waxman marched back to his dressing room where he sat brooding. Finally, there was a knock on his door, and when he answered, John Hirsch, recently appointed CBC drama head, was standing there with a dozen roses. "Al, what do they know about emotions?" Hirsch said, referring to the production staff. "Forget about them. I love you for what you've done. You're right. Now, please, come back to work."

"He had the same explosiveness as I did," Waxman says. "He and I were one. He was eccentric, but he was practical too. He didn't make them apologize. He just came to me and said, 'I'm apologizing. You're right. Everybody knows what you're doing for the guest stars. Please keep it up.' "

"John was always like a wild young flamingo, moving in all directions, looking, searching, always coming from or going to something," says Gordon Pinsent. "He was certainly the most awkward kind of dancer, but dancing was important to him. He wanted to get off the ground, not stay on it where everyone else was. He was always in flight, and so were our imaginations with him because he opened this wonderful door for us."

Hirsch brought his talented inspiration to the CBC in the mid-1970s, providing creative verve, bureaucratic single-mindedness, and storming through CBC management corridors focused totally on improving TV drama. Once when a colleague tried to talk to him about CBC budget problems, he said, "Don't tell me what the problems are. I don't want to know. If I hear and understand them, that will weaken my own preoccupation. I care only about drama. Nothing else."

After the CBC, he took his pyrotechnical talents to the Stratford Festival, where he was artistic director from 1981 to 1985. He died in 1989 at age fifty-nine.

"He was show business," says Waxman. "He had that volatile, emotional thing that should be really cherished and not dismissed."

Bruno Gerussi

Another volatile and emotional Canadian star was the late Bruno Gerussi, who'd had a successful dramatic career before vaulting into national prominence with "The Beachcombers," which enchanted Canadian TV viewers from 1972 to 1990.

"He was that cute, little, tough Italian playing Romeo," remembers Juliette, who knew Gerussi from his acting days in Vancouver in the early 1950s. Born in Medicine Hat, Alberta, Gerussi and his family moved to the West Coast when he was eight years old, and at fourteen he was working part time in B.C. sawmills for thirty-eight cents an hour. He acted in high-school plays and won a scholarship to the Banff School of Fine Arts. While he was there, he won another scholarship, this time to the Seattle Repertory Playhouse. After that he came back to Vancouver and began performing on CBC Radio and -TV, becoming, in Juliette's words, "the little boy wonder" of Vancouver's drama scene. Lured east in 1954 by the Stratford Festival, he became a leading performer playing, among other roles, Romeo to Julie Harris's Juliet. Gerussi, who was never overly impressed by stardom, was put off by the presence of so many English actors at Stratford. "Oh to be in England, now that England is here" was his comment at the time. He became friendly with one English actor, however, James Mason. The Stratford actors frequently played softball on a baseball diamond beside the theatre, and when he arrived to play his first game of softball, Mason's attire made him stand out from his jeans-and-sweatshirt-clad colleagues. "James came trotting out onto the field in cricket whites, elegant linen," Gerussi remembered. "Someone shouted, 'James!' and threw a ball at him. He reached up, caught it in his hand, but one finger went straight out. He'd totally dislocated his finger. I ran over and he said, 'Oh my God, Bruno this is dreadful. What'll I do?' I said, 'Keep still,' and I yanked the thing back in place while he yelped, and then I got some tape, and he went on to play the whole game. He played like a raving maniac and ripped his elegant whites to shreds."

Gerussi quickly became one of the stars of the Canadian acting community, working closely with Kate Reid, Frances Hyland, John Drainie, Tommy Tweed, and producers and directors Tyrone Guthrie, Andrew Allan, Esse Ljungh, and Norman Jewison. He was at Stratford for a decade, occasionally appearing in CBC shows and then hosting the CBC network morning show. Although he performed onstage in New York and toured the States, he didn't want to go to Hollywood because, he said, "I'd probably wind up just playing fat, little Italian gangsters." Instead, in part because he loved to eat, he wound up doing a TV cooking program called "Celebrity Cooks." It was a live show in which not everything went as planned. "I was once mixing something in a high-speed mixer and forgot to put the lid on," he said. "I just lost my concentration, and when I turned the thing on, stuff shot up in the air and came down on my head and all over my shoulders. It looked like a flock of seagulls had just flown over me and made their deposits."

Gerussi broke into TV stardom with "The Beachcombers," which began in 1972 and lasted eighteen years. Filming was done at Gibsons Landing, in British Columbia, and one aspect of the series of which Gerussi was particularly proud was in having roles played by native people. He became especially friendly with Chief Dan George, who was a role model for many young native performers. George had been around in show business for years and was always being asked for advice. Gerussi remembered hearing George in conversation with a serious young performer who wanted to know his philosophy of acting. The wise old chief's response was "Always take the money up front."

Gerussi used Chief Dan George in one "Beachcombers" episode just after the chief had done a movie with Clint Eastwood. On the movie set, he'd been frail, and an actress friend had accompanied him to take care of him, staying in a hotel suite next to his. Just before going to Gibsons Landing, *People* magazine had done an article mistakenly suggesting there was more than a nurse relationship involved. "I cut out the article," said Gerussi, "and made up a bunch of Wanted posters saying, 'Chief Dan George, Alias Sweet Lips-Smooth Talker, is on the loose. Lock up your daughters and your wives.' I put copies up all over the reserve at Sechelt where we were shooting a 'Beachcombers' episode. Dan thought it was great."

Gerussi, as Nick Adonidas, became one of the country's most popular personalities. "People say, 'I grew up with you,'" Gerussi remembered. "The impact of the show was just stunning and wonderful." But after nearly two decades, "stunning and wonderful" were not the words that leapt to Ivan Fecan's mind. "'Beachcombers' people had been used to doing their own thing without having any network control," says Nada Harcourt, then a close associate of Fecan. "Then everything came under Ivan's style. He wanted control and centralization. Bruno asked to have a love interest in the show, but we didn't think that would be appropriate. He also wanted to jump out of airplanes or hang-glide. He wanted to do death-defying stunts, and we were terrified he'd hurt himself. But it was just the way he was. When we said no, he'd get furious and say, 'Nick is very vital!'"

Gerussi was particularly angry when Fecan moved "The Beachcombers" from its prized Sunday night prime-time slot to the lower-profile Wednesday night period, where the program ran against NHL hockey on another channel.

"They promised a big advertising campaign, but it never came about," said Gerussi. "Of course, the audience numbers were going to drop. I knew the end was coming when they did that. They did it deliberately so that the numbers would drop and they could blame cancelling the program on the grounds that it wasn't popular anymore. That was an out and out fraudulent lie. Total bullshit!"

"Sure, ratings inevitably diminished, having moved out of Sunday night," says Harcourt. "But Fecan put in 'The Road To Avonlea' on Sunday nights instead of 'The Beachcombers,' and it was certainly the right decision because 'Avonlea's' ratings were huge."

That's not a sentiment Gerussi shared. "The moment a new guy comes in, he wants all the furniture changed," said Gerussi. "That's stupid! Fecan's artistic judgement was totally bizarre, totally lacking, and just very stupid. They wanted the money to do other things."

But with the backing of his boss, vice-president Denis Harvey, Fecan cancelled "The Beachcombers." "Ivan is one of the most astoundingly astute politicians I have ever known," Harcourt says of the driven, hard-working Fecan. "He's an astonishing figure in Canadian broadcasting. I don't think anybody will ever know his game plan. He's almost Machiavellian in his ability to come out on top. He is a tough manager. He wanted to create a star system as he did with 'Street Legal' and 'The Road to Avonlea,' and he knew he could handle a star system. You can only have a star system when your executives are tough as nails and in control."

Fecan, understandably, was leery about going to a farewell dinner given for Gerussi and his colleagues by the town of Gibsons. He finally was persuaded to go, accompanied by Harvey and Harcourt. Harcourt says that, just to be safe, Fecan organized a "getaway boat" that would pick up him and his network colleagues if they felt too uncomfortable. "He was a bit nervous, and the publicist was told to stay very close to Ivan because they feared threats," says Harcourt. "When the show was cancelled, the cast just puked on him, as is usual in such decisions. So we didn't stay too late, and we left on the getaway boat."

A similarly contentious ending happened with "Street Legal," although this time the axe-swinger was program head Phyllis Platt, not Fecan. Fecan, in fact, had been responsible for reshaping and popularizing the series when he inherited it on his arrival at the CBC. But, says Harcourt, who worked with both Platt and Fecan, "Platt said the show wasn't to her taste. She thought it was too shallow. She wanted to put her own stamp on the network and create a new series."

That observation is echoed by the show's sleek and sexy star, Cynthia Dale. "Phyllis Platt had taken over and wanted her own shows," she says. "It happens all the time; new regimes come in and they throw out the old regime's stuff. They want to put their own imprint on the shows."

Cynthia Dale

Cynthia Dale has seen many ups and downs in showbiz since she was a five-year-old chorus girl in *Finian's Rainbow* at Toronto's Royal Alexandra Theatre. "Even then, I was flirting with the boys in the band," smiles the vamp of "Street Legal." "At five years old, I was paying income tax, doing a lot of commercials, taking dancing lessons every day, and later doing Wayne and Shuster and Tommy Hunter shows. I'd be about nine then. I was a performer and had to hit my marks and know my lines. The hard part was going back to school because the kids would have seen me on air and made fun of me. Even the teachers would put me down. It was an awful childhood at school. I was like the kid who was always beaten up. I was working and going to dance lessons, so I was never part of the gang. I coped because I knew performing is what I wanted. I think I came into this world knowing this is what I wanted."

"She was a cute little kid in those early days," says Elaine Saunders. "But I tell you, she's smart. She knows if she's stepped into horse bucky. She's knows if she's in something that isn't right for her."

As a child performer, Dale also learned things can go wrong. In the middle of a stage-show dance number when she was twelve, her wig fell off and went flying into the audience. "It was the first time I consciously remember using the F word," she says. "I said it very loud and the audience heard it too. So did my mother, and it was the first time she ever knew that I knew that word."

Dale's real name is Ciurluini, but when she was six an agent told her mother that her children, who were all on the stage, needed a simpler name and he suggested Dale. So, Cynthia Dale she became, although she's never legally changed her name. "I could never do that to my father. I could never disown my name," she says.

"I grew up in the halls of the CBC. I was the token kid in many of the skits, the little kid with the big voice and a lot of spirit." As a child performer, on her breaks she would explore the sets in the rehearsal halls, getting lost among the carousels, rocking horses, and fancy wardrobes. "On the top floor of the Sumach Street building, where we did rehearsals, there was a commissionaire's office that had fabulous pictures on the walls of all the performers. That room was like magic for me. I wish I could see those pictures again." She met Juliette in the rehearsal halls, who, as Juliette usually did, handed out advice. She learned, too, from Wayne and Shuster. "They taught me timing," she says. "I had a dancer's discipline and I knew to sit and watch, to see the adults work out the beats in comedy and see what worked in being funny, where to put the emphasis, the pacing, and how to deliver the punch line. Johnny and Frank fought a lot over details, but that attention to detail is what made them great. It was always 'Make it better. Make it better.' I would sit there and listen and watch and learn."

If ever there was a child of television, Cynthia Dale is it, and as a teenager she was at rehearsals, shows, and dance lessons most of the time, working both on TV and the stage. She appeared in episodes of the series "To See Ourselves" and "Wojeck," and did a few feature movies and a number of stage productions. At one point, however, CBC-TV seemed to dry up for her. "For a while, it was hell for me," she says. "I couldn't get any parts. I couldn't even get arrested at the CBC."

She was in New York performing with Lally Cadeau in *Tamara* when the CBC offered her the role of Olivia, the conniving, smouldering femme fatale of "Street Legal." She was twenty-seven and had more than two decades of showbiz experience behind her. Her inspiration had come from her dance teacher, Gladys Forrester, who taught her about discipline, and Emily Carr, whom she portrayed as a young girl in a TV show and whose life taught her to be uncompromising and passionate about her work. "I'm accused of being too hard on people, expecting too much," she says. "I'm a rehearsal-holic. For the first two years of 'Street Legal,' C. David Johnson and I talked almost every night on the phone about our characters and scenes we were going to do the next day. It was quite relentless, but that's what made it a success: hard work."

Combining soap opera, legal clashes, and Canadian topicality, "Street Legal" took off, becoming the longest-running, most glamorous CBC-TV hour-long drama series ever aired and making Cynthia Dale a household name. For eight years and 124 episodes, the show was always near the top of the audience charts until Ivan Fecan left to join Baton Broadcasting. In stepped Phyllis Platt, a bilingual journalist and tough-minded manager, who took on the job as CBC-TV entertainment head and brought with her a discomfort about the show.

There were discomforts and tensions, too, between the actors and

Nada Harcourt, who was executive producer of the show for its last year. "The actors were basically a little bit out of control," says Harcourt. The stars were earning about $7,000 an episode, but that didn't offset their unease, including a dislike for the new CBC broadcast centre in downtown Toronto. "They had no parking spaces and they couldn't smoke," says Harcourt, "and they had moved away from their own little nest outside the CBC to the new building."

Harcourt had come up through the ranks at the CBC, working as a script assistant in news and as an assistant in "This Hour Has Seven Days" and Pierre Berton's "The National Dream." She also had been head of the children's department, where she began to develop a show on Anne of Green Gables, which she later took with her to the entertainment department. She worked in entertainment as a senior executive developing programs until being named as executive producer of "Street Legal." In short, Harcourt was a shrewd, battle-hardened veteran of CBC productions, while Dale was a tough, sharp, multitalented performer who knew exactly what she wanted. A clash between them was almost inevitable. In many ways, it was a clash of differing disciplines.

As far as Harcourt is concerned, what turned the program's backstage unease into open rebellion was an offer Dale had to do the stage show *Crazy for You*. "She wanted to do it more than anything in the world," says Harcourt. "But she was the star of our series, and she had a contract with the CBC."

While negotiating the matter, Harcourt felt that in case Dale did do the stage show, she would have to be written out of several scripts. "I took Cynthia out of three scripts, and when we finally told her no about doing the stage show, she came to my office and demanded to be put back in those three episodes as a star."

From that point on, relationships on the series degenerated into loud acrimony, threats, and bitterness. Behind her back, Harcourt was nicknamed Darth Vader. Fuelling the conflict were angry complaints from the performers over a senior story editor whom Harcourt had hired and then let go. "They hated her," says Harcourt. Then, she says, one of the stars found another had negotiated an extra two weeks' holiday time and "went berserk over it," causing more dissension.

There was more strife when Harcourt decided to lessen Dale's role in "Street Legal." "Cynthia previously had been the main character to cause trouble, usually sexual trouble in the show," Harcourt says. "The problem was there was no new way for any writer to come up with a way of doing what had already been done a million times. I couldn't get the writers to find new situations sexually for Cynthia. So we decided to have a battle about right-wing politics between two other characters and shifted the focus off Cynthia."

What particularly outraged Harcourt was a meeting Dale had with Platt. "She went over my head," says Harcourt. "I was absolutely livid. After that I just cut her dead and would not even speak to her. Before Phyllis, nobody had gone above the head of an executive producer."

Even prior to this incident, Harcourt had felt uneasy with Platt, in part because she suspected Platt disliked her because she had worked so closely with Fecan. "I don't think she liked me from day one," says Harcourt. "Frankly, Phyllis is a very good journalist and a very good manager. But, she hasn't got a clue about drama."

The central clash, however, was between Harcourt and Dale. "I made her life hell for the last year," Dale says. "And mind you, she made my life hell for a year as well. She totally wanted to change all the characters. She had a completely different idea of the show. She said to me, 'You can't be aggressive anymore. You have to slow down your walk. You can't act this way because you're a married character now. You have a baby. You can't be sexy.' The cast spent a lot of time going to Phyllis Platt complaining, saying we won't work with her."

As the 1994 season wore on, tempers were increasingly frayed, although there were no face-to-face shouting matches. There was, however, a flood of griping and complaints about the changing nature of the series.

Finally, both sides came to the brink. "The CBC was told by me and Eric Peterson that if Nada Harcourt came back next season, we would not come back on the show," says Dale. "It wasn't worthwhile. I was too creatively unhappy after being so creatively happy for years. The last year of 'Street Legal' was the most unhappy and worst creative experience in my life. They knew they had to find another executive producer."

"They" knew that from Harcourt too. At the same time as Dale and Peterson warned Platt, Harcourt told her she would resign when the season ended. "I want to warn you ahead of time," she told Platt, "I will not do the show again. Cynthia is the star, and I will not work with her. I want to give you ample time to get a new executive producer."

Instead, Platt killed "Street Legal" and replaced it with another drama series, "Side Effects," which itself died after a couple of years. "Side Effects," however, may not have had a fair chance. Platt told Harcourt that the series wasn't ready yet. She would have preferred to keep "Street Legal" on the air for another half or full season. "But I didn't give her the luxury of that with my decision to leave," Harcourt says.

Even after all the threats and bitterness of the last year of "Street Legal," the cancellation seemed abrupt to Dale and her colleagues. The word came in a conference call from Platt. "But," Dale says, "they didn't say thank you, didn't say goodbye, didn't say a thing. I understand shows have to be cancelled, but it's the way it's done. It's called class. They didn't owe us a job, but they did owe us some respect for what we had done. There are gracious ways of doing it."

The next series Cynthia Dale did, "Taking the Falls," aired on CTV. In it, Dale played a tough private eye. It died after one season.

The Friendly Giant and Mr. Dressup

Ending a long-running series is almost always traumatic for the stars and producers. Nada Harcourt recalls with anguish the cancellation of "The Friendly Giant," a show beloved by Canadian children for more than a quarter of a century. The first hint of the program's impending demise came when the program's star, Bob Homme, and his sidekick, Rod Coneybeare, received a facilities sheet indicating that no production resources would be provided to the show for the coming year. CBC reporter Sheldon Turcott got word of this and started to track down more details. He planned to report that night that "The Friendly Giant" had been killed. He talked to Homme, who told him, "I think I'm cancelled."

When CBC vice-president Peter Herrndorf heard that Turcott was asking questions, he wanted to stop the story. Harcourt, who was then head of the children's department, recalls that Herrndorf phoned her and said, "Take a cab to Bob Homme's house and tell him we're not cancelling the show. Just tell him that."

Harcourt went to Homme's home, gave him Herrndorf's message, and told him to stand by for further word on the show. When she returned to the CBC, she says, "Peter called me again and told me to go back out to see Homme once more to assure him yet again. 'The man's embarrassed,' I told Peter, and I added, 'He's sick in bed with a bad back and he doesn't want to see me. I'm not going out there again.'"

At that point the show had not been formally cancelled, although it was on its deathbed. But Turcott's questions had touched a raw nerve in the CBC bureaucracy, and Herrndorf, anxious to avoid bad publicity for cancelling "The Friendly Giant," called Turcott to say the show would continue. In his story that night, Turcott said the program had been in danger of cancellation but would carry on. The show's production staff, grateful for Turcott's efforts, presented him with a T-shirt stating, "I Saved The Friendly Giant." The rescue didn't last long, however. A year later the program was finally cancelled.

In sharp contrast to the bumpy ending for "The Friendly Giant," "The Beachcombers," and "Street Legal," it was a smooth sail into the sunset for "Mr. Dressup" when new productions for that show ended. After twenty-nine years on the air with his tickle trunk, his puppets, and his role as a gentle, playful uncle, Ernie Coombs decided to call it a day. As Mr. Dressup, Coombs had created one of Canada's most enduring and endearing TV characters, and a couple of generations of Canadians grew up with him. He came to Canada with Fred Rogers from the United States to develop children's programming in the early years of TV. Rogers later went back to the States to star in his own children's show, "Mr. Rogers' Neighborhood." Coombs stayed with the CBC in a show called "Butternut Square," which, in 1967, became "Mr. Dressup." "I really just wanted to entertain and educate kids," he says. "I see myself kind of like a wacky uncle."

When he did his last show in 1996, Coombs was treated like an icon. Deputy Prime Minister Sheila Copps, CBC president Perrin Beatty, and senior network executives all saluted him in a classy send-off.

"He touched the lives of countless Canadian children," said CBC vice-president Jim Byrd. When the technicians, puppeteers, and musicians spontaneously applauded at the end of the last taping, Coombs said quietly, "I love you all. You made me what I am today. You know that and I appreciate it."

"The Road to Avonlea"

The graceful end of "Mr. Dressup" was matched in tone by the ending of one of the most popular prime-time shows in Canadian TV history, the Sunday evening smash success, "The Road to Avonlea," which finished its seven-year run in 1996. Produced for the CBC and the Disney Channel by Kevin Sullivan, it was regularly watched by 2.5 million Canadians and millions more in the United States. It was sold to TV stations in 140 countries, everywhere from Bolivia to South Korea. The CBC and Disney wanted to keep it going, but fearing the series might go stale, Sullivan decided to end it. "The format of the show had probably peaked," he said. "I would rather leave on a strong note than a weak note." The series had reached the period just before the outbreak of the First World War, and that seemed like a good cut-off point.

"I know I'll miss it," said Gema Zamprogna, one of the stars who, as Felicity King, literally grew up on the series. "We're like a family. They're my life. To walk away and say goodbye was very hard." It was hard for all the stars of the series, but the cancellation left them with a wistful ache rather than filled with bitterness.

The long-running series grew out of the mini-series "Anne of Green Gables" in 1985 and its sequel two years later. Those earlier programs made a star out of Megan Follows, who played Anne, although at first Sullivan had been unsure of her in the title role. Nada Harcourt, the CBC executive handling the program, insisted on Follows, and within a year Sullivan had become a fan. As a child on the set, Follows and her young fellow actors would sometimes sneak into the make-up trailer and try on all the wigs worn by other performers. At one point Follows was doing a Hollywood movie and acting in "Anne" at the same time, juggling filming schedules and flying back and forth. "I was taking red-eye flights and staying up thirty-six hours at a time," she says. "I got food poisoning once on my way back from San Diego, and I barfed my way across the continent back to the set."

Most of the stars in the Lucy Maud Montgomery setting were

Canadians, but a few came from Hollywood for guest roles, including Christopher Reeve, Faye Dunaway, Dianne Wiest, Michael York, and Stockard Channing. "Faye Dunaway was fascinating," says Lally Cadeau, a star in the "Avonlea" series. "She's a very high-maintenance person. She would take five hours to do her hair and make-up. But she's got a great figure. If she hadn't had all that stuff done, she would have had this wonderful European face. It's been done two or three times."

The plastic surgery of another Hollywood guest star so impressed Cadeau that she had to know who her doctor was. "I found out it was Victoria Principal's husband, and he had done a great job on her face. It wasn't one of those where they put their foot on your back and sort of pull."

The Hollywood flavouring of the series was encouraged by the Disney Channel partners in the "Avonlea" series, and they also encouraged an old-fashioned, sentimental, almost syrupy, innocence in the scripts. Co-star Cedric Smith told one reporter, "The scripts got soapier and sappier."

"In one script Cedric, as my husband, would go off to the barn and sing to the cows and have a little drink," says Cadeau. "But that was cut out. It was a Disney decision. There was also a young sailor who was not allowed to smoke a pipe. They didn't like smoking." Jackie Burroughs says Disney wanted to soften her sharp-tongued character, Aunt Hetty. "They loved that sort of stuff, but we wouldn't let them make us totally saccharine," Cadeau says.

Still, with Disney paying half the cost of $1.2 million each episode, everyone paid attention to its desires. As Cadeau told entertainment writer Martin Knelman, this was commercial TV and "if the producers tell you to carry a duck, then you carry a duck, as long as they're writing the cheques."

Jackie Burroughs

Disney wasn't the only source of occasional discomfort for some of the "Avonlea" stars. Jackie Burrough's intense focus on developing her role in "Avonlea" was sometimes taken amiss by her colleagues. "I've heard that they think me bossy," Burroughs says. "I've heard I'm difficult to work with. I *am* bossy, actually. I want to do it the way I want to do it. It's easy to tread on other people's toes without even knowing it. If you're me, it is anyway, evidently. They may think I'm bossy and upstaging, but I don't mean it. I'm just taking my role to the limit."

Some felt Burroughs occasionally went beyond the limit. "You just never know what to expect from Jackie," says her co-star Lally Cadeau. "She cares deeply about the scenes. She knows a lot and she's been around for a long time. She's an interesting dichotomy of self-involvement and democracy. She's a humanitarian who doesn't give a damn about anybody.

"Sometimes she'll be in every one of your shots so that you never have a clean close-up. She'd twirl an umbrella behind you or get her hand on your shoulder or her head popping up over your shoulder. Once when Jackie was bobbing hysterically up and down in front of me, I said, 'Will you get out of my face.' She recoiled like a snake and slithered away, and she didn't talk to me for about two months."

Cadeau remembers Pat Hamilton telling her how alarmed she was at playing a scene with Burroughs. "I've got three days to be totally prepared for this scene with Jackie," Hamilton told Cadeau. "I don't want her to have any control." Cadeau says she was chagrined watching Gordon Pinsent act with Burroughs in one TV show. "She did a million-trillion bobs and weaves and banks around him, and Gordon just sat there," she says. "Maybe Gordon was overwhelmed or tired. It was kind of sad and you'd think, 'Come on, Gordon, fight back!' "

This kind of criticism always surprises the sharply focused, talented Burroughs. "I don't believe in upstaging," she says. "I really like working with actors. My wars are never with actors. People say I think like a director, but I wouldn't want to be one. I don't want anybody else to boss me, but I don't want to boss anybody else, either. I just don't like being controlled."

"Sometimes," says Cadeau, "she'll just decide she hates the director before he even arrives, and then she'll go for him like a terrier and will never let go for a second. She'll be on the set for the whole time saying, 'And then I want to be here, and then I want to be there, and then I'll move like this.' "

"I have to be involved in the entire project," says Burroughs. "I like to watch other people's scenes. I just couldn't come in and do my part.

It would be too lonely for me. But then I get bossy and get into terrible trouble because I have lots of opinions on how it's being shot, the lighting and everything. I'm being a nuisance to help the program."

Burroughs has been acting since she performed as a student in a play at the University of Toronto, directed by drama writer and future critic Herbert Whittaker. "Then I just sort of fell into things, summer stock and stuff like that," she says. "I never really wanted to be an actor. Being an actor is like being a girl. You have to sit there and wait to be asked. So if nobody asked me, I could say, 'I don't care. I didn't want to be at this party anyway.' "

Her first love is radio, where she worked with John Drainie, Lister Sinclair, Barry Morse, and others. "I always feel so related to radio," she says. "I love it. It's such a wonderful medium because people are so very free. You're all around that microphone together making this sound, making an illusion together. You're really pulling together, while on TV, everybody is trying to look good. It's just harder on television. There's more stuff in the way. The visual is more inhibiting. You're really vulnerable when the camera is looking at you and you're trying to be cool."

In radio, Burroughs found a special friendship among the performers that's lacking in television. "The kind of people who did radio were a breed apart," she says. "In radio, you're passionately involved, and when the show is over, you go off together in this great camaraderie and get pissed. You don't do that in television. In TV, you've got to be up at four in the morning and work until maybe nine at night. You're not going to be partying after that. Besides, TV is always so nervous-making. You're not so friendly. You're so self-involved, you don't have that extra mile to share with someone. It makes me nervous, really nervous."

Burroughs's first exposure to TV was a revelation for her. She was supposedly riding in a truck on a farm. "I remember that to simulate the truck moving they had people wiggle the truck from side to side and then had other people running by, holding trees and bushes. I remember thinking that even I could dream up something as technical as that."

The wizened, grand old CBC Radio building on Jarvis Street was a magic palace for Burroughs as she grew up in broadcasting. "There was just something about that old building," she says. "The old linoleum, all the old moulding, the crawly things on the floor, and the rats and the mice. The CBC was full of them. And the nasty, torn carpets, the creaky old equipment. You had to go a mile to go to the bathroom. And, you could smoke anywhere. It was wonderful!" Burroughs hates the sleek, modern, non-smoking new CBC building in Toronto and has been there only once to visit singer Rita MacNeil.

Although most performers complain about the absence of a star system in Canada, Burroughs is just as happy without one. "You don't have to pay the penalties for stardom," she says. "I don't feel worried about going on the subway, and I don't have to keep up a front, pretending I'm better off than I really am. Canadians don't bug you or, maybe, don't care that much. Here in Canada, it's kind of great because you have freedom to fail, since nobody remembers you anyway."

While Burroughs may be a dynamo of action on the set, she's a wisp of a woman, weighing at best about one hundred pounds, although she was pudgy as a teenager. Her oddball eating habits include one or more platefuls of potatoes and gravy and white bread every day, mashing them all together. "It's my favourite," she says. "And I always do everything I like." That includes twenty cups of coffee or more a day and, she says, "I'm a proud three-pack-a-day smoker of Benson & Hedges." She used to drink with exuberance, but no longer does, and for a while lived a fast-lane life with her now ex-husband, a prominent 1960s rock and roll musician. "Now I live a very existential life," she says.

Although she's been a star of Canadian radio, television, and film for more than a quarter of a century, Burroughs never made much money until her role as Aunt Hetty in "Avonlea." She still lives in one room in downtown Toronto's Yorkville area, but she's put all her savings from "Avonlea" into a house in a Mexican mountain village near Oaxaca. "I met a Mexican and I bought the land," she says. "His sister was the architect, and his cousin built it. And it was just like a dream. I gave them all my money because I know nothing about that stuff. I love it, and there is no phone. Thank you, 'Avonlea.' Thank you, Kevin Sullivan. Thank you, CBC."

Lally Cadeau

Jackie Burroughs's "Avonlea" co-star, Lally Cadeau, has been determined to be a star since she was a child. "I was an actress right from the word go," she says. On family car trips to Florida, she would imitate gas station attendants and motel clerks, and at Christmas would dance on the table for her family. At age ten, she played the young Elizabeth in *Elizabeth the Queen* at the Hamilton Players Guild. "I remember that frisson of being on the stage," she says, "that tremendous, bowel-gripping fear and then that absolutely thrilling excitement, which I've had ever since."

As with many actors, however, Cadeau finds being onstage more "bowel-gripping" than "thrilling" when she is playing herself rather than a character. "You can hide behind a character, it's like an armour, I suppose," she says. "But whenever I've done a live presentation as just myself, my knees knock just like an old doorknocker. I have to wear skirts of a certain width, crinolines are the safest things." She tries all sorts of tricks to get rid of her nervousness, such as going for a swim at the YMCA just before having to host a show, talking with friends, sipping coffee, and arriving late. "But the nervousness never goes away," she says. "The teeth go to chattering, then the knees, and then the hands tremble. It's all very embarrassing."

Cadeau loves radio acting because it is so freeing for a performer. "Its fabulous what you can do with a microphone," she says. "The characters you have inside of you, the feelings that you want to express that you can bring out through the voice, which you might be too self-conscious to do on TV. You can show shades and contours of a character that might be intimidating to do on television. TV is disturbing and frustrating to work in because it's just so quick. And in TV you're very much a functionary."

Like Juliette, Cadeau complains of TV directors using up-the-nostril shots. "You have to become a temperamental actress because those shots have never flattered anyone," she says. "But they do it consistently. No woman of any age wants to have that shot, especially if you haven't had plastic surgery."

While she has starred in radio drama and the theatre, it is television that made Cadeau nationally known, starting with her 1980-87 series

"Hangin' In," in which she starred as a social worker, and then on "Avonlea" from 1989-96.

Cadeau was anxious to quit both series at the end of their run because she wanted to move on to other drama challenges. She feels, however, as do most actors, that the CBC lacks appreciation for their work. "You'd get nothing from the CBC. Maybe they're afraid of being in show business," she says. "Maybe it's the bureaucracy. But one feels they will cross the street rather than run into you and say hello." The only exception she experienced was Peter Herrndorf, now heading TVOntario, who, she says, "would send you three dozen red roses and a note saying, 'I love you.' "

Stars Over Canada

There may be no star system in Canada, but there is no denying there are stars and that the CBC, sometimes in spite of itself, has been their firmament.

In a country of diminishing national symbols, the stars, as much as anything or anyone, for sixty years on the CBC have provided a common bond for Canadians, starting with Foster Hewitt, through the Happy Gang, Lorne Greene, Max Ferguson, Wayne and Shuster, Patrick Watson, Norman DePoe, Juliette, Kate Reid, Fred Davis, Al Waxman, Anne Murray, Cynthia Dale, Peter Gzowski, Barbara Frum, Peter Mansbridge, and hundreds of others.

In their voices and in their faces, they reflected Canada. For all their gaffes, frustrations, rivalries, and bruised egos, they helped provide a sense of national identity through the microphones and cameras of the CBC.

As Elaine Saunders says, "We all grew up with these people."

Appendix

Plus Ça Change

The following is a 1947 memo to CBC executives from chief news editor Dan McArthur:

To Whom It May Still Concern
UP SHIT CREEK WITH A P & A* PADDLE

When I came to the CBC eight years ago I was happier than I had been in years. I had spent a long dismal time doing work in which I had no interest, kissing the asses of people for whom I had neither liking nor respect.

When I came to the CBC in 1939 it was a happy release. For the first time since I had made my own living, I felt that it was not at the expense of my integrity as a human being. There was an atmosphere of aliveness and enthusiasm, of human understanding and companionship, of satisfaction in doing one's job, that was new in my experience. It made me slap-happy and I still look back on those months with the CBC in 1939 as something never to be forgotten. I remember how surprised and delighted I was with the first conference that I was called in on. It had to do with serious matters – the White Paper on Controversial and Political

---

*Personnel and Administration.

Broadcasts – and the people who were there took it seriously, too, but in a different sort of way. They were relaxed and casual, they joked and they made wise-cracks, but they got along with the job. This, I thought, is the way people should work together. I remembered business conferences that I had been forced to sit through, where a bunch of stupid bastards sat around trying to impress one another, and the less brains they had the more ponderous and self-important they looked. What a lot of shit it was; I was glad to clean it from under my heels.

Well, a lot of water has gone under the bridge since then and now the water has the same old stink. Now we are up Shit Creek too. The old happy enthusiasm has gone; instead we stew and worry and tie ourselves in knots of P & A red tape. To Hell with it. In a job that should be creative and dynamic, that needs imagination and sensitivity and flair, that can only thrive in an atmosphere of casualness and shared enthusiasms, we now live in something so beautifully organized that all the guts have been squeezed out of it, only a spark left of vital creative life. People still do their jobs and sometimes they do good things too. Most of the best things are done by people who are outside the CBC, who haven't had the bejeezus organized out of them – They haven't felt the cold touch of the P & A Department, that fungous growth that now covers the whole of CBC like a green mildew. Anyone who has a real spark of creative capacity needs handling with a light rein, and in the atmosphere of the theatre and not the Civil Service. Creative work needs discipline, but of a special kind. It has to be based on a deep and intimate understanding of what makes such things tick. It means that a man may be a bit of a screwball and sometimes a goddamned nuisance, but it all depends on the payoff. If he bats out something new and good every so often, it's swell. The thing is to keep him at it, to keep the good things coming while you quietly kill the turkeys before they take wing on the air. You do this without wounding him or killing whatever vital juice is in him. And that is a job that requires sensitivity and understanding, of knowing how to balance six pats on the back with a good swift kick in the arse, of maybe getting drunk with the guy and shooting the shit with him till the cows come home.

That's one thing. It's another thing to have to suck up to some fatass who has to justify a job with the P & A Department, to humiliate yourself by trying to explain in Basic English why something needs to be done about an operation of which they know nothing. To hell with it, I've done it too often and I won't do it again. Let me be specific. Last summer we tried to get a special type of fan recommended by the engineers to keep the hot dead air moving in the Central Newsroom. This newsroom is bad because it is half below ground and all the windows are on the level of the asphalt paving of the Jarvis Street parking lot. The air heats up and seeps into the newsroom and stays there. Try to read yards of teletype news copy and absorb its content and rewrite it in good radio style in an oven like that. Well, try it sometime. We requisitioned for this fan in July of 1946. Nothing happened, and then this summer, after one editor had been off duty for three days and another on the verge of collapse and the rest dopey from the heat, we start all over again to get this bloody fan. What do I find out? I learn that the 1946 requisition was killed by the P & A Department in Ottawa. One of its junior officials explained in a letter to the engineers in Toronto – that if they put a fan of this special type in the Central Newsroom they would have to do it in other places too. Actually – the Central Newsroom is a special situation because of its proximity to the parking lot. But special situations mean nothing to these buggers, what they want is uniformity and conformity, in newsrooms and in individuals, everything nicely grouped and graded from coast to coast and neatly filed at Head Office. If anything means death in a creative enterprise it is uniformity. We mustn't set a precedent about fans, so let a bunch of dopey heat-struck editors in the Central Newsroom grind out dull bulletins and fuck the listener, why worry about that? He only pays the license fee, the poor sap.

That's one example, only one. Jesus wept, the interminable memos I have written trying to explain to these P & A people that news editors can't double up on one another's jobs to take care of special leave to compensate for working holidays. Every year I've gone over this business and I'm goddamned if I go over it any more. If one of these lardarses would spend a week in a newsroom doing a trick, he might know what in hell I was talking about.

The real authority has all been drained off to the P & A Department, or the Administration, or whatever is Official and the antithesis of radio in any creative sense, drained off to people who have never contributed a single creative spark to the only important end of radio, the program end; who have never spent an hour on production because they haven't the knowledge or experience or capacity.

All this is humiliating, even to me in News, the least creative and perhaps in the long run the least important of all the program divisions, because unless people are going to get something out of life except stewing and being so goddamned serious about it, we need entertainment and a lot more of it and a lot better. If this creeping paralysis of P & A domination can't be checked, if we can't crack it up and get back the old dynamic and stimulating atmosphere, and restore the vital creative juices to the CBC, then to hell with it all. Just to be one of another batch of poor old dyspeptic bastards, stewing away in a stinking mess of P & A red tape, trying to figure up arguments to get approval for this or approval for that, then we're up Shit Creek and P & A has the paddle, and as far as I'm concerned I intend to jump in and swim for shore – Only one thing can give the CBC any real justification and that is the vitality and significance of its programs. That means an atmosphere in which enthusiasm and creative capacity can thrive, where the official type of mind will no longer dominate.

Can we get it back? Can we drain out the embalming fluid and pump in blood . . . maybe some new blood? I suppose there must be some hope; I must feel that way myself or I wouldn't have bothered to get this off my chest. Anyway, it's been a useful catharsis. It gives me as much personal satisfaction as having had a damned good crap.

D. C. McA.
July 12, 1947.

Sources

The principal sources for the book are the stars themselves and their colleagues. In a few cases, I drew material from other interviews and from published memoirs, as noted below. Some interviewees preferred to remain anonymous and, sadly, some have died since I interviewed them. The people I interviewed are: Roger Abbott, Toronto; Alex Barris, Toronto; Cameron Bell, Vancouver; Pierre Berton, Toronto; Allan Blye, Los Angeles; Lloyd Bochner, Santa Monica, California; Dave Broadfoot, Toronto; Don Brown, Toronto; Stanley Burke, Toronto; Jackie Burroughs, Toronto; Lally Cadeau, Toronto; June Callwood, Toronto; Norman Campbell, Toronto; Murray Chercover, Toronto; Bill Cunningham, Toronto; Cynthia Dale, Toronto; Jimmy Dale, Naples, Florida; Fred Davis, Toronto; Mary DePoe, Toronto; John Drewery, Ottawa; Max Ferguson, Millbank, Ontario; Allan Fotheringham, Toronto; Murray Frum, Toronto; Vickie Gabereau, Vancouver; Bruno Gerussi, Vancouver; Clyde Gilmour, Toronto; Robert Goulet, Las Vegas; Jim Guthro, Toronto; Peter Gzowski, Toronto; Barbara Hamilton, Toronto; Bill Harcourt, Toronto; Nada Harcourt, Toronto; Don Harron, Toronto; Denis Harvey, Toronto; Peter Herrndorf, Toronto; Art Holmes, Toronto; Ted Hough, Toronto; Tommy Hunter, Penetang, Ontario; Carroll Hyde, Naples, Florida; Steve Hyde, Naples, Florida; Frances

Hyland, Toronto; Norman Jewison, Toronto; Al Johnson, Ottawa; Juliette, Vancouver; Harvey Kirck, Toronto; Betty Kennedy, Milton, Ontario; Bill Langstroth, Thornhill, Ontario; Len Lauk, Vancouver; Charles Lynch, Hull, Quebec; Donald Macdonald, St. Mary's, Ontario; Catharine McKinnon, Toronto; Peter Mansbridge, Toronto; Larry Mann, Tarzana, California; Ray McConnell, Toronto; Trina McQueen, Toronto; Mavor Moore, Vancouver; Keith Morrow, Naples, Florida; Barry Morse, Toronto; Anne Murray, Thornhill, Ontario; Sydney Newman, Toronto; Jim Neilson, Vancouver; Leslie Nielsen, Toronto; Gordon Pinsent, Toronto; Harry Rasky, Toronto; Lloyd Robertson, Toronto; Gunnar Rugheimer, London; Morley Safer, New York; Paddy Sampson, Toronto; Elaine Saunders, Toronto; Frank Shuster, Toronto; Lister Sinclair, Toronto; Des Smith, Toronto; Len Starmer, Toronto; Mark Starowicz, Toronto; Lorraine Thomson, Toronto; Joan Tosoni, Toronto; Alex Trebek, Los Angeles; Pamela Wallin, Toronto; Patrick Watson, Toronto; Al Waxman, Toronto; Jack Webster, Vancouver; Brian Williams, Toronto; Austin Willis, Wetaskiwin, Alberta; Roy Wordsworth, Naples, Florida; Larry Zolf, Toronto.

Other Sources

Maclean's
Toronto Star
CBC-TV's "Linehan and Juliette"

BOOKS

Allan, Andrew. *A Self-Portrait*. Toronto: Macmillan of Canada, 1974.
Barris, Alex. *Front Page Challenge*; Toronto: CBC Enterprises, 1981.
Berton, Pierre. *My Times*. Toronto: Doubleday Canada Ltd., 1995.
Drainie, Bronwyn. *Living the Part*. Toronto: Macmillan of Canada, 1988.
Ferguson, Max. *And Now Here's Max*. Toronto: McGraw-Hill Co. of Canada Ltd., 1967.
Gzowski, Peter. *The Private Voice*. Toronto: McClelland & Stewart, 1988.
Hewitt, Foster. *His Own Story*. Toronto: Ryerson Press, 1967.

Hunter, Tommy. *My Story*. Toronto: Methuen, 1985.

Moore, Mavor. *Reinventing Myself*. Toronto: Stoddart Publishing Co. Ltd., 1994.

Nash, Knowlton. *History on the Run*. Toronto: McClelland & Stewart, 1984.

———. *Prime Time at Ten*. Toronto: McClelland & Stewart, 1987.

———. *The Microphone Wars*. Toronto: McClelland & Stewart, 1994.

Pinsent, Gordon. *By the Way*. Toronto: Stoddart Publishing Co. Ltd., 1992.

Rutherford, Paul. *When Television Was Young*. Toronto: University of Toronto Press, 1990.

Webster, Jack. *Webster!* Vancouver: Douglas & McIntyre, 1990.

Young, Scott. *Gordon Sinclair: A Life and Then Some*. Toronto: Macmillan of Canada, 1987.

———. *The Boys of Saturday Night*. Toronto: Macmillan of Canada, 1990.

Index